AWASH WITH ALE

2000 YEARS OF IMBIBING IN BATH

by

Kirsten Elliott & Andrew Swift

AKEMAN PRESS

Published by AKEMAN PRESS
www.akemanpress.com

© Kirsten Elliott & Andrew Swift 2004

ISBN 0 9546138 0 5

Designed by Niall Allsop in Bath
Printed by SRP in Exeter

Set in Frutiger, Perpetua and Trajan

ACKNOWLEDGEMENTS

Thanks to Colin Johnstone, the Bath City Archivist, and his assistants, Lucy Powell and Mary Blagdon for their help in tracking down many of the historical documents used in this book. Also to the staff of Bath Central Library, Bristol Reference Library, and the Somerset and Wiltshire Record Offices.

We are also indebted to Stuart Burroughs of the Museum of Bath at Work, Paul De'ath, and Jean Fry who read the manuscript of the book at an early stage and made a number of helpful suggestions. Also to Marek Lewcun of the Bath Archaeological Trust for information on Roman Bath.

CONTENTS

A day without wine, as the old saying goes,
is like a day without sunshine.

CHAPTER ONE

FROM TIME IMMORAL

He was a wise man who invented beer.
Plato

Alcohol has been one of the most powerful influences on the development of civilization. Why, then, has it been so sedulously ignored by most historians? Is it, perhaps, because alcohol has constantly threatened to drag civilization back into the mire? Or is it because – given all the trouble alcohol has caused – they think that, by ignoring it, they can retrospectively wish it away?

Some hope! Alcohol, dangerous though it can be, is an essential ingredient of a civilized lifestyle. A day without wine, as the old saying goes, is like a day without sunshine. A day without beer is not much fun, either. Recent research by Merryn Dineley, an experimental archaeologist, suggests that the greatest step forward in the history of mankind – the decision of our distant ancestors to stop being nomads and settle down – was due to a taste for beer. Relatively speaking, it did not happen all that long ago.

Humans spent at least 150,000 years as hunter gatherers. It was only around 10,000 years ago that they decided to settle down and start cultivating crops – in particular, wheat and barley. This, it now seems, was not because they wanted to make bread, but because they had discovered that sprouting grain could be fermented to make a drink with mind-bending qualities. It made them laugh, it made them cry, it gave them visions of beatific bliss, it made them fall over. It opened the gates that inexperienced, overeager and under-age drinkers have been kicking open ever since – the gates of heaven and hell. Heaven while imbibing the ambrosial nectar of the tree of the knowledge of good and evil, hell while handling its after-effects the next morning. On top of all that, when they threw the spent grain away, wild sheep, goats and cattle came along, scoffed it, and hung around for more, thus providing a ready source of meat. Why go on being hunter-gatherers when they'd got all that on their doorstep?

So it seems that civilisation may have been a by-product of ancient man's desire to get blasted. It would be the ultimate paradox. But the history of alcohol is full of paradoxes. Alcohol fuelled working class resentment and fomented riots, yet it also hindered the development of a coherent working class movement. Sedition and dissent flourished in inns and alehouses, yet, throughout history, innkeepers and brewers have been firmly on the side of the establishment. Brewers, in particular, were among the first fat cats on the industrial scene. And, while alcohol can be seen as a liberating force, it was one of the main factors which led to the institutionalised subservience of women in the late eighteenth and nineteenth centuries.

Concentrating on alcohol's impact on society through the ages may seem like rubbing the reader's face in the most sordid and murky aspects of our past. In a sense that is true, but, while the history of alcoholic indulgence (and over-indulgence) cannot be equated with the history of civilization, it is a vital part of it and one that has too often been ignored. There are many weighty tomes dealing with Bath's past that do not mention a single pub.

It is not only historians who ignore the Bacchic arts. The standard view of Bath in days gone by is of a quiet, genteel resort where visitors spent their time dancing, taking the waters, listening to music, indulging in a little harmless chit-chat and promenading alongside the river on sunny afternoons. This was an impression fostered by early guide books and cultivated by those responsible for the city's prosperity. Nothing likely to upset the refined sensibilities of wealthy visitors was to be mentioned. The pursuit of anodyne respectability was sometimes taken to bizarre extremes. In the mid-nineteenth century, for example, when cholera broke out in the lower part of the city, the Corporation denied all knowledge of it, for fear it would deter visitors. They only owned up when their request for funds to deal with it was turned down by the Government on the not unreasonable grounds that no outbreak had been reported. As late as 1928, Bath Corporation successfully covered up a typhoid outbreak in Bathwick, which led to five deaths, by muzzling the local press and buying up national newspapers in bulk and destroying them. As a result, the evidence for a view of Bath which contradicts the squeaky-clean one is difficult to find and depends almost entirely on long-forgotten documents and newspaper reports hidden away in record offices and libraries.

When it comes to novels about Bath, much the same applies. You will not find much about getting blitzed in Persuasion or Northanger Abbey, for example. Basing an understanding of Georgian Bath on Jane Austen's novels is as misleading, in its own way, as basing an understanding of Scottish

You will not find much about getting blitzed in Persuasion or Northanger Abbey society on the novels of Irvine Welsh. Jane Austen chronicled the lives of the people she lived among. Although she observed them with an unflinching eye, it was an eye that rarely strayed beyond her immediate circle. This is not a criticism, but a statement of fact. You may as well look in the novels of PG Wodehouse for a searing analysis of a lost generation traumatised by the First World War and haunted by the spectre of mass unemployment. Wodehouse – like Austen – was an entertainer. To use their books as mirrors of their society is like trying to clean your windows with a blancmange.

The rambling odyssey that follows is an attempt to redress the balance, to tell the story of a city awash – sometimes with cider, sometimes with wine, sometimes even with gin – but mostly with ale. And where better to start than with the Romans?

The big drink in Roman Britain was wine. The Romans not only brought wine with them but established vineyards in Britain as well. It is likely that the south-facing slopes above the Star Inn in Bath were first planted with vines by the Romans.

Bath – or Aquae Sulis as it was then known – was primarily a pleasure resort and wine would have flowed freely in the hot baths. Bathing was as much as a social occasion as anything else, and over-indulgence was commonplace. There were constant complaints about rowdy drinkers splashing about and making a nuisance of themselves. Sometimes, early temperance campaigners took matters into their own hands, smashing the drinking vessels of inebriated revellers. Although servants sometimes accompanied their masters to the baths, by and large they were reserved for the wealthy. The lower orders had to find their entertainment elsewhere.

We do not know how many pubs there were in Roman Bath, but in Herculaneum it is estimated that there were around 900. If Bath had even half that number, the place would have been packed with them. No doubt, like pubs throughout history, they would have ranged from the eminently respectable to the decidedly dodgy. And – especially in the dodgy ones – you would have been able to get a dodgy kind of ale.

Ale had been around for centuries before the Romans arrived. We know very little about what pre-Roman ale was like, but archaeological evidence from elsewhere in the British Isles suggests that hallucinogenic (and poisonous) plants such as henbane, hemlock and deadly nightshade were sometimes added to the brew. Such ales would not have been for everyday use, but reserved for religious ceremonies. Merryn Dineley suggests that the ritually smashed pots found at religious sites around Britain held these potent brews and were broken – like the plates in Greek restaurants – when their contents had been drunk. This raises the intriguing possibility that the first person to get out of his head in Bath was a shamanistic priest hell-bent on visionary communion with the spirit of the hot springs. This would, of course, give a much earlier date for the mixing of strong alcohol with hallucinogenic drugs in Bath than has hitherto been supposed. Sadly, it seems to be a theory we will never prove.

The Romans were in Bath for over 350 years – from 43AD to around 400AD – the same period that separates us from Oliver Cromwell. For much of this period, Bath would have been a multicultural melting pot. When excavations were carried out in

Walcot Street in 2000-2001, the body of a man – almost certainly a potter – buried there in the fourth century AD was discovered to be of Egyptian origin. There were undoubtedly many other foreigners in Bath as well – North Africans, Armenians, or Macedonians, perhaps, as well as immigrants from provinces closer to home, such as Germania, Hispania and Gallia. They would have included traders, freed slaves, artisans, retired soldiers and merchants, as well, no doubt, as a few chancers and criminals. Many would have settled down and married, their descendants becoming naturalised Sulians. How many stayed behind when the Romans left is anybody's guess – but by that time many immigrant families would have been here for generations, if not centuries, and had nowhere else to call home.

Where the Romans drank in Bath we have no idea. Nor do we know where the people who succeeded them drank. Doubtless, primitive ale houses were set up in the ruins of the Roman city. Doubtless too there were complaints, as there always

Where the Romans drank in Bath, we have no idea ...

AWASH WITH ALE

are, about the price, the quality, or the strength of the ale – and about drunken youngsters relieving themselves in the doorways of other people's wattle shacks before taking an ox cart for a joyride.

When the Romans left, the city formerly known as Aquae Sulis did not suddenly shut down or descend into anarchy. The Romans left behind a sophisticated Latin-speaking native population. For them, Bath was Akemancester, the southernmost city in the province of Wiccia in the kingdom of Mercia. But, once the Romans had gone, the land became prey to incursions by marauding Saxons. These culminated in a mighty battle at Dyrham in 577, in which the three kings of Wiccia were slain. The Saxons followed up their victory by sacking the three Wiccian cities – Akemancester, Glevum (Gloucester), and Corinium (Cirencester). The waters from Akemancester's hot springs spread out in a great pool over the fallen ruins of the Roman buildings, silt choked up the conduits and obliterated what had been one of Europe's top leisure resorts. Even the name of Akemancester was forgotten and the site was known simply as "Hatte Bathe" – hot bath.

Eventually the Saxon conquerors settled down and some sort of order returned to the land. They converted to Christianity, and, in 676, almost a century after the Battle of Dyrham, Osric, King of Mercia, established a nunnery at Hatte Bathe, possibly on the site now occupied by Fountain Buildings at the bottom of Lansdown Road. In the following century, King Offa of Mercia built a monastery which, by 781, was described as "that most famous monastery at Bath." These ecclesiastical buildings provided a focus for the re-establishment of a new settlement – not a city, perhaps, but certainly more than a few wattle huts.

If the Saxons drank wine, they kept very quiet about it. Ale, relegated to second place during the centuries of Roman rule, made a comeback. Ale loosened the tongues of bards and emboldened warriors to go into battle. It was drunk as a matter of course by the highest and the lowest in the land. If you fancied a change, there was always mead, or perhaps cider, but ale was the national beverage. When Abbot Aelfric of Cerne Abbas, in the tenth century, prepared his "Colloquy" – a series of questions and answers designed to teach novices Latin – he was only reflecting standard practice when he included the following exchange:

Q And what drinkest thou?
A Ale if I have it, or water if I have no ale.

Ale fuelled the somewhat maudlin strain of lament that characterised much Anglo-Saxon poetry. Saxon bards could always be relied upon to come up with something on the theme of "things ain't what they used to be." This passage from "The Wanderer" is fairly typical:

Where is the horse gone? Where the rider?
Bestowal of treasure, seats at the feast?
Alas, the bright ale-cup, the mailed warrior,
The prince in his splendour – those days are long sped
In the night of the past, as if they never had been.

They even wrote a poem about the lost splendours of Akemancester:

> *The citadel is breached, the work of giants crumbles.*
> *Roofs lie fallen, towers in ruins,*
> *Barred gates lie broken, frost frets mortar …*
> *Ceilings are shattered, gaping and crumbling,*
> *Eaten away by age. The men who built them,*
> *Long since departed, lie in earth's embrace.*
> *A hundred generations have passed away.*
> *This wall, now lichen-grey and red with age,*
> *Withstood for centuries the storms; but now it crumbles …*
> *Bright was the citadel, with many bath houses,*
> *Its high gables rang with martial sound,*
> *Mead-halls were filled with joyous noise.*
> *But all were foredoomed by fate.*
> *Many fell fighting, pestilence claimed the rest.*
> *All those valiant souls were laid low.*
> *Their ramparts ruined, their halls deserted,*
> *The city decayed …*
> *Here stone buildings stood, a hot stream*
> *Welled from the earth, caught in the bright bosom*
> *Of a stone-walled pool. There the baths were,*
> *Gloriously hot, never failing.*
> *Now the hot streams pour forth and flow away*
> *Over the grey stones.*

Bath in the early Saxon period was part of Mercia. Its religious foundations were endowed by Mercian kings and came under the jurisdiction of the Bishop of Wigornia (Worcester). Wessex – and the territory of the "Sumorsoetan" – lay on the other side of the Avon. Logically, it seems that Bath should have stayed in Mercia and eventually formed part of Gloucestershire. As Katherine Symons wrote in 1934, "a glance at the map of Somersetshire will show how curiously Bath and its Forinsecum Hundred lie isolated north of the Avon, in country that obviously ought to be Gloucestershire." Its transfer to Wessex – and its later inclusion in Somerset – was down to King Alfred. As part of a defensive strategy to defend Wessex from the Danes, he annexed Bath and turned it into a fortified city, at the same time as extending the boundaries of what later became Somerset westward beyond the River Parret and along the Bristol Channel coast almost as far as Lynmouth. And so it was that we were bequeathed the curiously-shaped county which lasted, more or less intact, for over a millennium, until, in the late twentieth-century, politicians and bureaucrats started dismantling it.

As England slowly and violently moved towards unification, Bath, on the border between Wessex and Mercia, became one of the most important places in the country. Its defences were consolidated, a mint was established, and, on Whit Sunday, AD 973, Edgar was crowned King of All England in its abbey.

Edgar not only has an important place in the history of Bath; he also has an important place in the history of drinking. He was the first in a long line of monarchs to decide that drinking was a bad thing. Edgar ordered that each village should have only one alehouse. Next, he tried to restrict the amount people drank in these alehouses. By doing so, he gave us a phrase that is still in use today. Back then, most alehouses could only afford one drinking vessel – a communal one which passed from hand to hand in convivial befuddlement. Drinking was a serious business, and toasts, drinking songs and other devilry to facilitate the raising of the wrist, led to a great deal of over-indulgence. Edgar decided to put a stop to this. He decreed that every drinking vessel should be of a standard size – the four pint "pottle." He also decreed that eight pegs should be placed inside each pottle (marking half pint divisions), with nobody allowed to drink down more than one peg at a time. The idea was that you would drink your half pint and pass the tankard on to your neighbour. Needless to say, it didn't work, and before long people were taking each other down a peg or two the length and breadth of Edgar's kingdom.

Passed from hand to hand in convivial befuddlement

CHAPTER 2

MERRIE ENGLAND

Perhaps a better name would be Feeling No Pain England. It seems that most people were the worse for wear most of the time. They drank ale morning, noon and night. There was no alternative. Water was dangerous, tea and coffee unknown. People kicked off the day with a few pints of "small beer" (so called to distinguish it from the "big beer" that came later). Drinking ale was not confined to the working classes – or the peasants as we were then known. Everybody, male and female, right up to the highest in the land, started off the day with a session which would put most modern drinkers flat on their backs. In 1512, Lady Percy, the wife of the Earl of Northumberland, downed a quart of ale and a quart of wine for breakfast, and nobody batted an eyelid.

That was on a normal weekday. When it came to high days and holidays they really let their hair down. But, although the Middle Ages were intensely religious, nobody seems to have suggested that knocking back copious amounts of alcohol was a bad thing. Monasteries had their own breweries, and church-ales (a forerunner of church fetes, although rather more fun) were regular fixtures. It is impossible to say with any certainty exactly how much people drank in the Middle Ages, but eight pints a day seems to have been a fairly standard allowance. Strengthwise, again it is hard to know for sure, but the consensus is that ale ranged from 4.5% to 7.5% alcohol by volume, with the weaker brews being drunk in the morning, and the stronger stuff reserved for later in the day.

Such universal over-indulgence helps to put the bizarre and barbaric behaviour of our distant ancestors into perspective. But there was often a heavy price to pay. Take the Battle of Hastings, for example. On the night before the battle, William's men prayed to God for victory in the coming fight. Harold's – without putting too fine a point on it – didn't. According to RV French, a Victorian chronicler of ale, the English, "had in the morning their brains arrested for the arrearages of the ingested fumes of the former night, and were no better than drunk when they came to fight." Looked at from that perspective, the Norman Conquest must go down as the longest hangover in history. One wonders what sort of limp excuses there were when the English – those who were left – staggered home:

Well, there was I was with the lads, somewhere down near Hastings, putting away a few pints of Saxon Skullsplitter – well, to be fair, we had just walked all the way from Yorkshire, so we were due a bit of a celebration – anyway this local ale, didn't taste like much, but we should have known from the name – someone told me it was only 4.8%, which obviously I could have handled, but I reckon it must have been more like 6.5%. Anyway, to cut a long story short, I woke up next morning with this blinding headache and all these geezers called Norman coming over the hill shouting at me in French. Next thing I knew, we'd lost the country.

The Normans were originally Norsemen from Scandinavia, but had lived in France long enough to acquire Gallic habits like drinking wine. And so, once again, England was overrun by a race of wine drinkers. It is from the Norman Conquest that the genteel English prejudice in favour of wine dates. The new ruling class, who came over with the Conqueror, stuck to wine, not just because they were used to it, but because it distinguished them from the second-class, ale-quaffing Saxons. They may have been happy enough to drink small beer for breakfast, but when it came to dinner, nothing but wine would do.

Vineyards were re-established all over Southern England in the centuries following the Norman Conquest, including those on the slopes of Lansdown. Production, however, lagged far behind demand. The dearth of references to home-produced wine over the centuries suggests that most of the wine drunk in this country has always come from abroad. By the late middle ages, wine consumption ran at around eight pints per head per annum, and wine accounted for a third of the country's imports. Much of it flowed in through Bristol, at the same time as cloth, the country's major export, flowed out. As peasants, who made up the bulk of the population, would rarely, if ever, have drunk wine, those who did drink it were obviously putting away much more than that notional eight pints.

Peasants continued to drink ale. The alehouses they drank it in were pretty grim affairs, but, when we're talking medieval, grim was pretty much the order of the day. Lavatories were virtually unheard of, streams through towns and villages were open sewers, and the plague was a frequent visitor. With the best will in the world, it is hard to find fault with Kingsley Amis's memorable description of the period in *Lucky Jim*:

> Those who profess themselves unable to believe in the reality of human progress ought to cheer themselves up by a short study of the Middle Ages. Had people ever been as nasty, as self-indulgent, as dull, as miserable, as cocksure, as bad at art, as dismally ludicrous, or as wrong as they'd been in the Middle Ages?

Hardly surprising that people went around half-cut to cope with it all.

Pictures of medieval alehouses are fairly stylised affairs. To get a better sense of what they night have looked – and smelt – like, we have to fast forward to the early 1600s and cross over to Flanders to look at the paintings of Adriaen Brouwer. He specialised in dimly-lit alehouse interiors filled with unpleasant drunks. One of his works, in the Dulwich Gallery, shows two red-faced men, in a state of advanced inebriation, downing copious draughts straight from a pitcher. Behind them, two other men are raucously singing. In the distance, groups of other imbibers concentrate on getting legless. All are oblivious to a solitary figure in the foreground, supporting himself against a post and contentedly relieving himself onto the flagstoned floor. If it was like that in the early 1600s, imagine what it was like a couple of hundred years earlier.

Not surprisingly, alehouse keeping was a fairly lowly occupation in the middle ages. Many alehouses were kept by women, known as ale-wives. Most brewed their own ale, but there were also common brewers who supplied alehouses with what was generally a superior – and dearer – product. In an age of lax or non-existent licensing, when most households brewed ale for their own consumption, many tradesmen or craftsmen sold ale to attract business and supplement their income. Blacksmiths, in particular, encouraged their customers to have a drink while they waited for their horses to be shod – the number of *Blacksmith's Arms* and *Horseshoes* still around today are a legacy of this ancient tradition.

Around the time that Henry VIII was working his way through the marriage market, John Skelton immortalised a brewster (a female brewer) in a poem called "The Tunning of Eleanor Rumming." It is too long to quote in full, but here, just to give you a flavour, is part of the section on how hens helped out with the brewing:

> *They go to roost*
> *Streyght over the ale joust,*
> *And dung, when it commes,*
> *In the ale tunnes.*
> *Then Eleanor taketh*
> *The mashe bowle and shaketh*
> *The hennes dung away,*
> *And skimmeth it into a tray*
> *Whereas the yeast is,*
> *Withe her maungy fistes.*
> *And sometimes she blendes*
> *The dung of her hennes*
> *And the ale together*
> *And saith "Gossip, come hither,*
> *This ale shall be thicker,*
> *And flower the more quicker."*

Hence the expression (still occasionally heard), "this beer tastes fowl." It makes Baldrick's recipe for the brown bits on the top of cappuccino sound positively inviting. Eleanor Rumming may have been based on a real-life brewster who kept a pub called the *Running Horse* at Leatherhead. It would be comforting to think that Skelton used poetic licence in his description of her, but he was probably just reflecting current practice. When John Aubrey visited Hereford over a century later, he discovered brewing practices that made Mrs Rumming's seen positively hygienic:

> Under the cathedral church at Hereford is the greatest charnel house for bones
> that I ever saw in England. In AD1650 there lived amongst those bones a poor

Betty the brewster just bade him good morrow

old woman that, to help out her fire, did use to mix the deadmen's bones. This was thrift and poverty, but cunning alewives put the ashes of these bones in their ale to make it intoxicating.

The most vivid description of what alehouses were like in the middle ages comes from William Langland's poem, *Piers Plowman*. This story of a Friday afternoon drinking bout, and the lost weekend that followed, shows that Chaucer did not have the field to himself when it came to medieval vulgarity:

> *Now beginneth Sir Glutton to go to his shrift;*
> *His course is to kirkward, as culprit to pray.*
> *But Betty the brewster just bade him good morrow,*
> *And asked him therewith as to whither he went.*

AWASH WITH ALE

"To holy church haste I, to hear me a mass,
And straight to be shriven, and sin nevermore."
"Good ale, have I, gossip; Sir Glutton, assay it!"
"But hast thou hot spices at hand in thy bag?"
"I have pepper and paeony seed and a pound of garlic,
And a farthingworth of fennel seed for fasting days."

Then Glutton goes in, and with him great oaths.
Cicely the shoe-seller sat on the bench,
The warrener Wat and his wife also,
Timothy the tinker with two of his lads,
The hackney man, Hick, the needle man, Hugh,
Clarice of Cock Lane, the clerk of the church,
Davy the ditcher and a dozen other;
Sir Piers the priest and Parnel of Flanders,
A fiddler, a ratcatcher, a Cheapside raker,
A rider, a rope-seller, dish-selling Rose,
Godfrey of Garlickhithe, Griffin of Wales;
And a heap of upholsterers, early assembled,
Gave Glutton, with glad cheer, a treat of good ale. . . .

There was laughing and lowering, and "let go the cup!"
They sat so till evensong, and sung now and then,
Till Glutton had gulped down a gallon and a gill.
He neither could step, nor without a staff stand;
Then began he to go like a gleeman's dog,
Sometimes aside, and sometimes arear,
Like that one that lays lines, young larks to ensnare.

As he drew to the door, then dim grew his eyes,
He was tripp'd by the threshold and thrown to the earth.
Clement the cobbler him caught by the middle,
To lift him aloft, and him laid on his knees;
But Glutton, that great churl, was grievous to lift,
And coughed up a caudle in Clement's lap;
So hungry no hound in Hertfordshire lane
As would lap up the leavings, unlovely of scent.

With all woe in the world his wife and his wench
Bore him home to his bed, and brought him therein.
And after this surfeit, he slept, in his sloth,
All Saturday and Sunday, till sunset had come.
Then woke he in wonder, and wiped both his eyes;
The word he first uttered was, "where is the bowl."

Inns started to appear alongside alehouses in the late middle ages. Many were originally run by local abbeys. Abbeys had a tradition of providing hospitality for travellers, but in the early days few people strayed very far from home. Most of those who did were pilgrims. As travel increased with the growth of the woollen industry, however, the abbeys found they could not – and did not want to – cope with the numbers of people who were travelling around the country for secular reasons. So they built inns. The *George* at Glastonbury and the *Talbot* at Mells were built by Abbot John Selwood in the late fifteenth century. The *New Inn* at Gloucester was built by Abbot John Twining at around the same time.

The *George* at Norton St Philip near Bath started life as a guest house for Hinton Abbey. Later, it developed into an important commercial centre, where merchants and traders met to do business, and goods were sold, bartered and transhipped. Inns such as the *George* maintained their role as the focal point of fairs and markets until well into the nineteenth century, when local authorities built cornmarkets, corn exchanges and market halls to encourage traders to conduct business in a non-alcoholic environment.

Information on medieval inns in Bath is very sketchy, but it seems that the abbey established a guest house on the north side of Bell Tree Lane, where St Catherine's Hospital stands today. Later known as the *Bell Inn*, it closed around 1770 and was demolished some 60 years later. By 1503, the *White Hart* had opened at the top of Stall Street, and other inns such as the *Angel* (now the *Rat & Parrot*) in Westgate Street and the *Christopher* (now *All Bar One*) in the High Street probably date from around the same period.

Although drunkenness was frowned upon in the middle ages, there is no evidence that drinking – even what we would today regard as heavy drinking – was regarded as in any way sinful. Our medieval ancestors may have been half cut a lot of the time, but such a state of affairs seemed perfectly natural. All that began to change in the mid-sixteenth century, when a bunch of reformers decided it was time to wipe the smile off Merrie England's face.

CHAPTER 3

UNMERRIE ENGLAND

Sir Toby Belch: Dost thou think, because thou art virtuous,
there shall be no more cakes and ale?
Clown: Yes, by Saint Anne; and ginger shall be hot i' th' mouth too.
Sir Toby: Th' art i' th' right. Go, sir, rub your chin with crumbs.
Shakespeare, Twelfth Night

The demonisation of alcohol seems to have begun sometime in the mid-sixteenth century, around the time that Henry VIII severed links with Rome and established the Church of England. This was not mere coincidence. Medieval Christianity was all-embracing, and that meant it embraced alcohol. Monasteries ran breweries and owned inns. Church festivals were opportunities for the whole parish to forget their troubles as specially-brewed barrels of ale were tapped. The Protestant Reformation put paid to all that.

Monasteries were dissolved and their inns sold off or given away. *The Bell* in Bath was granted to the last Abbot of Bath, William Gybbs, who had acquiesced in the suppression of the abbey. The *Talbot* in Mells, however, suffered an altogether more curious fate. The story goes that Richard Whiting, the last Abbot of Glastonbury, in an attempt to persuade Henry VIII to spare his abbey, made him a Christmas gift of the deeds of twelve manors, part of the abbey's estate. Among them were the deeds of the Manor of Mells, which included the *Talbot*. Mid-sixteenth century England was a lawless place and, to hide the deeds from any potential ne'er-do-wells, he put them in a pie before entrusting them to his steward, Thomas Horner. On his way up to London, Thomas looked inside the pie and transferred one of the deeds to his own pocket. Abbot Whiting's attempt to curry favour with the King proved fruitless and his subsequent intransigence led to his execution on Glastonbury Tor. Thomas Horner, having sat on the jury that condemned him to death, was later confirmed as Lord of the Manor of Mells in recognition of his services to King and Country. The poem written to celebrate his cunning is still popular today:

Little Jack Horner
Sat in the corner
Eating a Christmas pie;
He put in his thumb
And pulled out a plum,
And said, What a good boy am I!

It should be pointed out that the Horner family strenuously deny that the poem has any connection with Thomas Horner, who, they claim, bought the manor off Henry VIII after the dissolution of Glastonbury Abbey. They also maintain that, as the character in the poem is called Jack, it cannot possibly refer to Thomas, conveniently ignoring the fact that Jack was a common name for a knave right up until the nineteenth century.

Land ownership, education and business were all dramatically affected by the dissolution of the monasteries. Most people, however, were more affected by changes to the role of the parish church. The medieval church was at the centre of the community, the venue not only for religious services but also for festivities, celebrations, and church ales. Church ales were, as their name suggests, an opportunity for the people of the parish to get together in church and drink ale. Like today's charity-raising bashes, the proceeds from them went to the church or to a particular person, such as a clerk or a woodward (the officer entrusted with the care of the forest). Bid ales (or bede ales) were held for the benefit of parishioners who had fallen on hard times. Originally, they were held in church, but, when it was decided that churches should be reserved for solemn ceremonies, they moved out to the churchyard or to a nearby house. Many parishes built their own "church houses" and some of these survive as inns, especially, for some reason, in Devon.

Church ales did not disappear immediately, even though the church authorities did all they could to get rid of them. They survived, in the face of official disapproval until the early seventeenth century, when the magistrates finally outlawed them. In Somerset, the end came in 1608, with the Wells Quarter Sessions Court declaring that "church ales, clerk ales, woodwards ales, bid ales and all kinds of suchlike ales whatsoever be immediately from henceforth throughout the whole countie of Somerset utterly forbidden and suppressed." With the disappearance of church ales, local inns and alehouses assumed a far greater importance, and so it was that a peculiarly English institution – the village pub – was born. The difference was that the profits from the pub went not to some worthy cause but into the pockets of the landlord. The village pub replaced an institution which, although controlled by the church, was effectively a communally-owned inn-cum-welfare-institute. Since then, the concept has been revived in many forms. Friendly societies, lodges, and working-men's clubs all have a similar remit, the difference being, of course, that they only serve a very small – and generally male – section of the community. Ales were for everybody.

The secularisation of drinking had two consequences. First, it led to the demonisation of drink; second, it created the binge-drinking culture we are still struggling to come to terms with today. Those parts of continental Europe that maintained an allegiance to the Roman Catholic church have a drinking culture which is not only the envy of those who seek to reform our drinking habits, but also has striking parallels to the drinking culture of the middle ages, when drinking was accepted as a fact of life. The conclusion, hard though it may be for the zealots of reform to stomach, seems to be that the binge-drinking culture was created by the demonisation of drink. Telling somebody that drinking is immoral, anti-social and wicked is the quickest way to get them to prove you right, especially if they have got a spark of rebellion in them. Telling them, on the other hand, that drinking is absolutely fine seems unlikely to elicit quite the same response.

It is tempting, but almost certainly fanciful, to argue that Roman Catholicism, with its mysticism and idolatry, fulfilled an emotional need which Protestantism did not, and that the English took to binge drinking to fill the emotional void left by the Reformation. It is far more likely that binge-drinking was caused by a process of cultural fragmentation, in which drinking, along with a lot of other things that were accepted as part of life in the middle ages, were marginalised and demonised. Medieval Christianity was not some happy-go-lucky, laissez-faire creed – quite the opposite – but it was all-embracing in a way that the Protestantism was not – look at Chaucer's *Miller's Tale*, look at the misericords in great cathedrals – many of them verging on the pornographic – depicting the ups and downs of everyday life. Medieval society accepted that people drank – some drank too much, some made fools of themselves, but that was the way things were. Certainly, they were punished if they went too far – and there was always the prospect of eternal damnation to look forward to – but if they wanted to behave like animals, then so be it. When the Puritans came along, however, it was a very different story.

The first shot across the bows came in 1552 with an Act of Parliament requiring "keepers of alehouses and tippling houses to be bound by recogisance."* Up to this time, anyone could run an alehouse without a licence; magistrates only got involved if it was kept in a disorderly manner, when it became indictable as a nuisance. The Act was deemed necessary because of the "intolerable hurts and troubles to the common wealth of this realm [which] doth daily grow and increase through abuses and disorders as are had and used in common ale houses and other houses called tippling houses." Alehouse keepers had to provide recognisances or assurances that they would not "use any unlawful games, or keep disorders in their houses." Anyone considered unsuitable could be refused a licence. The statute did not extend to inns, as these were "for lodging travellers." However, if an inn degenerated into a mere drinking den, "and the master or innkeeper suffer men to sit tippling there in a disorderly manner, it shall be taken to be an ale house."

Quite why the Puritans who came increasingly to dominate religious and civil affairs in the wake of the Protestant reformation were so anti-drink is difficult to say. Perhaps they associated it with the bad old days when England struggled under the yoke of Roman Catholicism. Perhaps there was – as many of them claimed – a dramatic escalation in drunkenness in the latter half of the sixteenth century. However, even

---

* There had been an earlier Act, in 1495, which gave Justices of the Peace power "to put away common ale-selling in towns and places where they should think convenient and to take sureties of keepers of ale-houses in their good behaviour," but this was something of a panic measure, granting extraordinary powers to deal with outbreaks of civil unrest.

though society was changing at an alarming rate, nobody seems to have put this escalation down to the impact of social change, preferring to blame that traditional scapegoat, the dastardly foreigner. Just as tabloid newspapers in the 1980s blamed the rise of the lager lout on habits acquired on Spanish package tours, so commentators in the 1580s put the increase in drunkenness down to habits acquired fighting the Dutch. William Campden, writing in 1581, declared that:

> The English, who hitherto had, of all the northern nations, shewn themselves the least addicted to immoderate drinking, and been commended for their sobriety, first learn'd, in these Netherland wars, to swallow a large quantity of intoxicating liquor, and to destroy their own health, by drinking that of others.

Eleven years later, Thomas Nashe – no stranger to the alehouse himself – included an attack on drunkenness in *Pierce Pennilesse's Supplication to the Devil*:

> Let me descend to superfluitie in drinke: a sinne, that ever since we have mixed our selves with the Low Countries, is counted honourable: but before we knew their lingering warres, was held in that highest degree of hatred that might be. Then if we had seene a man goe wallowing in the streetes, or lie sleeping under the board, we would have spat at him as a toade, and called him foule drunken swine, and warned all our friends out of his company: now he is nobody that cannot drink super nagulum, carouse the Hunter's hoop, quaffe upset freze crosse, with healths, gloves, mumps, frolickes, and a thousand such domineering inventions. He is reputed a peasant and a boore that will not take his licour profoundly.

So there we have it. It was all the fault of the Dutch. And, in case you are wondering what super *nagulum*, Hunter's hoop and *freze crosse* are, just think of the stupidest drinking game you have ever taken part in and you will get the general idea.

The Dutch were also blamed for the rise of tavern culture in the late sixteenth century. Taverns, a cut above the average alehouse, selling wine as well as ale, were the superpubs of their day. Puritans loathed them. Bishop Earle was more restrained than most when he described the tavern as "a degree or (if you will) a pair of stairs above an alehouse where men are drunk with more credit and apology." Thomas Brown, on the other hand, was not impressed, condemning them as places where the "young quality retire to spend their tradesmen's money and to delight themselves with the impudence of lewd harlots free from the reflections or remarks of their own servants."

"What immoderate drinking in every place," spluttered another moralist. "How they flock to the tavern! As if they were born to no other end but to eat and drink, as so many casks to hold wine; yea, worse than a cask, that mars wine and is itself not marred by it." Bishop Earle, however, painted a picture of the tavern that is as seductive today as it must have been almost 400 years ago:

> Men come here to make merry, but indeed make a noise, and this musicke above is answered with the clinking below. The drawers are the civillest people in it, men of good bringing up, and howsoever we esteem of them, none can boast more justly of their high calling. 'Tis the best theatre of natures, where they are truly acted, not played. A melancholy man would here find matter to work upon, to see heads as brittle as glasses, and often broken; men come hither to quarrel, and come hither to

A house of sinne you may call it, but not a house of darknesse ...

be made friends ... It is the common consumption of the afternoon, and the murderer or maker-away of a rainy day ... A house of sinne you may call it, but not a house of darknesse, for the candles are never out; and it is like those countries far in the north, where it is as clear at midnight as at midday. After a long sitting, it becomes like the street in a dashing shower, where the spouts are flushing above, and the conduits running below, while the Jordans [chamber pots] like swelling rivers overflow their banks. To give you the total reckoning of it, it is the busie man's recreation, the idle man's business, the melancholy man's sanctuary, the stranger's welcome, the Innes of Court man's entertainment, the scholar's kindness and the citizen's curtesy.

Early taverns in Bath included the *Sun* in the High Street, owned by the Chapman family, the *Queen's Head* in Cheap Street, and the *Fleece* in St Michael's Place, off Westgate Street. All, unfortunately, called last orders over 200 years ago.

In 1585, England, with a population of just over three million people, had around 24,000 licensed premises – one for every 126 people. That was the ratio for the country as a whole. In urban areas the ratio was much lower. The magistrates in Coventry, for example, declared in 1544 that the "brewers and tipplers [alehouse keepers] be now increased and multiplied to such a great extent that a great part of the inhabitants of this city be now brewers or tipplers of ale." In London, Thomas Dekker observed that "a whole street is in some places but a continued alehouse."

Faced with what they perceived as an alarming increase in drunkenness, the authorities took drastic measures to reduce the number of licensed premises. Somerset magistrates started issuing a series of orders aimed to close disorderly houses in 1594. In 1618, there was a national clampdown on disorderly houses. Five years later, the Mayor of Bath proudly reported that he had not only suppressed all "unnecessary alehouses," but also regulated the strength of the ale brewed in them. This was just the beginning. In 1631, Somerset magistrates launched a draconian programme of wholesale suppression. Only two or three alehouses were to be licensed in each town, and then only if there were insufficient inns "to give entertainment to passengers." In the countryside, the only alehouses left open would be those along "great thoroughfares," and they would have to be at least five miles apart. There were also campaigns to water down the strength of the ale, giving rise to confrontations such as the following:

> Certain Justices of the Peace, being informed of the odious abuses committed by drunkenness in their jurisdictions did, according to their places and duties, meet at a market town and sat two days hearing information, and working reformation. At last, they concluded that the ale and beer were too strong, and therefore, commanded that from thenceforth smaller drinke should be brewed, whereby unruly people might go to bed sober. But one mad tossepot fellow being much aggrieved at this order . . . asked them if they had sat two days about the brewing of small drinke; to whom one of the Justices replied, Yes. Why then, quoth the drunkard, I pray you sit three days more to know who shall drink it, for I will have none of it.

In 1613, John Wood, the Mayor of Bath, announced another initiative:

> From henceforth noe person nor persons shall sell or retaile any beer or ale in his house as an aleseller or vituler but he shall take the same ale or beere from the Common Brewers or from one of them appointed to brewe in the Cittie aforesaid upon payne to forfeite to the use of the poore of the said Citie ten shillings for every sale made of any pennyworth of such ale or beere by any person or persons brewing or causing to be brewed and sellinge or causing to be solde in the Cittie aforesaid contrarye to this order – and if any such person as breweth be licensed to sell ale or beere this his licence (for sellinge or causinge to be sold) is presently made voyde and to be supprest ipso facto.

This policy of suppressing home-brewed houses, and concentrating production in the hands of a few common brewers, came directly from James I, who wanted to impose a tax on brewing and was aware of the impossibility of doing so if tens of thousands of small brewers were allowed to stay in business. However, Parliament not only declared the tax – and the suppression of home brewed houses – illegal; they also successfully opposed a similar move by his son, Charles I, in 1637. Despite John Wood's edict, home-brewed houses continued to be the norm until well into the next century. Only then, as larger breweries were established, did tied houses start to take over.

It is comforting to record, after this litany of edicts and clampdowns, that by the 1630s, far from there being fewer licensed premises than there were 50 years earlier, the number had doubled. True, the population had also increased dramatically – by around 60% – but this still meant that, while there had been one licensed house for every 126 people in 1585, there was now one for every 95 people.

The authorities did not just have licensed houses in their sights. Anything that encouraged people to have a good time was outlawed. In 1603, a proclamation prohibiting fairs was read in Bath. In 1634, the Corporation dismissed a Bath Guide with the Chaucerian name of Widow Broade after "she miscarried herself through drinking and so caused the Mayor to have several checks from the Lord Chief Justice." In 1628, William Prynne of Swainswick declared that, "of all the gross and crying sins which have of late … overspread our nation … there are few more common, few more dangerous, hurtful and pernicious than the unnatural, unthrifty, odious and swinish sin of drunkenness." Four years later, he wrote an attack on dancing and the theatre called *Histriomastix*. "Dancing," he said, "serves no necessary use, no profitable, laudable or pious end at all. It is used only from the inbred depravity, vanity, wantonness, incontinency, pride, profaneness or madness of men's depraved natures." He also cast aspersions on the Queen, for which he was stuck in the pillory and had the tips of his ears cut off. You'd like to feel sorry for him, but somehow you feel he was asking for it. Instead of shutting him up, however, this only succeeded in turning him into a martyr. He went on to be an ally of Cromwell and one of the leading lights of the revolution which unseated Charles I. It just goes to show where taking a firm line on drink can lead you, even if you do come from Swainswick.

Historians have argued the toss as to whether Cromwell was a good thing or not for the last three and half centuries. It seems fairly clear, however, that if you liked having a good time, were partial to the odd pint or six, and were not too bothered about going to church, life under Cromwell was not a barrel of laughs. Sunday prohibition got going in earnest. Travel on a Sunday – unless it was to or from church – was forbidden. You could even end up in the stocks if you went for a stroll in the country. All pub games were banned. Theatres closed, fairs, feasts and festivities were outlawed.* Bath fell on hard times, as this report from 1642 makes clear:

> The inhabitants of Bath express great griefs that they have had little company this summer … The poor guides are now necessitate to guide one another from the ale-house, lest they should lose their practice. The ladies that are there are fallen into a lethargy for want of stirring cavaliers to keep them awake … The poor fiddlers are ready to hang themselves in their strings for a pastime for want of other employment.

However, one thing the Puritans did not manage to do was stop people drinking. In fact, with so little else left to do, alcohol consumption actually went up.

---

* It is only fair to point out, however, that the Puritans also banned Morris Dancing, which just goes to show that nobody is all bad.

When I waked I found myself wet with my spewing

CHAPTER FOUR

IN GOOD KING CHARLES'S GOLDEN DAYS

... And so after drinking a pot of ale alone at Mrs Harper's I returned to Mr Bowyer's, and after a little stay more I took my wife and Mrs Frankelyn to Axe yard, which at the further end there were three great bonfires, and a great many gallants, men and women; and they laid hold of us, and would have us drink the King's health upon our knees, kneeling upon a faggot, which we all did, they drinking to us one after another. Which we thought a strange frolic; but these gallants continued thus a long while; and I wondered to see how the ladies did tipple. At last I sent my wife and her bedfellow to bed, and Mr Hunt and I went in with Mr Thornbury (who did give the company all their wine, he being yeoman of the wine-cellar to the King) to his house; and there, with his wife and two of his sisters, and some gallant sparks that were there, we drank the King's health and nothing else, till one of the gentlemen fell down stark drunk and there lay spewing; and I went to my Lord's pretty well. But no sooner abed with Mr Sheply but my head begun to hum and I to vomit, and if ever I was foxed it was now – which I cannot say yet, because I fell asleep and slept till morning – only, when I waked I found myself wet with my spewing. Thus did the day end, with joy everywhere.

Samuel Pepys on King Charles II's Coronation Day, 23 April 1661

Charles II (a.k.a. the Merry Monarch) was restored to the throne in 1660. So glad were people to see the back of the Puritans that they used patriotic sentiment as an excuse to get totally ratted. Worse still, they accused anyone who did not join them in endless toasts to the King of a lack of patriotism. Things got so bad that, within a few weeks, the Merry Monarch had to issue a very unmerry proclamation, before the whole country descended into a drunken brawl. He told his subjects that, far from it being necessary to get legless to prove their loyalty to him, such behaviour was likely to bring the country to its knees. He singled out for particular opprobrium "a set of men of whom we have heard much, who spend their time in taverns and tippling houses and debauches, giving no other evidence of affection for us but in drinking our health, and in inveigling against all others who are not of their own dissolute temper."

Nobody paid a blind bit of notice. They may have been too drunk for it to register. Not only did people use the Restoration as an excuse to drink more. Ale started to get stronger as well. In 1680, a Member of Parliament urged the government to legislate for "a reformation of ale, which is now strong as wine and will burn like sack."

Despite the best efforts of the Puritans and five years of Cromwell as Lord Protector, England still beat off the competition when it came to drinking. "The English beer is best in all Europe," a French Ambassador wrote in 1672. "It was necessary to drink two or three pots of beer during our parley; for no kind of business is transacted in England without the intervention of pots of beer." A Swiss traveller, César de Saussure, visiting England fifty years later, noted that:

> Debauch runs riot with an unblushing countenance. It is not the lower populace alone that is addicted to drunkenness; numbers of persons of high rank and even distinction are over fond of liquor.

Daniel Defoe, writing around the same time, declared that:

> Our drunkenness as a national vice takes its epoch at the Restoration or within a very few years after … Very merry, and very mad, and very drunken, the people were, and grew more and more so every day.

It is curious how, throughout history, people have always said that drinking was not a problem until a few years ago.

Leaving aside the question of when drunkenness became the national vice, there are certain things that can be dated back to the years after Charles II's restoration. One of them was the introduction of stagecoaches. The first coach from London to Bath – one of the first in the country – arrived at the *White Lion* in the High Street (where the northern extension of the Guildhall now stands) in 1667. It was announced as follows:

FLYING MACHINE

> All those desirous to pass from London to Bath, or any other place on this
> road, let them repair to the *Bell Savage* on Ludgate Hill in London, and the
> *White Lion* at Bath, at both which places they may be received in a stage-coach
> every Monday, Wednesday and Friday, which performs the whole journey in
> three days (if God permits), and sets forth at five o'clock in the morning.
> Passengers to pay one pound five shillings each, who are allowed to carry
> fourteen pounds weight – for all above to pay three-halfpence per pound.

That fare in today's terms would be around £130, on top of which there was the cost of two nights' bed and board at inns en route. All that to travel just over 100 miles in three days. You could almost walk it in that.

In 1686, the War Office, under the direction of William Blathwayt, produced a national survey of the accommodation available at inns throughout the country. The information was required so that he would know how many soldiers could be billeted in each town. Bath weighed in with 324 beds and stabling for 451 horses. By the end of the seventeenth century, there were at least 22 inns in Bath, over half of which were less than 50 years old. The best of these were the *White Lion*, the *Bear* in Cheap Street, the *White Hart* in Stall Street, and the *Christopher* (now *All Bar One*) in the High Street. Others included the *Three Crowns & Sceptre* in Cheap Street, the *Catherine Wheel*, the *Noble Science*, the *Greyhound*, *the Unicorn*, and the *King's Arms* in the High Street, the *George* near the Hot Bath, the *Angel* (now the *Rat & Parrot*), the *White Swan*, *and* the *Golden Ball* in Westgate Street, the *New Inn*, the *Three Tuns*, and the *Bell* in Stall Street, the *Plume of Feathers* and the *Rose & Crown* in Southgate Street, the *Three Horseshoes* and the *Three Cups* in Northgate Street, and the *Black Swan* in Broad Street.

These early inns were far from the hospitable places they later became. Celia Fiennes' description of the inns she encountered on her travels around England at this time gives a good idea of what travellers had to put up with:

> The lodgings so bad, two beds in a room, some three beds and four in one room, so that if ye have not company enough of your own to fill a room they will be ready to put others in the same chamber, and sometimes they are so crowded that three must lie in a bed. Few people stay above two or three nights, it is so inconvenient.

The sexes were not always segregated in these communal bedrooms. On the road to Dover in 1635, a traveller called Lieutenant Hammond recorded falling in with a party of French visitors, among whom was "a light and sprightly Mademoiselle." He lodged with them at the *Fleur de Luce* in Canterbury, where they "had free mirth and good content ... They were all weary as well as I, especially that pretty she-rider who at that time held it no nicety, nor point of incivility, to disrobe and bed her little tender wearied corpse in our presence."

And here, somewhat closer to home, is another traveller's description of the inn at Nether Stowey in 1649:

> Mine host was sufficiently drunk, the house most delicately decked with exquisite artificial and natural sluttery, the room besprinkled and strewed with excrements of pigs and children; the walls and ceilings were adorned and hanged with rare spider's tapestry, or cobweb lawn; the smoke was so palpable and perspicuous that I could scarce see anything else, and I could scarce see that, it so blinded me with weeping.

After waiting in vain for a supper which never came, he turned in for the night, only to be attacked by "an Ethiopian army of fleas so plump and mellow that they would squash to pieces like young boiled peas. For my further delight, my chamber pot seemed to be lined within with crimson plush."

Even well into the eighteenth century, the supposed Golden Age of the Coaching Inn, there were many who found the standard of accommodation left much to be desired. One disgruntled traveller wrote that:

> the innkeepers are insolent, the ostlers are sulky, the chambermaids are pert, the waiters are impertinent, the meat is tough, the wine is foul, the beer is hard, the sheets are wet, the linen is dirty, and the knives are never cleaned. I look upon the inn as the seat of all roguery, profaneness and debauchery; and sicken of them every day.

And, in case you are thinking that the inns in Bath must have been a cut above those in out-of-the-way places like Nether Stowey, here is John Wood's description of the lodging houses and inns he found when he came to Bath in 1725:

> The boards of the dining rooms and most other floors were made of a brown colour, with soot and small beer to hide the dirt, as well as their own imperfections.

At this time, despite several royal visits, Bath was far from being the elegant resort it later became. When Dudley Ryder visited in 1716, for example, he was surprised to see "so many fine ladies walking through the streets" of what was still "a country town"

The medieval city which had been built upon the ruins of the Roman settlement had kept within the walls – except for ribbon development along Southgate Street, Broad Street and Walcot Street. As walled cities went, Bath was near the bottom of the league. London was the largest, with its walls enclosing an area of 330 acres. Next came Winchester with 138 acres. Other major cities such as Chichester, Colchester, Exeter and Leicester, had between 100 and 125 acres. Bath had just 24.

Until around 1600, a large proportion of those 24 acres was given over to gardens or waste ground. Then, a population boom, combined with the growing popularity of Bath as a spa, led to a rash of new building. Palatial dwellings, such as that which now houses the *Grapes* in Westgate Street, started to appear. Bath's population, which stood at around 2,000 in 1660, had risen to 5,000 by the end of the century. The Corporation was keen to see new development kept within the city walls, so that they could keep control of it. As a result, Bath soon got very crowded. When Pepys visited in 1668, he found the city "clean, though the streets generally narrow." By the end of the century, with double the number of people crammed into the same space, Bath was bursting at the seams. Given our ancestors' standards of hygiene and sanitation, the smell must have been appalling. Bath was, however, fast becoming the country's top resort. It was clear that something radical would soon have to be done to relieve its overcrowding.

The introduction of regular stage coach services was just one of the innovations which had a major social impact in the late 1600s. Many things we take for granted today first became commonplace in the years following the Civil War – tobacco, coffee and gin, for example.

Tobacco first arrived in England in 1565. For many years it was little more than a curiosity, although some believed it had medicinal properties. Among these was France's ambassador to Portugal, Jean Nicot, from whom nicotine takes its name. In the early seventeenth century, tobacco started to be used as a recreational drug, and, perhaps because it was generally sold at taverns and alehouses, its users were said to "drink" it. Not everybody was in favour of Sir Walter's weed, however. King James I, for example, loathed the stuff. It was an "invention of Satan," he fulminated, "a custom loathsome to the eye, hateful to the nose, harmful to the brain, dangerous to the lungs, and in the black stinking fume thereof nearest resembling the horrible Stygian smoke of the pit that is bottomless." Alehouse keepers were told that they were not to "utter, nor willingly suffer to be utter'd, drunke, or taken any tobacco within [their] house, cellar, or other place thereunto belonging." With that sort of publicity, it is hardly surprising it took off. By 1633 the government had given up trying to ban it and taxed it instead.

The popularity of tobacco and the growth of a highly competitive market led to a rapid fall in prices. By the end of the Civil War, a pipe of tobacco was within reach of all but the most penurious alehouse toper. For the next three centuries, smoking would be the almost inevitable accompaniment to a pint. Home-grown tobacco supplemented the imported variety until the late eighteenth century when its production was banned in an attempt to boost the American economy.

In 1789, the government attempted to raise money by forcing publicans to take out licences to sell tobacco. As with most government initiatives, it did not take long for people to find a loophole. The *Bath Chronicle* reported on 17 December 1789 that "in many places the innkeepers and publicans have resisted the taking out licences for dealing in tobacco by giving away that commodity and selling their pipes."

Over the years, tobacco-smoking rituals, now totally forgotten, developed in Bath's alehouses and taverns. A writer in 1898 recalled the tobacco-smoking rituals of the mid-nineteenth century:

> The old, brightly-coloured, brass tobacco box, where you had to insert the copper in the aperture before you could open the lid to obtain the fragrant weed, and the long alderman carefully laid out in the Japanned tray, together with the spills, which were contained in a narrow receptacle formed in the handle of the tray, were indispensable adjuncts at many of the inns, but now they are all luxuries of the past. So unknown a thing is the old tobacco box that, like the obsolete tinder box, thousands would be unable to understand what it was actually used for. The only houses where I know the long clay is used now is at Mr George Biggs, New Orchard Street, and Mr Tanner, at the *Full Moon*.

Today, the 400-year-old link between tobacco and alcohol looks finally set to be broken. Ireland's ban on smoking in pubs – inconceivable just a few years ago – has encouraged those who favour a similar ban here to step up their campaign. Perhaps, when the "no smoking" signs finally go up, snuff-taking – that neglected alternative to the cigarette – will make a comeback. If it does, the *Star Inn*, with its tins of complementary snuff on the shelf in "death row," will be ready

Coffee was introduced into England in 1648 and the first coffee house opened in London two years later. Despite their name, coffee houses offered a variety of beverages. In 1669, an Italian visitor noted that, in addition to coffee, "sherbet, tea, ale, cock ale[*], beer etc." were generally available. Bath's first coffee house opened around 1679. Like tobacco, coffee met with considerable opposition. A brief but intense pamphlet war broke out in the 1670s, in which women spelled out their objections to the roasted bean. The *Women's Petition Against Coffee Houses*, published in 1674, declared that men came home from the coffee house "with

---

[*] In case you are wondering, yes, cock ale was made with a cock.

nothing moist but their snotty noses, nothing stiffe but their joints, nor standing but their ears." Which, if nothing else, is an interesting variation on the age-old theme of brewer's droop. "Certainly," the pamphlet went on, "our countrymen's pallates are become as fanatical as their brains; how else is't possible they should apostasize from the good old primitive way of ale drinking, to run a whoreing after … a little base, black, thick, nasty bitter stinking, nauseous puddle water."

Despite this, coffee houses remained popular meeting places for men about town. A 1755 guide to Bath informed visitors that "the two principal coffee houses are that kept by Mr Morgan in the Grove, called *Morgan's Coffee House*, the other kept by Mr Richard Stephens, called the *Parade Coffee House*, on account of its fronting the Grand Parade." By the 1770s, coffee-house culture was in decline. When Matthew Bramble visits one in Smollett's *Humphrey Clinker*, published in 1771, he finds it full of decrepit old men, among whom he is dismayed to discover several former acquaintances. Coffee houses hung on for several more years, however. As late as 1791, Mr Blew from the *Star & Garter* in Pall Mall moved to Bath to open the *Argyle Coffee House & Tavern* next to Pulteney Bridge. By the 1830s, however, when they had finally disappeared, the temperance movement started opening a new type of coffee house aimed at working men, in an effort to get them out of the pub.

The impact of tobacco and coffee, however, were as nothing compared to that of the third member of this unholy trinity – gin. So tremendous was its impact, in fact, that it deserves a chapter all to itself.

CHAPTER FIVE

MADAM GENEVA: THE PERILS OF GIN

Don't tell my mother I'm living in sin,
Don't let the old folks know:
Don't tell my twin that I breakfast on gin,
He'd never survive the blow.
AP Herbert

Twice in British history gin has threatened to bring the country to its knees – or, to be more accurate, to have it lying flat on its back, mumbling incoherently, with a stupid grin on its face.

Gin was first brought into this country by soldiers returning from an expedition to the Netherlands in 1586 – the same expedition, you will recall, that introduced them to "immoderate drinking." It was far from being an instant success. For the next hundred years, the only spirit readily available in England was brandy. Although brandy took its name from a Dutch word – "brandewijn" (burned wine) – it came from France. By 1673, consumption of brandy had grown to such an extent that a petition was presented to Parliament calling for imports of it to be banned:

> Before brandy, which is now become common and sold in every little alehouse in England in such quantities as it now doth, we drank good strong beer and ale, and all laborious people (which are far the greater part of the kingdom) their bodies requiring, after hard labour, some strong drink to refresh them, did therefore every morning and evening used to drink a pot of ale or a flagon of strong beer, which greatly helped the promotion of our own grain, and did them no great prejudice; it hindered not their work, neither did it take away their senses nor cost them much money, whereas the prohibition of brandy would … prevent the destruction of His Majesty's subjects, many of whom have been killed by drinking thereof, it not agreeing with their constitution.

The petitioners overplayed their hand by calling for a ban on tea, coffee and chocolate as well, thus revealing their true motivation to be protecting the grain market rather than safeguarding the health of the nation. The petition also introduced an argument that would soon become familiar – everything was fine so long as the drinking classes stuck to beer; it was when they started to drink spirits that things got out of hand.

Despite the power of the farming lobby, the petition was rejected and consumption of brandy continued unchecked.

All that changed with the Glorious Revolution of 1688, when James II was packed off to France and William III came over from Holland, bringing gin with him. Gin not only took its name from a Dutch word – "jenever" (juniper) – it came from Holland as well. William, keen to stimulate trade with his native country, decided to encourage his new subjects to switch from brandy to gin.

When England's monarchs have attempted to curb people's drinking habits, their efforts have – as we have seen already, and will see again – been a dismal failure. When, like William III, they have attempted to encourage people to drink more, they have succeeded beyond their wildest dreams. William not only persuaded the English to pour Dutch gin down their throats, he encouraged them to make it themselves. This was good news for the farming lobby, as gin, unlike brandy, was made from grain. William reckoned that, if he promoted the distillation of gin in England, there was a fair chance people would stop drinking brandy altogether. So, in 1690, he abolished the distillers' monopoly and announced that anyone could start a distillery by giving ten days notice to the excise.

Pandora's box had nothing on William's. By 1714, two million stills were in operation. By 1735, the number had shot up to five million. At the time, the population of England & Wales stood at just over six million. And, while you are reeling from the implications of that statistic, here's another to ponder. Production of spirits went up from half a million gallons a year in 1684, to two million by 1700, to five million by 1735, and to 20 million by the 1740s. That is over half a pint of gin a week for every man, woman and child in the country.

It did not take a genius to realise that things were rapidly getting out of hand. Stopping people knocking back gin was a lot more difficult than getting them to start. Legislation to cut production and raise prices only encouraged distillers to go underground. Illicit gin – closer to methylated spirits than to what we know as gin today – was invariably disgusting and often lethal. The gin distiller's art, purifying raw spirit by repeated distillation, flavouring it with juniper berries and leaving it to mature, eventually producing a liquor which slipped down like silk and imparted a warm glow of bonhomie and *joie de vivre* to the tippler, was for the toffs. Salt and quick lime could do the job in a fraction of the time. As for flavouring, there was no need for maturation. Chuck in a handful of something or other, give a quick stir, and stand well back. A recipe published in an eighteenth-century publican's handbook involved 120 gallons of raw spirit, a splash of turpentine, half an ounce of sulphuric acid, half an ounce of bitter almonds, a gallon of lime water, a gallon of rose water, eight ounces of alum and a pint of wine spirit. It would probably have had a kick like a rabid giraffe with an attitude problem. You would have risked blindness and who knows what else by drinking it, but one thing is beyond doubt. You would have ended up drunk. And if you think that sounds bad, imagine what the concoctions that did not make it into the recipe books were like.

As an escape from the terrifying realities of life at the bottom of the social heap, gin was cheap and oblivion was guaranteed. "It charms the unactive desperate and crafty of either sex," wrote one contemporary, "and makes the starving sot behold his rags and nakedness with stupid indulgence, or banter both in senseless laughter and more insipid jests." All too often, oblivion was permanent. Reports of people dying in their twenties and thirties from persistent drinking or an incautious binge – or from accidents caused by being paralytic – were commonplace.

All of this, of course, would have had an effect on beer, even if William had not upped the duty on it at the same time as opening the floodgates to cheap gin. Production of small beer, for example – staple fare for most people because of the dangers of drinking water – dropped by 12% between 1684 and 1710. Over the same period, gin consumption rose by 400%. In the early eighteenth century, if you were poor and wanted to get drunk, beer did not really come into the equation. In 1736, the *Daily Post* reported that, "for a halfpenny, a man may get a dram of gin, tho' he has not always three-halfpence to purchase a pint of porter." Hogarth's *Gin Lane* with its famous sign – "Drunk for a Penny, Dead Drunk for Two, Clean Straw for Free" – was not a joke but the reflection of a frightening reality. The less famous companion piece, *Beer Street*, which shows everybody happy and prosperous as they quaff tankards of wholesome, foaming ale, shows how bad things had got. Such a picture would have been unthinkable a century earlier, when beer was seen as the root of all evil. Compared with the gin menace, however, the bibulent days of befuddled Old England seemed a lost world of peace and plenty.

Although the impact of gin upon Bath has received little attention compared with the effect it had on London (largely because Bath's newspapers did not start until after the worst of the gin craze was over), there is no doubt that it was a social menace of the first order. In 1736, for example, when one of a series of draconian (and largely ineffective) anti-gin acts was passed, the London *Daily Gazette* reported the binge that preceded its implementation:

> It was observed that … several retailers' shops were well crowded, some tippling on the spot, whilst others were carrying it off from a pint to a gallon, and one of these shops had such a good trade that it put every cask they had upon the stoop, and the owner, with sorrowful sighs said, "is not this a barbarous and cruel thing that I must not be permitted to fill them again!" … Such has been the lamentations that on Wednesday night gin's funeral obsequies were performed with formality in several parishes and some of the votaries appeared in ragged clothes, some without, and others with one stocking … We hear from Bath that Mother Gin has been lamented in that city in much the same manner.

Two years later, when the magistrates attempted to control illegal gin-selling by offering bounties to informers, the *London Evening Post* reported that Bath had been troubled by "a vile fellow, who informed against fifteen persons for retailing spiritous liquors."

The novelist Henry Fielding, who was also a London magistrate, had no doubt that the dramatic increase in crime in the first half of the eighteenth century was due to gin. "Gin is the principal sustenance for more than 100,000 in [London]," he wrote in 1751. "Many of those wretches there are who swallow pints of this poison within 24 hours, the dreadful effects of which I have the misfortune every day to see, and to smell too." If his estimate was correct, that meant that one in seven Londoners were permanently out of their heads on gin. Not all of them would have been adults. Stories of children dying from a lethal draught were commonplace, and babies were often poisoned through their mother's milk.

Bath was second only to London as a resort for the beau monde (and the mauvais monde). From the late seventeenth century on, thousands of people flocked to the city, often from far afield, either in search of work or to beg or steal from wealthy visitors. As a result, a large proportion of the city's population were rootless. Many were in desperate circumstances. They were far more likely to be tempted into the self-indulgent oblivion of the gin bottle than people who were part of extended, settled families. On Holloway, where hundreds of vagrants were crammed into verminous, insanitary hovels, gin flowed freely. Death, whether accompanied by violence, starvation, drunkenness, disease or accident, was a frequent, and sometimes a welcome, visitor. The squalor of the lives eked out on that dark hill is beyond all imagining.

One striking feature of the gin menace is that it was associated, by those who sought to regulate it, with women rather than men. Witness the central figure in Hogarth's *Gin Lane* – a toothless, drunken hag, with a new-born babe falling from her heedless arms. Gin was personified as Madam Geneva, while beer – John Barleycorn – was held to represent all the solid, masculine virtues which the rise of gin had so enfeebled. "Almost at every herb stall," wrote a commentator in 1751, "[women] will find a private room backwards, where they may take their glass in secret very comfortably." Even today, gin still sometimes goes under the name of "Mother's Ruin."

The accusation that women were the chief victims of the gin epidemic was rubbish. Men drank as much gin as women, if not more so. The myth of female over-indulgence was, however, very convenient for the male-dominated establishment, who started a campaign of vilification against female drinkers. It was outstandingly successful. Even today a drunken man is far more acceptable – even though he may be shunned or treated as a figure of fun – than a drunken woman. Compare the honour paid to hell-raisers such as Oliver Reed, Richard Burton or Gazza with the attitude to a female celebrity who takes to the bottle. In the eighteenth century, as capitalism kicked in, the spectre of the drunken woman was one of a number of ways in which the establishment disempowered women.

Tracts warning about the dangers of women hitting the bottle were everywhere. "When a woman once takes to drinking, I give her over for lost," one writer declared in 1726. Hysterical stories of babies poisoned as they suckled at their mother's breast – although based on fact – were blown up out of all proportion. In 1737, the influential *Grub Street Journal* suggested a campaign to ban the sale of spirits to women. "The wives of genteel mechanicks," wrote one correspondent, "under pretence of going to prayers in their apartments, take a nap and a dram, after which they chew lemon peel to prevent from being smelt." Not all the writers of these tracts were men. In 1750, Elizabeth Haywood published *A Present for Women Addicted to Drinking, Adapted to All the Different Stations in Life, From a Lady of Quality to a Common Servant*. The

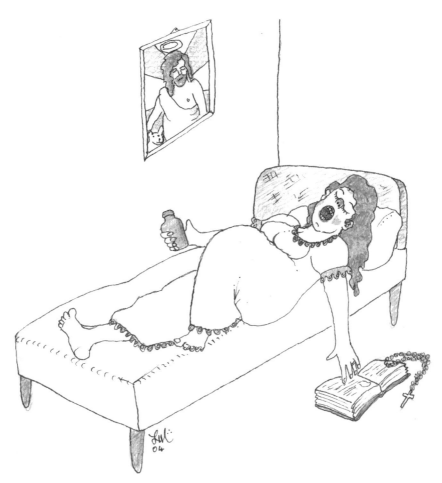

The wives of genteel mechanicks, under pretence of going to prayers in their apartments, take a nap and a dram

treatise was necessary, she declared, because of "the prodigious progress made by this vice of female drinking within these few years." Among the pastimes she suggested for young ladies who wished to kick the bottle were "painting, japanning, colouring of prints, or whatever else will fix the attention, and take off that inclination for indolence which made for the other vice." There were no such qualms two centuries earlier when Lady Percy had downed her liquid breakfast.

At the same time as all this was happening, however, major economic changes were taking place. Nowhere were they happening faster than in the brewing industry. Traditionally, brewing had been a small-scale, lowly occupation, generally carried out at the local alehouse. Many alehouse-keepers-cum-brewsters were women. There were common brewers, but these were the exception. Their ability to expand was limited by primitive technology. In the eighteenth century, however, a series of technological innovations made large breweries viable. There was big money to be made, but it was dependent on getting people to stop drinking beer brewed in the local alehouse and start drinking beer from breweries instead. And so the men whose capital was tied up in the breweries had to squeeze the small operators out, be they men, or – as was very often the case – women. One of the ways the new capitalists achieved their objectives – not just in brewing but across a wide range of trades and occupations – was by fostering a culture in which women ceased to have the economic freedom and power they had hitherto enjoyed. This is not to say that there was a golden age of equality before the eighteenth century – that is why women did jobs that men avoided, like alehouse keeping – but there were far more women in business, albeit in a small way, in 1750 than there were in 1850. The image of the weak woman, who would give into temptations like that of the gin bottle if left to her own devices, was brought to fruition by the grim-whiskered paterfamilias of Victorian England, but it had its roots in the England of Defoe and Fielding. And it was gin that helped to set the whole thing in motion.

The genie of gin fever was slowly squeezed back into the bottle William III had so casually uncorked by a whole raft of legislation, both local and national. It took a long time, however. In 1758, Henry Fielding's brother, John, wrote confidently that "gin is now so dear, or else so very bad, that good porter gains the pre-eminence, and I doubt not, but at year's end, there will be found a considerable increase in the consumption of that commodity." Thirty years later, however, Bath magistrates were still signifying "their determination to the retailers of spirits, that after the present year no licence would be granted, allowing the retail of spirits in small quantities; – so that the worst of all nuisances (the petty gin-shops) will, by this resolution, be abolished." The problem died down, but it never really went away, and there were still tragedies like this one reported in the *Bath Chronicle* in 1800:

> Monday, a boy about nine years of age in Walcot having got to a gin bottle, took
> so copious a draught as to cause his death within a few hours.

And then gin fever flared up again. Once again, the government was to blame. Calls for free trade led to drastic reductions in the tax on spirits in 1825. Within months, over 8,000 new spirit licences were taken out. Once again, gin was much cheaper than beer, and drunkenness soared.

Calls for abstinence in the early nineteenth century usually applied only to gin. Beer – taken in moderation – was seen not only as acceptable but as a means of weaning people off gin. The Duke of Wellington, as we shall see later, came up with a solution that not only made matters worse, but ended up by demonising beer as well. It was left to reformers like Charles Dickens to identify the real source of the problem:

> Gin drinking is a great vice in England, but wretchedness and dirt are greater,
> and until you improve the homes of the poor, or persuade a half-famished wretch
> not to seek relief in the temporary oblivion of his own misery, with the pittance,
> which divided among his family would furnish a morsel of bread for each,
> ginshops will increase in number and splendour.

He wrote that in 1836. It was to be another 40 years before gin consumption began to fall. When it did, it was due not to legislation, but, as Dickens had predicted, a gradual improvement in the condition of the working classes.

AWASH WITH ALE

CHAPTER SIX

AND THE WALLS CAME TUMBLING DOWN

> You must know that I find nothing but disappointment at Bath. which is
> so altered, that I can scarce believe it is the same place that I frequented
> about thirty years ago … This place, which Nature and Providence seem
> to have intended as a resource from distemper and disquiet, is become the
> very centre of racket and dissipation … A national hospital it may be, but
> one would imagine that none but lunatics are admitted; and truly, I will
> give you leave to call me so, if I stay much longer at Bath.
> *Tobias Smollett, Humphrey Clinker, 1771*

Smollett was not the only one to bemoan the rapid expansion of Bath in the
eighteenth century. Jonathan Swift, for example, wrote that:

> this town is grown to such an enormous size, that above half the day must be
> spent in going from one place to another. I like it every year less and less.

Fair enough, you may think, until you realise that he wrote it in 1736. Not only was
there no Royal Crescent – there was no Circus. Apart from a few houses in Gay
Street, there was little to the north or west of Queen Square except fields. There was
no Pulteney Bridge, and, if there had been, it would only have led to a few small
farms and cottages. Kingsmead Square and Avon Street were recently built, and they
too looked out over green fields. Widcombe, it is true, was a sizeable weaving town
in its own right, but it is hardly the sort of place Jonathan Swift would have visited.
His comments, though, serve as a benchmark for the massive expansion of the city
which occurred in the years following 1736.

Bath had survived the Civil War relatively unscathed. When Samuel Pepys visited
in 1668, he reported that "the walls of the city … are good, and the battlements all
whole." Bath was, in fact, one of the best preserved medieval and Tudor towns in
the country. Today, "best preserved" means listed building orders and heritage trails.
In those days, it meant ripe for development. John Evelyn probably spoke for the
majority when he described Bath's streets as "narrow, uneven and unpleasant."

The first half of the eighteenth century saw considerable development outside
the old city, but the walls – and the gates – remained in place. Then, in an orgy of
unfetterment, the Corporation sanctioned their demolition. The end came suddenly.

In January 1753, the Corporation was still discussing the possibility of constructing "footways" through the North, South and West Gates. Eighteen months later, they ordered them to be torn down. The South Gate went in 1755, the North Gate in 1764, and the West Gate in 1767. Only the little-used East Gate survived. It can still be seen at the head of a shuttered alley below the Empire Hotel.

By the mid-1700s, the walls, which only a century earlier had been strengthened as Parliamentarians fought Royalists for control of the kingdom, were an embarrassing anachronism. Bath's population had shot up to around 10,000, and there were more visitors than ever before. The city which John Wood had described as "a maze of only four or five hundred houses, crowded within an old wall in the vicinity of the Avon" had spread far beyond its original bounds.

George Trim started the ball rolling in 1707 by building Trim Street, with a bridge breaching the city wall. That was only the beginning. Kingsmead Square, Avon Street, St James's Parade, Beauford Square, Queen Square, Gay Street, North and South Parades all followed as speculators and builders vied with each other to erect ever-grander lodging houses for wealthy visitors. Even then, the Corporation proceeded with caution. When Daniel Milsom leased a plot of land by the city wall for building in 1739, it was "on condition that he [did] not build upon the town wall nor have any way out of the ground."

Nothing, however, could stop the city's relentless growth. The demolition of the gates spurred yet more development. By 1800, Bath's population stood at 33,000 – six times greater than it had been in 1700 – and it was the tenth largest city in the country.* Expansion outside the walls was matched by redevelopment within. Most of the redevelopment took place in a piecemeal way, rather than as part of some grand design, so that the ground plan of the medieval city, with its narrow streets and alleyways, survived largely intact while its buildings disappeared.

The buildings that were not pulled down were refronted. Conventional wisdom has it that the refronting of old buildings in the late Georgian period was carried out in order to bring them up to date. Analysis of council records from the period, however, suggests that this was rarely, if ever, the case. Old frontages came down so that buildings could be set back and streets widened. The majority of the old houses lining the city's principal streets – Broad Street, Cheap Street, Northgate Street, Stall Street, Upper Borough Walls, Walcot Street, and Westgate Street – were either rebuilt or refronted. As a result, even frontages from the early eighteenth century, such as that of the *Saracen's Head*, are rare. The streets that resulted may still have been narrower than the council would have liked, but they were a lot wider than they were before.

It was not only secular buildings which were rebuilt. All the medieval churches, except for the abbey, went as well. St James's was rebuilt in 1716, and again in 1768, St Michael's in 1742, and again in 1836. The disused church of St Mary's by

---

* To put this into some kind of perspective, Bath today is so far down the league table in terms of size that, even in the South West, it lags behind towns and cities such as Bristol, Plymouth, Swindon, Bournemouth, Poole, Cheltenham, Exeter and Gloucester.

AWASH WITH ALE

the Northgate was pulled down in 1771; the old chapel of St Michael's Within the Walls went around the same time. In 1803, at the end of a century of redevelopment, Robert Southey could write that, "if other cities are interesting as being old, Bath is not less so for being new. It has no aqueduct, no gates, castle or city walls, yet it is the finest and most striking town I have ever seen."

Seven years later, an American visitor remarked that Bath "is certainly very beautiful … We remarked a circular place called the Crescent, another called the Circus – all the streets straight and regular. This town looks as if it had been cast in a mould all at once; so new, so fresh, so regular."

Bath is still an endlessly fascinating city – even if it is no longer new. Wandering its streets, there is always some new perspective or architectural detail to see, some new trick of the light to admire. But just as fascinating is the knowledge that, in the dark earth below, lie the remains of another city, swept away in an orgy of enterprise to create the city we see today. The chances are that, if the old city had survived, it would still be a national treasure, but would lack the unique magnetism which has earned the city that replaced it world heritage status.

In the early stages of Bath's expansion, the growth in the number of alehouses more than kept pace with the increase in population. At the beginning of the eighteenth century, there were 58 inns and alehouses, one for every 86 people. By 1749, the number had rocketed to 150, one for every 67 people. That, however, marked the high point as far as pubs per person were concerned. While Bath's population continued to grow, the number of licensed premises started to fall. By 1760, there were only 136. Two years later, there were 120. After that the number started to creep back up again – to 129 by 1772, and to 163 by 1780. By 1798, however, it had fallen dramatically, to just 100. Two years later, the number had recovered somewhat, to 116, but that was still only one pub for every 284 people.

The decline in the number of Bath's pubs was mirrored in other cities. In Cambridge, for example, between 1792 and 1814, there was a net loss of 22 pubs. Had the number of pubs kept pace with the increase in Cambridge's population, it would have risen by around 200. We will look in a later chapter at the reasons for this decline in pub provision. For now, we will leave you with a final thought. In 1806, one in 31 houses in Bath was a pub. Although this may seem an incredible instance of over-provision to us, for a veteran drinker at the time it would have seemed a tragedy, for in 1743, a mere 63 years earlier, the ratio had been one in ten.

The number of alehouses may have declined in the eighteenth century, but another kind of licensed house – the coaching inn – went from strength to strength. In 1765, less than a century after the first regular coach service from London turned up at the *White Lion* after a journey of three days, the journey time was reduced to a single day. Admittedly, you had to leave at two o'clock in the morning and did not arrive until five in the afternoon, but it was a major improvement. In 1784, there was another major step forward, when John Palmer introduced mailcoaches, which took a mere 13 hours for the journey from London. The arrival of the first mailcoach was celebrated with a shindig at the *Three Tuns* in Stall Street:

Wednesday evening last, on account of Mr Palmer taking possession of his new appointment in the Post Office, several of his friends and promoters of the plan dined at the *Three Tuns* ... and spent the day with the greatest harmony and festivity. In the evening the house was superbly illuminated. The *Lamb Inn* was likewise as elegantly lit up, with a profusion of variegated lamps. Over the door a transparency was displayed, representing Fame blowing her trumpet, from which hung a scroll with this inscription – "May the Mailcoach ever flourish." In one of the windows an ingenious artist had made a Chinese sketch in which the Mailcoach was represented on full speed; at stated intervals a highwayman made his appearance with an intent to stop the coach – and on the guard firing his blunderbuss the man and his horse were seen to fall and lay sprawling on the ground. This device occasioned great entertainment to an immense crowd of spectators assembled on the occasion.

The primary function of today's inns and hotels is to provide accommodation and refreshment for visitors. The same was true of the inns which sprang up in the sixteenth century, taking over the role once performed by the monasteries. By the end of the eighteenth century, however, this function had taken a back seat. Fortunes were made by innkeepers, not from the accommodation they offered, but from the coaching services they operated. Most fashionable visitors to Bath used inns as little as possible, opting to stay in lodging houses instead. As early as 1700, Ned Ward, arriving on the coach from London, obtained lodgings for himself and his two lady companions on the day he arrived. Most other visitors only stayed at an inn on their first night in Bath unless they had difficulty getting lodgings. Some also put up at an inn on their last night if their coach left particularly early the next morning. It is likely that, in the late eighteenth and early nineteenth centuries, many of the larger coaching inns made little or no profit from their supposedly core functions of providing bed and board, using these instead to entice customers to use their coaches.

To find a modern comparison, we have only to look at railway stations. Large railway stations cost a lot to run, but railway companies make no money from them (apart from peripherals like buffet and newspaper franchises); they do, however (at least in theory) make money from the trains that run between stations and which could not operate unless the stations were there. It was much the same with many coaching inns, whose owners were less interested in the inns themselves than in the coaching businesses they could operate from them.

The coach services listed in the 1755 *Guide to Bath* were still rudimentary. There were two coaches a day to Bristol – from the *Angel* in Westgate Street and the *White Hart* in Stall Street. Coaches for London ran three times a week – on Mondays, Wednesdays and Fridays – from the *Lamb Inn* in Stall Street and the *White Hart*. They left at six in the morning and arrived at five o'clock on the following afternoon. During the summer, there was a coach to Exeter every Friday morning from the *Lamb Inn*, with an overnight stop at Bridgwater, and a coach to Oxford every Thursday from the *White Hart*, with an overnight stop in Cirencester. There were also two coaches a week to Salisbury from the *Full Moon* at the bottom of Southgate Street, which managed the journey in one day.

Demand frequently outstripped supply and there was often a lengthy wait to get a coach at popular times. The only alternative was to hire a private carriage, as the Rev James Woodforde discovered in 1775:

> The Bath Coach for tomorrow for Oxford is quite full, so that I forfeit my half-guinea that I paid some time back, and must go to Oxford some other way. However, I met with a young gentleman from Devon at my inn, who is going to Oxford, by name Coleridge of Ottery St Mary, and we agreed to take a chaise tomorrow between us for Oxford … He spent the evening with us at the *Angel Inn*.

By 1839, two years before the railway opened from London, services had been transformed beyond all recognition. Five inns ran coaches to London. There were two a day from the *Castle* in Northgate Street, two from the *Greyhound* in the High Street, three from the *White Hart* in Stall Street, three from the *York House Hotel* and six from the *White Lion* in the High Street, two of which were mailcoaches. Although a couple of services still included an overnight stop at Reading, most did the journey in a day, one taking only nine hours for the trip. Three services, including the two mailcoaches, only went by road as far as Twyford, from where passengers were conveyed to London by the Great Western Railway.

Mailcoach services no longer started from the *Three Tuns*, which had closed in 1804, but from the *White Lion*. The first of the day was the 5.30am to Bristol, which had travelled overnight from London. This was followed by the 6.30am to Falmouth. Another mailcoach from London arrived in the afternoon, going on to Bristol at 3.30pm. At 6pm the mailcoach for Birmingham and the north left, followed by the two mailcoaches to London which left at 8pm and 8.15pm, each taking a slightly different route.

Many of the other services from the *White Lion* were operated by named coaches. The *Sovereign* ran to Weston-Super-Mare at 7.30am, the *Rocket* to Southampton at 8pm, the *Vampire* to Exeter at 8.30pm, the *Phoenix* to Poole at 9pm, the *Wellington* to Weymouth at 9pm, the *Rose* to Clevedon at 2pm and the *Accommodation* to Chippenham at 5pm. There were also unnamed services to Cheltenham at midday, Devizes at 5.30pm, Brighton at 8.30pm and an hourly service to Bristol.

The *Golden Lion* in Southgate Street also had an hourly service to Bristol, as well as daily services to Southampton and Chippenham and two named coaches – the *Eclipse* and the *Age* – running to London.

The *White Hart* in Stall Street had twelve coaches leaving between 7.30am and 10am. The line-up was as follows:

7.30am	Cheltenham
8.00am	Brighton (with an overnight stop at Southampton)
8.00am	Falmouth
8.00am	London (in nine hours)
8.15am	York (by the *Mercury*)
8.30am	Poole (Mondays, Wednesdays & Fridays)

8.30am	Lyme Regis (Tuesdays, Thursdays and Saturdays)
9.00am	Oxford & Cambridge (by the *Colegian*)
9.00am	Portsmouth (by the *Celerity*)
9.45am	London (with an overnight stop at Reading)
10.00am	Holyhead (with overnight stops at Cheltenham & Shrewsbury)
10.00am	Weymouth (by the *John Bull*; Tuesdays, Thursdays and Saturdays)

Then, apart from hourly coaches to Bristol which continued throughout the day, there was a lull until 3pm, when a coach set off for Cheltenham, followed by one for Warminster at 6pm, an evening coach for Birmingham and the *Regulator* for London at 7.30pm.

But it was the *York House Hotel* which offered the most extensive service. Apart from fast coaches to London at 7.45am, 9.30am and 8.15pm, and departures for Bristol at 9.45am, midday, 12.45pm and 3pm, coaches for the following destinations left between 8.30am and 9.45am:

8.30am	Barnstaple
	Edinburgh
	Holyhead
	Lyme Regis
	Minehead
	Sidmouth
8.45am	Birmingham
	Holyhead
	Liverpool
	Plymouth
9.00am	Bridport
	Cirencester
9.30am	Oxford
9.45am	Worthing

The coaching era reached its height just before its demise. More people were travelling and the inns were busier than ever, but everybody knew that within a couple of years it would all be over, as passengers abandoned stagecoaches for the railway. There would, of course, have been people who carried on regardless, as though the railways would never be a serious contender for long-distance traffic, just as there were people who were convinced that the internet was a flash in the pan or that mobile phones would never be any more than a yuppie fashion accessory. But anyone with half a grain of sense knew that, as soon as the railway arrived, the coaching era was as good as over. It is hard to overestimate the effect the coming of the railway had on Bath. Overnight, it devastated not only the coaching business but also the inns that relied on that business.

The standard of inns and taverns had, of course, improved immeasurably since Celia Fiennes and her contemporaries made their pioneering journeys around the country. Dr Johnson, whose friend and biographer, James Boswell, stayed at a long-gone inn in Walcot Street called the *Pelican*, once said that "there is no private house in which people can enjoy themselves so well as at a capital tavern … You are sure you are welcome; and the more noise you make, the more trouble you give, the more good things you call for, the welcomer you are … No, Sir, there is nothing which has yet been contrived by man by which so much happiness is produced, as by a good tavern or inn."

Interesting that the great Dr Johnson should be an early proponent of kicking up a storm with a load of alcohol in his stomach. But here he is again on the joys of oblivion:

> As soon as I enter the door of a tavern, I experience an oblivion of care, and a freedom from solicitude; when I am seated, I find the master courteous and the servants obsequious to my call, anxious to know and ready to supply my wants; wine there exhilarates my spirits and prompts me to free conversation, and an interchange of discourse with those whom I must love; I dogmatise and am contradicted; and in this conflict of opinions and sentiments I find delight.

Exactly the sort of aggressive, argumentative, opinionated drunk you really want to bump into when you nip into the pub for a quiet drink – an eighteenth-century cross between Gyles Brandreth and Oliver Reed. That is not to say Dr Johnson was unaware of the effect alcohol could have. "Wine," he said on a different occasion, "makes a man better pleased with himself; I do not say that it makes him more pleasing to others." He also recognised that there was an art to being drunk, declaring that "a man who exposes himself when he is intoxicated has not the art of getting drunk." Difficult to argue with that.

What raised the good Doctor above his fellow tipplers is that he could not only put it away; he could justify putting it away in a manner that brooked no argument. Take this fabulous put-down recorded by his friend, the Reverend Percival Stockdale:

> I called on Dr Johnson one morning, when Mrs Williams, the blind lady, was conversing with him. She was telling him where she had dined the day before. "There were several gentlemen there," said she, "and when some of them came to the tea table, I found that there had been a good deal of hard drinking." She closed this observation with a common and trite moral reflection; which, indeed, is very ill-founded and does great injustice to animals: "I wonder what pleasure men can take in making beasts of themselves." "I wonder, madam," replied the Doctor, "that you have not penetration to see the strong inducement to this excess; for he who makes a beast of himself gets rid of the pain of being a man."

It is the sort of reply most people only think of on the bus home.

Although Dr Johnson was keen on taverns, he seems not to have been a fan of alehouses. In his *Dictionary* of 1755 he defined an alehouse as "a house where ale is publickly sold; a tippling house … distinguished from a tavern, where they sell wine." Fair enough, but them he appended to the definition a quotation from a writer called South:

There they sit promiscuously in common dirty rooms

One would think it should be no easy matter to bring any man of sense in love with an alehouse; indeed of so much sense, as seeing and smelling amounts to; there being such strong encounters of both, as would quickly send him packing, did not the love of good fellowship reconcile him to these nuisances.

The picture of Adriaen Brouwer's rustic drunkard quietly relieving himself into the corner of a smoke-filled alehouse seems to spring unbidden to mind when reading such descriptions. A few years earlier, in 1731, a visitor to England, Don Manuel Gonzales, summed up the difference between taverns and alehouses in terms that recall Mr South's description:

The principal taverns are large handsome edifices, made as commodious for the entertaining of a variety of company as can be contrived, with some spacious rooms for the accommodation of numerous assemblies. Here a stranger may be furnished with wines, and excellent foods of all kinds, dressed after the best manner; each company and every particular man, if he pleases, has a room to himself, and a good fire, if it be wintertime, for which he pays nothing, and is not to be disturbed or turned out of his room by any other man of what quality so ever, till he thinks fit to leave it.

And though the taverns are very numerous yet alehouses are much more so, being visited by the inferior tradesmen, mechanics, journeymen, porters, coachmen, carmen, servants and others whose pockets will not reach a glass of wine. There they sit promiscuously in common dirty rooms, with large fires, and clouds of tobacco, where one that is not used to them can scarce breathe or see; but as they are a busy sort of people they seldom stay long, returning to their several employments, and are succeeded by fresh sets of people of the same rank of men at their leisure hours all day long.

Or, as another writer put it, less charitably, four years earlier:

The vile obscene talk, noise, nonsense and ribaldry discourses together with the fumes of tobacco, belchings and other foul breakings of wind, that are generally found in an ale-room ... are enough to make any rational creature amongst them almost ashamed of his being. But all this the rude rabble esteem the highest degree of happiness and run themselves into the greatest straits imaginable to attain it.

Smell was indeed a problem in the eighteenth century. If we could travel back 250 years, it would be the first thing we would notice. And it would not just be a nasty niff. It would hit us like a wall and have us fumbling for the fast forward button to carry us retching back to the twenty-first century. Matthew Bramble, in Tobias Smollett's *Humphrey Clinker*, gives us an idea what Bath smelt like in 1771. There was, he wrote,

a compound of villainous smells, in which the most violent stinks, and the most powerful perfumes, contended for the mastery. Imagine to yourself a high exalted essence of mingled odours, arising from putrid gums, imposthumated lungs, sour flatulencies, rank armpits, sweating feet, running sores and issues, plasters, ointments, and embrocations, Hungary Water, Spirit of Lavender, Asafoetida Drops, musk, hartshorn, and sal volatile; besides a thousand frowsy steams, which I could not analyse. Such, O Dick! is the fragrant ether we breathe in the polite assemblies of Bath.

That was in the Assembly Rooms. Outside, and especially in the streets leading down to the river, where horses and pigs – as well as humans – answered the call of nature willy-nilly, and dead cats and dogs rotted in the gutters – the smell was much, much worse. But, for the most odious odours of all, you would have to creep down to some dank alley's end, where, in a drinking hovel far beyond the rule of law, the full implication of the eighteenth-century's ignorance of hygiene would break over you like a brown tsunami.

But, if we could get over the smell, we would find a city which was growing at an unprecedented rate. Bath boomed in the eighteenth century for three reasons – first, there were the hot springs and the tourist industry, stimulated by royal patronage, which had sprung up around them; second, was Bath's proximity to Bristol, England's main port and the conduit through which much of the country's wealth flowed; third was the rise of a wealthy middle-class. We tend to think of eighteenth-century Bath in aristocratic terms – and indeed many aristocrats did come to Bath – but the main point about it was that anybody with enough money (or, like Beau Nash, with enough cunning) could make it in Bath. London society was hidebound by centuries of tradition, much of it centered on the Royal Court. Bath was a blank slate on which the rules had yet to be written, its King an upstart Welshman with a talent for gambling. Here is Matthew Bramble's opinion of Bath society:

> Every upstart of fortune, harnessed in the trappings of the mode, presents himself at Bath, as in the very focus of observation. Clerks and factors from the East Indies, loaded with the spoil of plundered provinces; planters, negro-drivers, and hucksters, from our American plantations, enriched they know not how; agents, commissaries, and contractors, who have fattened in two successive wars, on the blood of the nation; usurers, brokers, and jobbers of every kind; men of low birth and low breeding, have found themselves suddenly translated into a state of affluence, unknown to former ages: and no wonder that their brains should be intoxicated with pride, vanity, and presumption. Knowing no other criterion of greatness but the ostentation of wealth, they discharge their affluence, without taste or conduct, through every channel of the most absurd extravagance; and all of them hurry to Bath, because here, without any further qualification, they can mingle with the princes and nobles of the land. Even the wives and daughters of low tradesmen, who, like shovel-nosed sharks, prey upon the blubber of those uncouth whales of fortune, are infected with the same rage of displaying their importance; and the slightest disposition serves them for a pretext to insist upon being conveyed to Bath, where they may hobble country-dances and cotillons among lordlings, squires, counsellors, and clergy ... Such is the composition of what is called fashionable company at Bath; where a very inconsiderable proportion of genteel people are lost in a mob of impudent plebians who have neither understanding nor judgement, nor the least idea of propriety or decorum; and seem to enjoy nothing so much as an opportunity of insulting their betters.
>
> Thus the number of people and the number of houses continue to increase; and this will ever be the case, till the streams that swell this irresistible tide of folly and extravagance shall either be exhausted, or turned into other channels, by incidents and events which I do not pretend to foresee.

For substantial periods during the eighteenth century, Bath resembled nothing so much as a succession of massive building sites. The amount of money spent on the buildings of eighteenth-century Bath was roughly equal to that spent on building the cotton mills which fuelled much of the growth in Britain's economy during the same period. In November 1788, for example, the *Bath Chronicle* reported that there were "no less than 2,000 new houses in projection, besides those that are actually begun."

Although Bath portrayed itself as a place of refinement, where the sick could regain their health amid scenes of wholesome civility, the reality was somewhat different. Take this description of what the city was like under Captain Webster, Beau Nash's predecessor as Master of Ceremonies:

> He was no sooner invested with the title and authority of Master of Ceremonies than, after in 1704 organising a series of balls at the Town Hall at half a guinea a head, he proceeded to provide facilities for gaming. The effect of this move was immediate. The spirit of gaming daily increased, and the common people

soon became intoxicated with the same notion. They neglected their ordinary occupations, resorting to public-houses, and spent their time in an idle and dissolute manner. They became riotous and intemperate; frequent disturbances happened between the inhabitants and gentlemen's servants; and at that time the common people entertained a notion that Bath was a lawless place, and that no Act of Parliament extended or had power to enforce laws beyond King's-Down Hill. On this supposition they continued their unlawful proceedings for some time with impunity.

Under Beau Nash things improved drastically, but eighteenth-century Bath was certainly no place for the faint-hearted. Take, for example, the festivities to celebrate George II's coronation in 1727. Bearing in mind that poverty and malnutrition were endemic, it was clearly asking for trouble to carry a huge roasting dish, twelve feet long and six feet wide, containing a whole oxen, into the middle of the Market Place. But, just to ensure that things got out of hand,

> there was a great deal of money stuck into the ox as it was roasting, and about 100 rich stones, which made the populace so eager to come to the cutting of it up, that they jumpt over the gentlemen's shoulders, some whereof got into the very dish, and were over shoes in gravy; one of them being more eager than the rest was thrust into the belly of the ox and almost smother'd, and the fat flew about in such a plentiful manner, that the gentlemen were obliged to quit the table.

Next time somebody tells you that the eighteenth century was an age of genteel refinement, just read them that passage, and wait for the fat to fly.

The rich and famous, who visited the Pump Room and the Assembly Rooms, and whose stories have come down to us in memoirs, novels and diaries, formed only a tiny proportion of those who came to Bath. They were outnumbered – hundreds of times over – by those who came to serve or profit from them. They ranged from middle-class tradesmen and craftsmen, through servants and coachmen, down to vagabonds, prostitutes and beggars. Few of them left any memorial behind them and they are seldom discussed, except in passing, in histories of eighteenth-century Bath.

What united the vast majority of them, however, was a love of drinking. The alehouses or taverns they frequented would have ranged from highly respectable establishments, where friendly societies met, to low dives where drunkenness were endemic and standards of hygiene would have put your average pigsty to shame. Much public house trade came from domestic servants and coachmen. Pubs gave servants the chance of companionship and an opportunity to swap stories. John MacDonald, in his *Memoirs of an Eighteenth-century Footman*, recalls a typical evening at the pub:

> I was one of the company, which was very genteel, from noblemen and gentlemen's houses ...The evening was spent very agreeably by the company at country dances, cards and drinking. Supper was at eleven o'clock. After supper the company came into the drawing-room and began again.

That particular pub was run by an ex-servant. Many domestic staff made the transition from servant to publican. This was hardly surprising. Not only were there thousands of servants in Bath, but their skills were ideally suited to running pubs. A correspondent in the *Morning Post* in 1777 noted how "the menial servant, tired of his master's company and midnight revels, becomes the landlord of a snug public house." Many ex-servants who had taken pubs advertised their previous occupations and employers in the Bath papers as a form of testimonial. There was a degree of one-upmanship in all of this, and an implication that, if you supped at a particular tavern, you would be treated, if not like a lord, at least like a member of the minor gentry.

In 1819, Pierce Egan remarked on the high standards of Bath's better pubs:

> Eating houses or cooking shops, which are so numerous in London, are not to be found in Bath. Throughout the whole city there are not above three in number, and those with inferior accommodation. The visitors, in general, are of too high a cast to encourage such *pauvre restaurateurs*. Several of the public houses have good ordinaries.

It was not just the better class of servants who took to running pubs as a reviewer of Patrick Colquhoun's *Observations and Facts Relative to Public Houses* pointed out in 1797:

> When we consider who are the sort of persons who occupy public houses of every sort, from the best inn on the Bath Road to the lowest small-beer pothouse, or hedge alehouse, they are servants of all descriptions; the butler and the housekeeper, the footman and the lady's maid, the coachman and the cook, the gardener and the dairyman, the groom, or stable boy, with the nursery-maid, or kitchen-maid, the carter and the ploughboy with maidservants of their own rank, whether they have acquired an independent competency by cheating their masters and mistresses, or by long and faithful service, all direct their settlements for life to a public house.

Waiters from Bath's inns and assembly rooms also took their skills with them and opened pubs. At the lower end of the spectrum, tradesmen such as shoemakers, carpenters, or blacksmiths also supplemented their incomes by selling beer. At the bottom of the heap were those establishments where the sale of alcohol was very much a sideline and most of the income came from criminal activities. Running a house of ill repute was a favourite activity, as was running a gambling den, but there were many others.

Many pubs catered for two – strictly segregated – classes of customer: respectable tradesmen in the parlour, the hoi-polloi in the tap room. The *Cross Keys* in the Orange Grove, with criminals on the ground floor and policeman on the first, was a particularly notorious example, but there were many others. An Italian visitor to England in 1669 wrote that, "there are an infinite number of beershops where every sort of drink in the country is sold; of these I have counted as many as 32 kinds. These places are not very extravagant and they are almost to be found full downstairs, crowded with the rabble, and upstairs with every condition of man from artisan to gentleman."

Such segregation applied right across the board. Most of Bath's larger inns, as they expanded, opened establishments called taps nearby, for servants, liverymen, and tradesmen. These were pubs in their own right and often licensed separately.

Criminals on the ground floor and policeman on the first ...

Some of them simply took the name of the inn they were attached to, such as the *White Lion Tap* and the *York House Tap*. Others had names which indicated the type of clientele they catered for, such as the *Jolly Footman* or the *Horse & Groom*. The *White Hart Inn* in Stall Street boasted two taps – the *Jolly Footman* and the *Sadler's Arms* – catering for two distinct classes of servant.

The use of the word tap – which survives in the name of the *Bath Tap* in St James's Parade – harks back to the days before bars and beer engines, when beer barrels were lined up against the wall of one of the less prestigious rooms in an inn and "tapped." Beer was carried from this room to the other, more comfortable, public rooms, while those who had only nipped in for a quick pint or were too muddy or scruffy to be allowed to mix with more respectable customers stood and drank it on the spot. By a logical progression, alehouses which catered for the kind of people who frequented taps were called taps as well. Even when beer engines and beer cellars started to appear, the word tap continued to refer to bars or pubs where the sartorially or olfactorily challenged were expected to drink. Very few tap rooms have survived, but at least two can still be seen in rural Somerset – one in the splendid pub at Huish Episcopi, near Langport, officially known as the *Rose & Crown* but universally referred to as *Eli's*, and another at *Tucker's Grave*, the miraculously preserved roadside cider house between Faulkland and Norton St Philip.

As well as licensed houses, there were unlicensed ones. At the beginning of the eighteenth century, unlicensed premises almost certainly outnumbered licensed ones, especially in rural areas. In Bath and other cities it was more difficult to get away with it, but you did not have to go very far outside the city walls to find an unlicensed house. In the stews of Avon Street they would have been thick on the ground as well. They were known, for obvious reasons, as "hush shops." In 1735, the Corporation, clearly worried about the amount of unlicensed drinking, came up with a solution that has a curiously modern ring to it. They agreed:

> that the present Mayor and his successors shall for the future be indemnified … for granting his warrants for distraining the goods of any person who sells ale without licence within the jurisdiction of this city, or of suppressing such alehouse that shall prove disorderly.

But, while unlicensed houses – and many licensed ones – were dens of darkness and iniquity, almost unchanged from the sort of place run by Eleanor Rumming, at the more respectable end of the market things got markedly better. During the reign of George II, partitions began to appear in alehouses. Some alehouses acquired stables and started operating as inns. Others were adopted as meeting places by Jacobite clubs, masonic lodges, friendly societies, trade associations and political parties. The distinctions between alehouses, inns and taverns started to blur.

Despite the fabulous wealth which fuelled Bath's expansion in the eighteenth century, poverty was an ever-present problem. Beggars were everywhere, and despite a policy of zero tolerance, backed up by floggings and imprisonment, they did not go away. Eighteenth-century law enforcement was harsh. In 1767, for example, "two men, who had been begging for some time in this city, pretending to be lame, etc., were whipped out of town … having been found to be notorious imposters."

The problem was that other towns and cities had harsh regimes as well, and with such rich pickings on offer in Bath, it is hardly surprising that beggars kept returning. Their descendants were still coming back a century later, trying everything in their power to gain sympathy. In 1828, for example, "a man who was exposing his diseased feet in Norfolk Crescent … to excite compassion [was] committed by the magistrates to three months imprisonment." Eleven years later, a new technique, roundly condemned by the *Bath Chronicle*, was being used – children sent out to beg by their parents. Despite the draconian measures taken to deal with the problem, it refused to go away. In December 1851, for example, the *Bath Chronicle* reported that "the police have been engaged during the last fortnight in ridding the city of the swarm of beggars who had apparently settled here for the season. Several of them have been committed to prison as incorrigible, while a larger number have decamped."

AWASH WITH ALE

Although poverty was constantly present in eighteenth-century Bath, there was generally enough work – and enough money – around to ensure that most people managed to keep body and soul together. That changed in the last decade of the century. In March 1793, the Bath City Bank in the Abbey Churchyard temporarily stopped payment because of a "late general run on the house." A week later, the Bath & Somersetshire Bank failed and Bath was plunged into the worst financial crisis in its history. Virtually all building work stopped, money ceased to flow and thousands were thrown out of work. The reasons for the crisis were, as always, complex. A major factor was the cost of the war with France, which was to continue, on and off, until 1815. But there was another factor, unique to Bath. High Society, led by the Prince Regent, had discovered the joys of Brighton. Bath was no longer the most fashionable place in the country. It had always been a juggling act, maintaining the city's reputation as the top British resort. Now, suddenly toppled from the number one spot, it faced an uncertain future. The turnaround in its fortunes could not have come at a worse time.

Although the well-to-do suffered in the slump, many of them experiencing spectacular bankruptcies, it was, as always, the poor who suffered most. To make matters worse, there were a series of bad harvests and severe winters. By 1801, the price of a loaf of bread had risen to one shilling and eleven pence – more than a labourer's daily wage. At the time, around 3,000 pounds of flour was used in Bath every week by the gentry to powder their hair. If it had been used to make bread, it would have fed around 600 starving people. That gives some idea of the gulf between rich and poor in what, it is salutary to remind ourselves, was Jane Austen's Bath. Poor relief on an unprecedented scale had to be organised so that people did not starve in the streets or freeze to death in their hovels. In 1801, for example, "four tons of rice, convertible, when dressed, into twenty tons of food, were distributed in weekly portions among three thousand poor families." To this was added 60,000 quarts of soup, 200 sacks of potatoes and 317 tons of coal.

This was the Bath Jane Austen didn't write about. The gulf between the people she associated with and those at the bottom of the heap is, for us, unimaginable. The poor had nothing to look forward to, no dignity, no cause for hope, no prospect of comfort. Francis Place, "the radical tailor of Charing Cross," summed up the condition of the working man in the early nineteenth century as follows:

> None but the animal sensations are left [to him]; to these his enjoyments are limited, and even these are frequently reduced to two – namely sexual intercourse and drinking … It is not easy for any one who has not himself been a working man, accurately to estimate the agreeable sensations produced by the stimulus of strong liquor … yet so constant are these effects, that he who has scarcely any other means of excitement producing enjoyment, will in almost all cases … endeavour to produce them as often as he has the power, and dares venture to use it.

Bath was the first place in the country to be dependent on a seasonal economy based on tourism. It was originally a winter resort. In the early eighteenth century, its season ran from October to March, when fashionable society decamped to Tunbridge Wells for the summer. Although the notion of a season grew less rigid as the century progressed, as late as 1771, Jeremy Melford, in Smollett's *Humphrey Clinker*, could write in mid May that,

> The music and entertainments of Bath are over for this season, and all our gay birds of passage have taken their flight to Bristolwell, Tunbridge, Brighthelmstone [Brighton], Scarborough, Harrowgate, etc. Not a soul is to be seen in this place, but a few broken-winded parsons, waddling like so many crows along the North Parade.

Bath in the summertime was all but deserted, with August – as Joseph Haydn found when he visited in 1794 – being the quietest month of all.

When the leaves began to fall, the rich visitors returned, bringing with them not only their servants, but a caravanserai of hangers-on, ranging from the eminently respectable (tradesmen, portrait painters, dancing masters, and the like) to the eminently unrespectable (mountebanks, beggars, prostitutes, and so on). When the rich visitors left at the end of the season, many of those who had followed them – especially those at the less desirable end of the spectrum – stayed behind, unable or unwilling to leave. With the rich no longer around, they lacked the wherewithal to support themselves. The tradesmen had no one to sell to, the beggars no one to beg from. The prospect of the eventual return of the *beau monde* was enough, in many cases, to sustain them, but when the *beau monde* started to tire of Bath, the future suddenly looked very grim indeed.

Two hundred years ago, Bath faced an uncertain future, with long-term decline a distinct possibility. It is something that many British seaside resorts have experienced in the last 50 years, as visitors have decamped to warmer climes, and once grand hotels and refined guest houses have been turned into bed and breakfast hostels or seedy flats.

There were parts of Bath which, due to a combination of bad planning and bad luck, suffered a decline just as dramatic in the eighteenth century. Rows of houses built south of the old city walls, in the first wave of expansion, as lodgings for fashionable visitors, rapidly became slums as the problem of their proximity to the river became apparent. They were quickly superseded by better lodgings built on the hills north of the city. Although Bath never lost popularity or gentility to the extent that many once popular seaside resorts have done, by the early nineteenth century the bad parts of Bath were as bad as anything you could have found anywhere. Here, to give some idea what they were like, are some extracts from a Government Report on the "Sanatory Condition" of Bath in 1845:

> There is no plan of Bath, with proper levels, for building, sewerage, or other structural purposes. There are Commissioners for the out-parish of Walcot, who have powers under a local act to construct sewers, and somewhat more than one-fifth of the city comes under their jurisdiction for this purpose. For the remainder of the city there is a total absence of public powers for drainage and sewerage, a singular state of things for so large a town …
>
> The upper part of the city is well drained; but several streets in the lower part, from their situation and from negligence, are insufficiently drained.

There are sewers, but imperfect.

Many poor houses are defective in necessaries.

There are no public necessaries.

Many house drains bad.

The drains are covered but frequently obstructed …

Some of the courts and alleys were found dirty and ill-cleaned, and cabbage leaves, peas-cods, and other refuse of that kind thrown into them …

In the worst houses [there are] twelve families, frequently four persons in a room …

Perhaps the most telling statistic in the report comes near the end, where the average age of death for the various classes in the city is listed. For the gentry it was 59, for tradesmen it was 32, and for artisans and labourers it was 31. These figures, shocking though they are, are misleading because of the incidence of infant mortality. The rich, better fed, better housed and better looked after, did live longer, but the average working man or woman – if they reached maturity – could expect to live well into their fifties, if not longer. Infant mortality among the working classes, however, was appallingly high. In Lyncombe & Widcombe, the worst area, almost 50% of children died before they were five years old. Well over a third died before their first birthday. Immediate causes of death included "convulsions, asphyxia, bowel complaint, consumption and inflammation of the chest," but the real causes were, of course, the filthy conditions most of them had to endure, with chronic malnourishment thrown in for good measure. You wonder if people who call for a return to Victorian values really know whereof they speak.

A Bengalese, dressed in the costume of his country,
was charged with creating a disturbance

CHAPTER SEVEN

IMMIGRANTS

Karew Laffin, a Bengalese, dressed in the costume of his country, was charged with creating a disturbance at the *White Lion Tap* [in Bridge Street], and resisting the police. The defendant complained of being ill-used in the house, but a policeman stated that he saw him taking liberties with a young woman. He was discharged on promise of leaving the town.

Bath Chronicle, 2 July 1846

Karew Laffin's ejection from Bath is not as untypical as may be thought. Many itinerant travellers who turned up in the city soon moved on, helped on their way by harsh vagrancy laws. Throughout history, the authorities in Bath have taken a dim view of impecunious visitors – especially when they got drunk and made a nuisance of themselves. In the early seventeenth century, the Corporation even established a Bridewell or House of Correction at the top of what is still called Bridewell Lane. Here paupers from outside Bath were subjected to a prison-like regime to encourage them to leave the city. Despite the Corporation's efforts, however, they still kept coming – and many of them stayed.

Immigration – as opposed to invasion – really only got under way after the Norman Conquest. The first group of immigrants to turn up in any significant number were French Jews. In the two centuries following the Norman Conquest, Jews were vital to the English economy. This was because the medieval church regarded usury – otherwise known as moneylending – as a sin. Christians who became moneylenders risked social exclusion and eternal damnation. Given those sort of disincentives, it is not surprising that few Christians chose moneylending as a career. This created a problem for people who wanted to borrow money. The solution was simple – borrow money off Jews. In the twelfth and thirteenth centuries, Jewish immigrants established themselves as moneylenders in major towns and cities throughout the kingdom. Some became very rich. They also became increasingly unpopular. It was less a question of religious intolerance, more one of high rates of interest and what was regarded as sharp practice.

Today, dissatisfaction with financial institutions leads to a letter to the banking ombudsman. In the thirteenth century, action was more direct. Growing persecution culminated in 1290, with Edward I's expulsion of all Jews – who by then numbered around 15,000 – from the country. The ban on Jewish immigration was only lifted by Oliver Cromwell over 350 years later, in 1655.

In the late seventeenth century, Jewish immigrants again started to settle in Bath. Many more passed through as itinerant salesmen. Among them was one Hart Jacob, a Jewish jeweller, who had his entire stock stolen while staying at the *White Hart* in Avon Street in 1764. The thief was another foreigner – "Joseph Manuel, about 17 years of age, with black hair, had on a light-coloured coat, patched with many colours, a very old hat and speaks very bad English." In 1830, a visitor to Bath recorded a visit to another lodging house:

> Many of the lodgers were in the room; they were chiefly Jew pedlars occupied in relating the various successes of the day. Some of them were Poles.

The Jewish community in the city grew to such an extent that, in the 1820s, a synagogue was opened in the old theatre in Kingsmead Street. This, like the purpose-built synagogue opened in Corn Street in 1842, has long gone, and the only tangible reminder of the Jewish presence in Bath in the nineteenth century is the Jewish cemetery next to the *Forester's Arms* at Combe Down.

After the expulsion of the Jews in 1290, moneylending was taken over by Italian merchants from Lombardy, who laid the foundations of modern banking. The Lombards dominated the European wool trade in the late middle ages. Bath's pre-eminence as a wool and weaving centre means that Lombards, as well as merchants from other parts of Europe, must have been regular visitors to the city. Some of them may even have settled here.

In the early fourteenth century, large numbers of weavers from the Low Countries, fleeing warfare and religious persecution, also started to settle in England. By the mid-fifteenth century, they numbered around 16,000 – almost one percent of the population. Many of them settled in East Anglian weaving towns, which had strong trading links with the Low Countries. A significant number, however, made their way to weaving centres in the West of England, including Bath. The Jews and the Lombards had made no discernible impact on English drinking habits. This new wave of immigrants, however, was to have an enormous impact.

The beer they were used to at home contained hops. English ale, on the other hand, was unhopped. Finding the native brew not to their taste, they started brewing their own, importing hops from the Low Countries to do so. For a time, drinking this new style of beer was confined to the immigrant community, but soon increasing numbers of Englishmen started to acquire a taste for it as well. Hops did not just flavour beer. They also clarified the wort, gave the beer a good head, and helped it keep longer. It was this last characteristic that found it friends in high places. Supplying armies in the field meant, among other things, ensuring that they had enough to drink. It was clearly preferable to provide them with beer, which lasted several weeks, rather than ale, which lasted only a few days. So when London's ale brewers, concerned about competition from immigrant beer brewers, started a rearguard action against hopped beer, no less a person than Henry VI came to its defence:

All brewers of biere [are] to continue to exercise their art as hitherto, notwithstanding the malevolent attempts that were being made to prevent natives of Holland and Seland and others who occupied themselves in brewing the drink called biere from continuing their trade, on the ground that such drink was poisonous and not fit to drink, and caused drunkenness, whereas it was a wholesome drink, especially in summer time.

With that sort of backing, it is hardly surprising that hopped beer swept all before it. Even the size of beer barrels changed. The English ale barrel of 30 or 32 gallons was replaced by the standard Dutch barrel which held 36 gallons. Although we may regard kilderkins and firkins – the terms used for half-size and quarter-size barrels – as quaint old English terms they come from the Dutch words kinderkin and vierdekijn.

Hopped beer did not replace unhopped ale overnight. William Shakespeare – ever the traditionalist – only mentions beer four times in his plays, while ale gets 16 mentions.* Yet beer had many advocates – take Reynold Scot's 1574 treatise, *A Perfite Platforme for a Hoppe Garden*:

If your ale may endure a fortnight, your beer through the benefit of the hop shall continue a month, and what grace it yieldeth to the taste, all men may judge that have sense in their mouths. And if controversy be betwixt beer and ale, which of them shall have the place of pre-eminence, it sufficeth for the glory and commendation of the beer that, here in our own country, ale giveth place unto it and that most of our countrymen do abhor and abandon ale as a loathsome drink.

John Gerard, in his *Herbal* of 1597, also weighed in on the side of beer:

The manifold vertues in hops do manifestly argue the holesomeness of beere above ale; for the hops rather make it a phisicall drink to keepe the body in health, than an ordinarie drinke for the quenching of our thirst.

There were, inevitably, some dissenting voices. Andrew Boorde, for example, a founder member of Ye Campaigne for Reale Ale, sixteenth-century style, would have none of it. Ale, he wrote, in his *Dietary of Health* of 1542,

is made of malte and water; and they the which do put in any other thynge to ale than is rehersed, except yest, barme or godesgood, doth sofysticat theyr ale. Ale for an Englysche man is a naturall drinke. Ale must have these propertyes: it must be fresshe and cleare, it muste not be ropy or smoky, nor it must have no weft or tayle. Ale should not be dronke under five days olde.

Beer, on the other hand,

is made of malte, of hoppes, and water; it is the naturall drynke for a Dutche man, and now of late dayes it is much used in England to the detryment of many Englysshe people; specially it killeth them the which be troubled with the colyke; and the stone and the strangulion; for the drynke is a cold drynke, yet it doth make a man fat, and doth inflate the bely, as it doth appere by the Dutch men's faces and belyes.

Not surprisingly, given such entrenched opinions, it took over 200 years for hops

---

* Ale, however, is overshadowed by wine, which he mentions 73 times.

to be universally accepted. Even late in the eighteenth century, some drinkers were still fighting a rearguard action in support of unhopped beer. According to the Bath Chronicle of 17 September 1789, John Wesley was among them:

> In the reign of James I, says Mr Wesley, an Act of Parliament was passed "prohibiting the use of that poisonous weed called hops." Though this act has not been repealed, the use of this poisonous weed has been again introduced, and is continued on a general supposition that it is very wholesome and that malt drink will not keep without it. Mr Wesley considers the use of hops for preventing malt liquor turning sour as absolutely palpable a falsehood as ever was palmed upon mankind. He has himself proved that ale brewed without hops has kept for six months as well as that with hops; and insists that neither hops nor any other bitter is necessary to preserve it for any length of time.
>
> Forty years ago, Mr Wesley says, not a quarter of the hops was used that there are at present, and the ale then had a soft, sweetish taste, such as a decoction of barley unadulterated should have; but which is now rendered harsh, bitter and unwholesome. Wort is well known to be an excellent remedy for the scurvy, gout and stone; with the addition of hops this excellent remedy is turned to poison ... He considers the revenue raised by hops as a poor compensation for the loss of thousands of his Majesty's subjects by the grievous and mortal diseases caused by their use.

The earliest beer brewers used hops imported from the Low Countries. The ban on hops mentioned by Wesley was, in fact, no such thing. Officially described as "an acte for avoyding of deceit in selling, buying or spending corrupt or unwholesome hoppes," it was aimed at importers bringing "impure hops" into the country. It was estimated at the time that English brewers were being defrauded to the tune of around £20,000 a year, which gives some idea of the scale of the hop import market. It took some time for English growers to master the art of hop cultivation, but, when they did, the import trade gradually dwindled away. For a time, hops were grown wherever the climate allowed. Bath had a "hop meadow" on the Lower Bristol Road in Bath, just past the *Belvoir Castle*, although there is no record of when it was established, nor, indeed, of when it ceased production. Hops from certain areas of the country soon came to be favoured by brewers, however. In 1762, for example, hops from Farnham in Surrey were advertised for sale in Bath at the *White Swan* near St Michael's Church. Despite its name, this was not a pub, but a grocery-cum-off-licence which supplied spirits, tobacco, cheese and butter to the trade. By the late eighteenth century, hop growing was confined to a few counties where conditions were especially favourable. Records from 1835 show that 60% of British hops were grown in Kent, 31% in Sussex, and 6% in Herefordshire. Other counties (among which Somerset did not feature) contributed a mere 3%.

In the sixteenth and early seventeenth centuries, immigrants from the Low Countries were followed by refugees from France. Around 80,000 Huguenot refugees arrived in this country between 1560 and 1720. Although they had no impact on the history of beer drinking, they brought with them, not surprisingly, a predilection for wine. Many Huguenots settled in Bath. Among them was a young woman called Sally Lunn who settled in Lilliput Alley and supplied rolls to Spring Gardens. Others included a jeweller called Pierre Goulett, and Monsieur Phillott, whose grandson became a prominent member of the Corporation and the landlord of the *Bear Inn* in Cheap Street.

Another group of immigrants, who began to arrive in small numbers from the mid-sixteenth century onward, as the slave trade got under way, came from Africa. Although very few of them settled in England, there were still too many for Elizabeth I. In 1601, she called for the "great number of negars and blackamoores which are crept into this realm, most of them infidels, who are fostered and relieved here to the great annoyance of her own liege people [to be] with all speed avoided and discharged out of this Her Majesty's dominions."

Elizabeth's attempt to stem the tide of immigration from Africa failed, and by the beginning of the eighteenth century there were around 20,000 Africans in England. Most of them were living in London and the major ports, although a significant number lived in Bath. Some were the servants of wealthy visitors whose money came from sugar plantations in the West Indies – like the "two negroes, belonging to a Creole gentlemen," who disturbed the rest of Smollett's Matthew Bramble by playing French horns outside his room. What little we know of them comes from snippets like this from the Bath Journal of 10 February 1755:

> Wednesday last a black girl (servant to a gentleman in the square) was buried at Walcot Church. There were six black men to support the pall, and several others of the same complexion attended the corpse as mourners.

Three years later, the *Bath Journal* carried a laconic, and rather chilling advertisement:

> Thirteen-year-old negro boy for sale, enquire Mr Budge, Coach Maker.

Even more disturbing is the following "wanted" notice, which appeared in February 1767:

> Eloped from his master, a negro man, near 22 years of age, about five feet eight or nine inches high, well proportioned, and has a scar on the upper lip just under the nose. Had on when he went off a blue cloth livery coat with crimson cuffs and collar, waistcoat and breeches of the same colour, with white metal buttons. He was seen on the Bath road from Bristol on Wednesday last and is supposed to be gone for London. Whoever stops the said negro is desired to send to Mr Joseph Windsor at the *Angel Inn* near the Bridge, Bath, who will pay all reasonable charges attending.

Some of these absconders were never recaptured. Some became gentlemen of the road. In 1823, a council official reported that he had detained "a man of colour named James ... a rogue and vagabond wandering abroad and begging alms contrary to the form of the statute in that case made and provided."

Certainly, black paupers and beggars were a common sight as early as the mid-eighteenth century. In 1787, a government initiative called the Sierra Leone Scheme, tried to rid the country of "the incredible number of black men in every town and village" by refusing them relief unless they agreed to settle in Sierra Leone. This was effectively enforced repatriation – and so ineptly was it carried out that over 85% of those who took up the offer died within four years. The three ships chartered by the Government left England with 309 black passengers and 59 white women, the wives or widows of black men. Thirty-five of them died on the journey. Disease, starvation, and attacks from native inhabitants saw off most of the rest, so that, four years later, there were just 60 left. It is a shameful – and little known – episode of Britain's history.

Bath in the eighteenth century was a melting pot, and its proximity to the great port of Bristol meant that it was magnet for immigrants from overseas. With the exception of London, Bristol and Liverpool, Bath probably had the highest proportion of foreign residents in the country. Many, of course, were wealthy visitors, eager to enjoy the delights of England's most fashionable city. Although few stayed very long, many of those who followed them here became permanent residents. Foreign pastrycooks, jewellers, hairdressers, dancing masters, perfumiers, all settled in Bath to pander to the needs of their expatriate countrymen and to provide English visitors with a bit of foreign sophistication.

Although Bath has a rich immigrant tradition, the flow of people into the city from abroad has been tiny compared to those who have migrated to the city from elsewhere in the British Isles. Most of the people who came and settled in Bath in its eighteenth-century heyday probably lived no more than a day or two's walk away, tempted off the land by the prospect of rich pickings in one of England's fastest growing cities. Bath's population rose from around 5,000 to over 30,000 during the eighteenth century – a 500% increase. At any time during that period, incomers would have outnumbered Bathonians many times over. Only in the manufacturing cities of the Midlands and the North was there anything approaching such rapid growth. In Birmingham, for example, the population rose from 10,000 to 74,000 in the eighteenth century. Old provincial centres like York, Chester, Exeter and Norwich, on the other hand, hardly grew at all, and the majority of their inhabitants had family roots going back generations.

So, if we are to look for comparisons with the social life and social problems of Bath in the eighteenth century, it is to the new manufacturing centres, rather than to established cities, that we must turn. Bath's primary role as a tourist resort distinguished it in many ways from the powerhouses of the early industrial revolution, but it shared with them fundamental problems of assimilation, accommodation, and public order.

Many of those who came to Bath in the eighteenth century were tradesmen, craftsmen, servants or manual labourers who quickly fitted into the expanding city. It was not a difficult place to make friends. Many other people were new arrivals as well, just as eager to settle in and make a decent living for themselves. For those with enough business acumen or cunning – such as Ralph Allen from Cornwall or Beau Nash from Wales – the sky was the limit. Anybody connected with the building trade, if they had the ability to sub-contract, deal with developers or worm their way into the Corporation's favour, could make huge sums in a very short time – and lose them just as quickly if their luck ran out.

If those who had been here longer resented the arrival of all these incomers, there was more than enough company to compensate for their hostility. Most socialising went on in pubs. Many pubs were associated with a particular trade and served not only as social centres, but also as places where people could get to hear about work. Employers often recruited in pubs. Sometimes, landlords doubled as employers, and not only hired men in the pub to work on a particular contract, but paid them there as well. Upstairs, accommodation was generally available (as it still is in many pubs today) for those newly arrived in town, or those of no fixed abode. Other pubs served as social centres for servants or those connected with the coaching trade.

But, alongside this tidal wave of workers, Bath was awash with the great unwashed, or, as the Victorians called them, the undeserving poor. In the eighteenth century, most penniless migrants to Bath made for Holloway, where they found space on a communal doss-house floor before trying to get a share of the riches they had heard about. Some of them never made it. Between 1763 and 1824, over four out of five people claiming poor relief in Bath came from outside the city. Most came from Somerset, Gloucestershire or Wiltshire, but around a quarter came from farther afield. Some of them never tried to make it. Beggars, muggers, burglars, con artists, pimps and prostitutes – all came to Bath to ply their illicit trades.

In the late eighteenth century, the Avon Street area, spiralling ever further downhill, took over from Holloway as the doss-house centre of Bath. By 1842, an official report condemned Avon Street in the following terms:

> Everything vile and offensive is congregated there. All the scum of Bath -- its low prostitutes, its thieves, its beggars – are piled up in the dens rather than houses of which the street consists.

Another report, written three years later, indicates the living arrangements of those who flocked to Avon Street:

> During the season in Bath, when there is a considerable influx of visitors, the vagrants are the most numerous, and it is to be feared that indiscriminate charity somewhat prevails at this place. A large proportion of these vagrants is represented to be of the worst kind. They pay about 3d per night for their beds, placed in small, ill-ventilated rooms. The beds are usually occupied by two, but occasionally a larger number is crammed into them, without much respect for sex or age. . . . To relieve deserving poor travellers, a gentleman [of the Monmouth Street Society] attends daily (Sundays excepted) to hear the applications of poor travellers. He gives them (if considered deserving) a loaf of bread and some soup, under promise to leave the town.

It was in these overcrowded slums that much of the friction between incomers and established residents occurred. The worst street was reckoned to be Little Corn Street, nicknamed Little 'Ell. It is said that people in Avon Street liked Little Corn Street because it gave something to look down on. The incomers who seem to have been the cause of the most friction – partly because of their numbers and partly because they were easily identifiable – were the Irish. Although Irish immigrants came to Bath throughout the eighteenth and early nineteenth centuries, it was the Irish Potato Famine, starting in 1845, which caused their numbers to shoot up. Almost a million people died in Ireland during the famine. Not surprisingly, many of those who survived were desperate to leave.

Up to this time, immigration into Bath had been a steady flow from all directions. Now the city had a crisis on its hands – a mass of desperate and destitute people all from the same place. Not surprisingly there was trouble. The *Bath Chronicle* fulminated about the tidal wave of Irish immigrants flooding in and gave prominence to stories like this one of a wild Saturday night in Avon Street:

> Richard Barratt, an Irishman, was charged with being drunk and disorderly in Avon Street on Saturday night. It appeared that a crowd of people were assembled before the door of the *Fountain* public house, in consequence of some outrage committed by the prisoner, while he was at a window upstairs, threatening the mob outside. Presently afterwards some woman connected with him hurled a lump of coal upon their heads. Some of the crowd, in retaliation, smashed the window, when the prisoner rushed out of the house, furiously wielding a poker, and followed the people down the street, attempting to strike indiscriminately, as he proceeded.

The influx of Irish immigrants in the mid-nineteenth century helped to popularise two drinks – Guinness and whisky – which until then had been minority tipples. Guinness was an Irish version of London porter, which, strangely enough, became popular in England just as London porter started to lose ground to pale ale or bitter. Whisky, originally known as usquebaugh (water of life), was available as early as 1747 at the *Bath Punch House* in Green Street, along with other delicacies such as "right citron," "shrub" and "Batavian Arrack." It was not until the mid-nineteenth century, however, that it really caught on. One of the first people in Bath to stock it in bulk was Charles O'Beirne of 5 Monmouth Street, who styled himself a "Brandy & Spirit Merchant, and Importer of Irish Whisky." Eventually, in the 1880s, Scotch whisky started to eclipse the popularity of Irish and attain the popularity it has retained ever since.

Despite all the panic, the Irish who arrived in Bath fleeing the potato famine were soon assimilated into Avon Street's rich social mix, and pubs like the *Shamrock* were accepted as part of the way things were. In Bath today, pubs such as *Flan O'Brien's* and *O'Neill's* keep a very different type of Irishness alive.

CHAPTER EIGHT

RIOTOUS ASSEMBLY

And when night
Darkens the streets, then wander forth the sons
Of Belial, flown with insolence and wine.
John Milton, Paradise Lost, 1667

It is a seeming paradox that, while the licensed trade has always been reactionary in its politics, pubs and alehouses have always been seen as hotbeds of sedition. Brewers have traditionally supported the Conservative Party, yet, whenever civil unrest has reared its tousled head, it is fair bet that a good deal of ale went down its throat before it took to the streets baying for blood. John Downame, writing in 1613, certainly thought so. "When the drunkard," he declared, "is seated upon the ale-bench and has got himself between the cup and the wall, he presently becomes a reprover of magistrates, a controller of the state, a murmurer and repiner against the best established government."

Rioting has a long, if not particularly distinguished, history. When the price of bread shot up, when the government introduced an unpopular bill, when employers introduced new working practices or laid workers off, the standard answer was "take to the streets." In 1622, for example, the High Sheriff of Somerset wrote that, "the multitudes of poor spinners, weavers, etc., in the county, now without work, tend to mutiny." Corn carriers were stopped on the road by large mobs and threatened with physical violence unless they agreed to hand over their loads.

Weavers, who made up a substantial part of Bath's population, had a particularly bad reputation. United by a common cause, in a labour-intensive industry subject to fluctuations in the market, they were among the first urban proletariats. And, of course, they were fond of the odd drink. In 1751, a correspondent in the *Gentleman's Magazine* reported that weavers drank much more than village labourers. Drink undoubtedly fuelled the outrages of 1726, when weavers took direct action to persuade their employers that cutting wages was a bad idea. In May 1726, they marched into Trowbridge "in riotous manner," waving great clubs, "with high crowned hats on and with their faces smooted." They "broke into the workshops of several masters who oblig'd their men to work under price and cut a great many fine broad cloths out of the looms and even into small fragments and pieces and then went off again without being known or molested." When riots broke out in Bristol in August, *Farley's Bristol Newspaper* noted calmly that several weavers had been shot "but not mortally." In December it was the turn of Melksham and Bradford on Avon, when "journeymen weavers … arose in great numbers and forced themselves into the houses of several clothiers and master weavers, breaking their looms in pieces, etc. etc."

In the following year, 1727, the colliers rose up, objecting to newly erected turnpike gates which they had to pass through when taking their coal to market. This pushed their costs up and threatened to put them out of business. Colliers from Kingswood and Bussleton took direct action, demolishing four of the gates:

> That at Totterdown, in the Bath road, being erected again, they went the next day
> to view it, and finding it not to their minds, demolished it again the second time,
> and swear, they'll bring no coal into the city, nor suffer any turnpikes in their
> roads, till they were exempted from paying toll.

When four of the demonstrators were arrested, a mob gathered outside the gaol and threatened to break it down and release them. A year later it was the turn of the weavers again, 500 of whom rose "without Lawford's Gate" and burnt 30 looms before going on to wreak havoc at Chew Magna, Pensford and Keynsham.

Drunken mobs were still going round the country wrecking turnpikes over 20 years later, as this report from the *Bath Journal* of 7 August 1749 indicates:

> Last Wednesday morning, about 11 o'clock a great number of people from
> Kingswood and other parts of Gloucestershire destroyed the turnpike house
> at Toghill, about four miles from this city and burnt all the timber belonging.
> They then went to the public house at Toghill and drank a great deal of liquor;
> afterwards to the public houses on Lansdown, from thence to Bitton, and crossed
> the river at Keynsham, where they continued, and at Busselton, all that night; and
> have been almost ever since, wandering about the country raising contributions.

It was not just turnpikes that incurred the wrath of the mob. When the Avon Navigation opened to Bath in 1727, bringing Shropshire coal into the city, local miners reacted by damaging the locks. These attacks culminated in the destruction of the lock at Saltford, described by John Wood in his *Description of Bath*:

> Between the hours of eight o'clock on Thursday night and four o'clock on Friday
> morning, the 15th and 16th of November 1738, the lock at Saltford was almost
> destroyed by persons unknown; who left two threatening papers, which declared
> in substance that an attempt was made only by 300 men, as the beginning of
> much greater mischief that was intended against the navigation by as many
> thousand, unless an immediate stop was put to the sending of any more coals
> by water.

Rioting by working men in defence of their livelihood was one thing. As the eighteenth century wore on, however, sedition assumed a more sinister aspect. Discontent spread from specific grievances to wholesale condemnation of the *status quo*. Revolution was in the air and alehouses were its breeding ground. In 1776, John

Disney blamed the spread of popular disturbances on "unnecessary and ill-timed" meetings in alehouses. In the same year, full records of licensed houses began to be kept in Bath and the council issued the following diktat:

The Publicans in the City of Bath are to take notice that NO LICENCE will be granted for the future to any person whose house is open to associating journeymen carpenters, taylors or others.

The authorities were clearly getting worried.

In February 1776, it was observed "that the number of rogues and vagabonds, beggars, and other idle and disorderly persons, daily increase, to the great scandal, disgrace, loss and annoyance of this Kingdom." The Privy Council drew up a series of laws "relating to rogues and vagabonds (and others)" The list of those who came within the scope of the new laws was a long one. It included "all those who not having wherewith to maintain themselves, live idle, and refuse to work for the usual wages, and all beggars that go from door to door, or place themselves in the street or passages to gather alms . . . all fencers, bearwards, common players of interludes, minstrels, jugglers, and those pretending to be gypsies, or wandering in the form of Egyptians, and all pretenders to tell fortunes, or impose on the unwary, by pricking in the belt, hat, or shall play or bet with dice ... all petty chapmen and pedlars who travel without licence; all those who wander abroad, lodging in alehouses, barns, outhouses, or in the open air, not giving a good account of themselves, and all who wander abroad and beg, pretending to be soldiers, mariners, or seafaring men." For all this motley crew the punishment was "to be imprisoned, fined and publicly whipped."

In spite of all these precautions, the Gordon Riots broke out four years later. The Gordon Riots are a largely forgotten bit of our history, but they were probably the closest this country ever came to a full-blooded revolution. More damage was done in London during one week of mob rule than in Paris during the whole of the French Revolution. Hundreds of properties were destroyed and 290 people killed. The initial protest against the Catholic Relief Act, led by the rabble-rousing Lord George Gordon, took place on 2 June 1780. It soon got out of hand as the mob took it as an excuse to protest, not just about the alleged threat of Catholic domination, but about a system they saw as iniquitous and corrupt, where they were always hungry, always one step away from the gallows or a convict ship, while others lived a life of ease. As so often before and since, however, they vented their anger on a minority group. It is a story with a sickeningly contemporary ring to it. Catholic immigrants from Ireland and Holland, who had settled in the East End of London, were competing for jobs in the tanning and weaving industries, just as those jobs were starting to disappear due to the introduction of new technology and an influx of cheap imports from the East Indies. But, although they bore the initial brunt of alcohol-fuelled mob violence, it soon escalated into a general orgy of destruction.

For the best part of week, London was to all intents and purposes under mob rule. Anyone appearing in the streets without a blue ribbon to show their allegiance to the Protestant cause and a ready "No Popery" on their lips was liable to be beaten up or lynched. Stage coaches from London arrived in Bath with "No Popery" daubed on their sides. Protection money was extorted from householders to stop their houses being burnt down. Newgate, King's Bench and Fleet Prisons were stormed and their prisoners liberated. Not until 9 June, when troops began to arrive in the city in large enough numbers to reimpose some sort of order, did the tumult start to die down. At which point, the tocsin of revolution rang in Bath, and was duly reported in the *Bath Chronicle*:

> Friday evening a most alarming riot happened here, which was begun by a footman and some boys breaking the windows of a house where the Roman Catholic priest resided, adjoining to a new Chapel, newly built for persons of that religion.* In a very short time, as night came on, they were joined by a great number of people, most of them strangers, and armed with carpenter's tools, who broke open the chapel doors immediately and began gutting it and throwing the materials out of the window. The Magistrates and other peace officers assembled as quick as possible, but ere they could exert themselves the mob had increased to such a multitude that every effort to disperse them was ineffectual. The riot act was read and some persons seized, but instantly rescued. The Magistrates and many respectable citizens used every possible exertion to prevail on the mob to disperse, but without effect. Major Molesworth with a few of the City Volunteers hastily collected went into the Chapel, to the imminent hazard of their lives, and so far prevailed with the rioters as to be suffered to put out the fire several times, which they repeatedly kindled for its destruction. About 20 more of the Volunteers were soon after got together, and Capt. Duperre, at the request of the Mayor, headed them and led them into the Chapel, with their pieces not loaded. The instant they entered the building the mob rushed in upon them on all sides, and a pistol was fired at Capt. Duperre, which fortunately missed, and as fortunately destroyed an old rioter who had been once before wounded at an insurrection at Trowbridge – but it so incensed the mob, who supposed him shot by one of the Volunteers, that they immediately fired the Chapel, and the corps having received a few wounds and finding it utterly impossible to resist so large a body, made a slow and good retreat. The Chapel and about six or seven houses that surrounded it were entirely burnt by about four in the morning, when this desperate rabble, by the repeated and laudable exertions of the Magistrates and citizens, were prevailed upon to disperse, without carrying the remainder of their diabolical plan into execution, they having declared their determination to fire the old chapel and the houses of several Roman Catholics residing here.
>
> As soon as the Mayor and Corporation saw the impossibility of so numerous and desperate a mob being quelled by the civil power, amounting to some thousands, they sent expresses to Wells, Devizes, etc., and to the Commanding Officers of the troops there to come to their assistance … It is impossible to say too much in commendation of all the officers both horse and foot for their

* The chapel was on the south side of Lower Borough Walls, adjacent to St James's Burial Ground.

AWASH WITH ALE

uncommon expedition on this occasion. They understood from the messengers that the town was fired in several places, and how desperate and large a body they were to encounter, which the flames they saw from the neighbouring hills seemed to confirm – yet the danger only served to hasten them to our relief. Most of the Corporation stayed up all night to watch the city and receive the officers at their arrival, whom they very properly invited to an elegant dinner. By the disposition of the troops and peace officers everything here now is perfectly quiet. It is universally agreed that the leaders in the riot were persons sent from London, the gutting and firing the Chapel was executed with amazing haste and regularity, and not a single person in the city was insulted except those who attempted to seize them.

It seems that the villains who have chiefly headed the riots in London have a list of every Roman Catholic Chapel and School throughout the Kingdom, particularly of every new one, and have dispatched their emissaries to go from town to town and destroy them. It is therefore necessary for the Magistrates of every city, from the unhappy example of this, to be most strictly on their guard, and desire the inn and lodging house keepers to give notice of every suspicious person that comes there – particularly as the suddenness of this disaster was such that the utmost prudence could neither foresee or prevent.

Among the residents in Bath at this time was the novelist Fanny Burney. She had been particularly alarmed by news of the London riots because her family home was in St Martin's Street, an area with many Roman Catholic families. On 6 June, her father had only prevented his house being burnt down by shouting out, "No Popery," to the mob. The following day, he had tried to take his precious library to what he thought would be the relative safety of his sister's house in Covent Garden, but was unable to get through the hostile crowds in his coach. Fanny's friend, Mr Thrale, with whom she was staying in South Parade, was, although not a Catholic, sympathetic to the Catholic cause and had been labelled a Catholic in the Bath papers. When rioting broke out in Bath, they decided to get out of the city as quickly as possible. The day after the burning of the Catholic Chapel, they made for Brighton, from where they planned to escape to France if the rioting continued to spread.

The Gordon Riots not only frightened many visitors and would-be visitors away from Bath. It made many residents consider leaving as well. A letter written to the Mayor a month later by Francis Bennett, a linen merchant who had himself been Mayor seven years earlier, sums up the mood of many citizens:

It is with horror and grief I inform your worship that Gordon's mob, who lately destroyed the Romish chapel and building adjoining thereto in this once famous and most beautiful city, threatens likewise to destroy many more before it be long, if Providence don't interfere; therefore, kind sir, let me earnestly beg the favour of your worship to put yourself and this almost ruined city in a proper posture of defence before it is too late, as your worship and the ever worthy Mr Phillott at the *Bear* are in imminent danger ... It is true I spent many thousands in this city, and that with a great deal of pleasure and satisfaction, and would be heartily sorry to leave it on account of a destructive and rebellious set of ruffians, as it is the only part of England I like best, therefore, if I thought that I could live in peace and safety, should, with many more worthy and respectable gentlemen of my acquaintance, rest contented and fear no danger. Those ungrateful, and wicked miscreants, I am credibly informed, intend, as soon as the town is a little quiet and evacuated of its present trifling force, and the militia encamped, to assume their former destruction, with double force, and are certain to gain their most abominable point if not timely repelled by force and justice.

Whether Mr Bennett was justified in his fears is impossible to say, but clearly the Council had to be seen to be doing something to restore confidence. Somebody had to pay, and that somebody was John Butler. This, as reported in the *Bath Chronicle*, is the story of his trial:

John Butler was arraigned at half past nine [on Friday 30 August]. He was indicted for that he and others (twenty more) unlawfully assembled on the 9th of June and began to demolish the house of John Brewer in the Parish of St James.

Mr Batt shortly opened the indictment, after which Serjeant Davy went into the case fully. He began with lamenting the late riots, which threatened not only Government itself, but the whole society at large. What induced the prisoner to take the part he did, he could not say, but would, from charity, suppose he was actuated by a zeal for the Protestant religion.

There was, he observed, a reciprocal duty between the King and the subject: the subject owed allegiance to the Crown, and the Crown protection to the people; the people, if they do not pay allegiance to the Crown, are not intitled to protection. In the present case, the Crown was not able to afford the protection to be wished. The riots began in London, and were too great to be suppressed by the Civil Magistrates; this made it necessary for the King to call in the aid of the military. Bath being a place of resort for the sick or for pleasure, there was no military there: Government had never quartered any there, and therefore riots there are more alarming than in other places; a riot there ought to be immediately attended to, and the perpetrators punished. There are two considerations: First, the story of what happened at Bath; Second, the share the prisoner took in it. The Serjeant then proceeded to state the particulars of the late riot at Bath, and the share the prisoner took, who, he informed the jury, was perhaps the first instigator, by huzzaing, waving his hat, and crying, "No Popery, down with Popery," at the head of the mob, pursuing Mr Brewer, who is a Romish Priest, through the streets, till he ran into a house for protection and was driven out, and from thence pursued to the gates of the Guildhall, where he found protection.[*] Butler began with his own hand by throwing stones, and when he had done this, left the mob to complete the business he had begun.

If any were eminently to be distinguished from others, it was the man who

---

[*] The learned Serjeant, or the person who took the minutes of his speech, is here mistaken. The beadles at the hall door refused Mr Brewer admittance; and he took refuge next door at the *White Lion Inn*, whence he escaped the pursuit of the mob.

AWASH WITH ALE

first incited, who first began, and who first stirred up, the mob to do the mischiefs which afterwards were effected. Butler was a footman, and, till this affair, his character, he believed, was untainted. The Serjeant next observed, that in treason and riots, like those stated in the indictment, character was of no use, but in other common charges, such as sheep-stealing, etc., character might go a great way. If the accusation be proved to be true, the jury would discharge their duty by finding him guilty; if not, the Serjeant said he should rejoice with the best and warmest of the prisoner's friends in their acquitting him.

Samuel Wheeler deposed that he knew the prisoner and saw him in the evening of the 9th of June, in his master's house, between six and seven. The witness lived with Mr Baldwin in the Crescent, was footman there, and was speaking with the prisoner of the riots in London. The prisoner asked him how the affairs went on in London, he told him he heard chapels were demolished. The witness said it was a pity chapels were demolished. The prisoner said it was no matter whether the chapels were demolished or not. The witness thought it a pity in such troublesome times. The prisoner said he supposed the witness was a Roman Catholic. The witness replied, "it is no matter what religion I am of; I am no Roman Catholic." The witness saw him again about half past eight, in Pierrepoint Street, afterwards in the Market Place going homewards, but saw him in no other street; when he saw him in Pierrepoint Street he was with a parcel of boys, about 30 or 40, crying, "No Popery." He believed the prisoner cried, "No Popery," but could not distinguish his voice from the rest. He did not see him wave his hat. They were chiefly boys or between boys and men.

John Cottell said he lived in Stall Street and was a shoemaker by trade. A little after eight in the evening on the 9th of June, he saw the prisoner at his door, but the first time he saw him he was coming down Belltree Lane [Beau Street]. Mr Brewer was before him, the prisoner behind. The witness went down to the bottom of the Alms Lane, where the building was, which was afterwards destroyed; he saw many people, among whom was his journeyman and others removing their goods. When he got into Stall Street, he saw Mr Brewer running along the lane and into Stall Street, the prisoner following him with 30 or 40 boys with him. Mr Brewer ran into his shop, the witness followed him; he said he came in for fear of the people. The witness asked him what was the matter, for he seemed much frightened by the people before his door; he asked him to walk into the parlour, which he did; the witness went from the parlour to the door and said to the prisoner, "for God's sake, what do you want, you don't want to murder the man?" The prisoner said, "you are no Roman Catholic, turn the Popish son of a bitch out." He had his hat waving in his hand and cried, "No Popery;" then it seemed general among the whole mob, "turn him out, turn him out;" he thought it in vain his speaking to them, as they did not go away. He then returned to the parlour to Mr Brewer, who, having heard what passed, went out at the same door he came in, and went up the street, and the prisoner with the mob followed him. Mr Brewer ran as far as he could see him, which was halfway up the street, all crying "No Popery," the prisoner and all cried so; he then lost sight of him, and in a few minutes the prisoner returned, running very fast, and the boys with him, but not so many as before; they came down Belltree Lane and were running towards the chapel.

John Horton, Chief Constable, deposed, that he saw the prisoner between eight and nine o'clock coming down Westgate Street with 30 or 40 boys and grown people; that he came huzzaing, waving his hat and crying, "No Popery." The witness went to him, and asked him the meaning of those people being there, and told him, 'twould be attended with bad consequences, and productive of much mischief; bade him go home and mind his business; he made no answer, but cried, "No Popery," and repeated it two or three times; he spoke to him again, and one of the men jostled him and his brother officer, Mr Smith; he then said again to the prisoner, "you don't know the consequence that will arise, it may be very fatal to the town." The prisoner said, "you will know more by and by," then waved his hat, huzzaed, cried, "No Popery," and went away towards St James's Parade and towards the Chapel; the mob followed him to the amount of 50, 60, 70, much increased.

Charles Davis deposed that he saw the prisoner on the 9th of June in the afternoon, between three and four o'clock, blowing a fife, and walking slow, no mob about him then. Between eight and nine in the evening, in Cheap Street, opposite the opening to the Churchyard, he saw Mr Brewer running, and the prisoner and boys following him, very quick; the witness then went home, and had not been there above ten minutes, before he heard a noise at the Romish Chapel, and boys breaking the windows at the east end with stones, dirt, etc., that there were between 50 and 100 people. He went from the crowd to endeavour to get some constables to suppress the riot; the prisoner was very active running about among them, seeming to encourage them, had his hat in his hand, and was huzzaing. The witness was away a quarter of an hour for assistance; when he returned he saw the mob very active in breaking open the doors; that he saw the door broke open, and immediately some returned with benches and other things into the street; that they went on from that time progressively in destroying everything; that there was a communication from the Chapel to Mr Brewer's house, through which he believes the mob got; that after burning the furniture, etc., in the street, the Chapel and five dwelling houses were set fire to and burnt. The Mayor came about eleven o'clock, and the volunteers to the number of 20 or 30 men, but they were not sufficient to disperse the mob; that the prisoner was very active, waving his hat and huzzaing.

Cross examined – he never saw the prisoner after his return; the last time he saw him was when the boys were breaking windows; he did not see him at the time of the fire.

William Tucker deposed that (standing with Mr Davis) he saw the prisoner on the 9th of June between three and four o'clock in the afternoon, playing a fife in a blue livery, as he passed Westgate Buildings; that he played horribly bad, which made them notice it; about nine in the evening he heard a noise in the street and saw the prisoner, but not Brewer. He heard some people say, there's the man hunting the priest; that he seemed to be at the head of some boys, waving his hand, but could not hear him say anything because he was not near enough; that he heard a noise at the Chapel about ten minutes after, went down, and saw the prisoner at the head of some boys, standing upon some mortar or rising ground to make himself conspicuous, waving his hat and crying out, "No Popery," while the boys were breaking the windows; saw no man take any active part, but saw a boy throw a stone and knock him down, and said, "what do you do here?," when he was immediately surrounded by three, or four, or six men, in carmen's frocks; two or three of them said, "you had better go away, or you will be used ill;" that he took their advice and went away, leaving the prisoner still on the same rising ground; he returned to the place again in about four or five minutes, but did not see the prisoner; the mob had increased, the windows were broke, and the door either was broke open, or they were breaking it open, and were taking out the benches, etc., and making heaps in the street; that he saw a variety of household furniture burnt on St James's Parade, and that the Chapel and houses were afterwards burnt.

Cross examined – he saw nothing of the prisoner after his return and does not know whether the prisoner was there when the house was broke open.

Thomas Baldwin, architect, deposed, that he saw the prisoner between half after ten and twelve o'clock near the Chapel; the people were then pulling down the house, that the prisoner was then 60 yards from them, standing as an idle spectator, and the mob destroying the cornice.

Cross examined – he said he could not speak to any other time than from half past ten to twelve; the witness did not stay there above two or three minutes; that the mob extended a great way, and he was near the prisoner when they were pulling down the cornice.

Mary Hughes deposed that on the 9th of June she saw the prisoner in the Churchyard near the Pump Room and several boys with him, all following Mr Brewer, who was running as fast as he could, the mob all crying out, "knock him down," but she would not swear that the prisoner said it, without she had heard him alone; there were three or four people between the prisoner and Mr Brewer. Mr Brewer ran by her very fast and tore her gown; she was much frightened, stayed to rest, and something after nine went towards the Chapel and saw the prisoner there, huzzaing, and a great number hammering at the door; the prisoner waved his hat and huzzaed, but she did not see the prisoner do anything. She did not see Davis or Tucker there.

Mr Hennagan deposed that he had known the prisoner a year, saw him first in the Market Place, and heard him huzza; there were many people with him between eight and nine o'clock; that he saw no more of the prisoner till he saw him at the Chapel, which was five or six minutes after the mob had broke the windows by throwing stones; that he saw the prisoner opposite a blacksmith's shop near the Chapel, and saw him throw some stones or brickbats at it; he saw him heave two stones, cannot speak positively to more, is perfectly sure of the person of the man, but cannot say whether the stones reached the building.

John Ridley deposed that on the 9th of June he saw the prisoner about a quarter before nine o'clock, at a building adjoining the Romish Chapel, boys breaking the windows, throwing volleys of stones, the prisoner huzzaed with them, and encouraged them, standing on a lump of mortar, and said, "fire away, boys," that he was there till he saw the peace-officers with their staves, and saw the prisoner then run away.

Cross examined – he ran away before the house door broke open, a little before nine or about nine.

Mr William Robinson, architect, deposed, that he built a long room called a Chapel; that the communication between the Chapel and the dwelling house was by three doors, one below, two above stairs; all one building, all carried up together, and all in Brewer's possession; he saw it after the fire, all the carpenter's work consumed, walls greatly damaged, windows and doors destroyed, and nothing but walls remaining.

Cross examined – Mr Brewer was understood to be the person to officiate there; the room was intended for a Chapel to perform divine service, and no other purpose; and the gallery for the purpose of coming into the Chapel …
For The Prisoner

Elizabeth Rickets: "I live with Mr Baldwin; on the 9th of June I saw the prisoner come in at a quarter past nine, and laid the cloth for supper, waited at supper, and went to bed twenty minutes before eleven; he was never out of the house after he came in at a quarter past nine."

Cross Examination: No apprehension that he would be arrested, no other particular reason than laying the cloth for remembering; when he went upstairs to bed, she went after him and looked at the clock, took exact notice, and generally looks at the clock when she goes to bed; her master and mistress generally go to bed after, but cannot say when they went to bed. She left nobody up but her master and mistress and the housekeeper; she took more notice that night of the hour than ever she did before: she is sure it was exactly twenty minutes, and that he went out at half past eight, and came home at a quarter past nine; he was not out all the afternoon, but with a letter to the post between four and five, and returned in half an hour. The family dined in the parlour at three, and then the prisoner dined with the servants, and it was after four when he put the things away, and then went with the letter, and was not away more than half an hour, and then was not out any more till half past eight, and returned at a quarter past nine. He was never out all the day or night but in going to the post office, and from half past eight till a quarter past nine, and never out after supper. It is about half a mile from the Crescent to the Chapel and post office near there, and is very sure it was full half an hour past eight before he went out in the evening.

Mrs Jane Powell, housekeeper: About four o'clock, the prisoner went to the post office, was away half an hour, she thought he made haste. At half past eight, he went out, she looked at her watch, as she was going out herself; she did not come in till 20 minutes before ten; he was then in. At half past eleven, people said he was at the head of a mob; she went up to his bedroom and called, "John, are you abed?" He answered, "yes." He said no more, nor she said no more. She looked into the room again about twelve, her mistress desired her to go up, telling her that she had heard he was in the mob; that she met her master, told him of it, and that he went up himself to see. She was sure the prisoner was not out after supper.

Mr Baldwin was from six to ten o'clock on the 9th of June on a visit at a neighbour's house; he returned at ten; the prisoner let him in at the door; his wife had done supper; a Lady told him there had been a great confusion, that he went out to see the place and returned in half an hour. Supposed, notice had been given a day or two before, there would be a riot, to the magistrates. That his wife told him somebody had said his servant was in the mob; that he understood it was a message from Mr Wiltshire to him, and said he went upstairs at eleven and saw him in bed; that he did not remember the maid's speaking to him on the stairs or meeting her. The prisoner had lived with him between two and three years; was sober, civil, diligent, and honest, and that he had never had a more valuable servant in his life. That he went to bed between one and two; did not know whether any of the servants were at the door, but that the housekeeper sat up till all were abed.

Rev Mr Pearce had known the prisoner twelve years; gave him a good character; he had lived with him two years.

Mr James Haynes gave him a good character, as a sober, honest servant, and never out one night while in his service, or given to riot or quarrel. A written character was produced and read, of a gentleman with whom he had lived some years, speaking very respectfully of him.

The learned Judge here summed up the evidence with great candour and impartiality, making very pointed and apt observations on the whole of it. The Jury, after five minutes conversation, found the prisoner guilty; but recommended him to mercy.

The trial lasted from nine in the morning till three in the afternoon.

Mr Brewer, the priest who was pursued through the streets, did not give evidence at the trial. Some time later, however, he jotted down his version of events for posterity:

I am the unfortunate Roman Catholic clergyman, who was hunted from place to place and pursued through several streets the evening of the Bath riot: it was with great difficulty I escaped from falling a victim to the fury of the mob. Being here the public minister for people of our persuasion I am well known and was openly attacked in the street that evening by one Butler, who is mentioned in the incendiary letter and was then servant to Mr Baldwin, a gentleman living in this town. After pursuing me at the head of the mob he led them to my house and chapel, both which, together with the furniture and books, were entirely

> destroyed. The unhappy man was afterwards tried and hanged on the spot, though from motives of delicacy I did not give evidence at his trial.

Such was the bizarre nature of eighteenth-century justice, that feelings of delicacy could excuse the victim of a serious assault from giving evidence at a trial that ended with the defendant being sentenced to death.

Seven other men were tried alongside John Butler. All were acquitted. Robert Saxty, who was present when the chapel was burnt down and cried out "No Popery," got off by claiming that he had only cried out "to save himself from being insulted." One of the witnesses, the drummer belonging to the Bath Volunteers, corroborated his story, adding that he had himself been knocked down and had his drum kicked in for refusing to cry, "No Popery." In an act of breathtaking audacity, Saxty placed a notice in the following week's *Bath Chronicle* thanking the witnesses who had turned up in court "to give evidence of his innocence, and to whom Mr Robert Saxty returns his sincere thanks for their kind and friendly attendance."

Charles Hewlett and William Brown were acquitted due to lack of evidence. William Mortimer, Richard Samys and James Sugar were all discharged on a promise of future good behaviour. Peter Butcher, whose trial came on last, was also acquitted, even though two witnesses swore positively against him. Mr Brewer's maidservant said that she saw him, at about 10.30pm, "enter the dining-room bed-chamber with a piece of railing, which she supposed to be the top of one of the Chapel seats, and that he destroyed with it the window and frame of the said room." A 16-year-old lad also said that he "had met the prisoner on the landing-place leading from the Chapel to the dining-room, with a piece of railing in his hand, and that he had heard him damn Popery, but saw no more of him." However, "John Wilkins, dyer, and another person swore that they were in company with Butcher from five o'clock till three-quarters past ten at a public house in Bridewell Lane; after which the prisoner went to Mr Bell's, at the *Raven*, who also deposed that he accompanied him to the fire, and that he never left him till past twelve o'clock."

When John Butler's sentence was announced, "he sunk into a fit, and remained in a state of insensibility a long time." Three days later, on Monday lunchtime, a gallows was erected on a plot of waste land a stone's throw from the old chapel, near where the *Hobgoblin* now stands. Butler left the prison in Grove Street at noon, accompanied in the cart by his two brothers, "each supporting by turns his drooping head upon the fraternal bosom, manifesting the truest affection and the acutest sorrow." At the Guildhall, 400 special constables, sworn in on the day after the riot, joined the melancholy procession. Trouble was clearly anticipated, and the authorities were taking no chances. The Bath Volunteer Regiment and the Scots Greys were in Queen Square, ready to swing into action if the call came. The bells of the city tolled as the cart with its unhappy burden passed through the streets. "His whole behaviour," noted the *Bath Journal*, "corresponded with the decency that marked every part of his conduct prior to the unfortunate transaction that occasioned his exit … The ceremony of his fate was rendered additionally awful by the agony of mind and feebleness of body which the shock of his sentence and the sense of his ignominious death had indicted."

When he reached the place of execution, the Rev Mr Philipps got into the cart and prayed with him "with great devotion" for full half an hour. At his request, a letter written just before he left the prison was read out to the crowd by the Rev Philipps:

I, John Butler, now under sentence of death, do solemnly declare in the presence of God, before whom I shall soon appear, that the evening of the ninth day of June last, I returned to my master's house at a quarter after nine, and never went out again till eleven o'clock the next morning; so help me God.

JOHN BUTLER

Signed and declared by the above John Butler,
as his dying words, in the presence of us, this

  28th day of August, 1780,
  Wm. Philipps, Minister.
  J. Smith.
  Wm. Pontin.

Then, "taking the last farewell of his brothers, he was turned off, surrounded by many thousands of weeping spectators. After hanging about half an hour, his body was taken down, put into a coffin, and carried away in a hearse to be interred in his native parish near Wells. He was about 26 years old."

Three weeks later, a poem, "written on the day of the late execution, at a very beautiful spot, laid out for the entertainment of the public, near Bath," appeared in the *Bath Journal*:

Far from the curious mob that crowd the streets,
I seek the shelter of this cool retreat;
This tranquil scene, for sacred quiet made,
Where the fresh zephyr breathes around the shade;
And while the world to yonder city go,
To gaze upon a spectacle of woe,
With anxious heart to this recess I fly,
And feel a generous sorrow bathe my eye,
E'en as the florid landscapes round me glow
I drop a tear upon the vale below,
I bless that hill which screens me from the wind,
I hail that wood that shuts me from mankind:
And innocence, with nature, seems to roam;
Here rave no tumults, riot strays not here,
But peace smiles softly, tho' the city's near:
Smooth glides the waters as you pass along,
And pleasure warbles in the linnet's song;
Fair, within reach, the ruddy fruits are seen,
And Autumn decks with various flowers the green:
The artist here from labour may repose,

And see health cultivate the blushing rose,
Here nature for the sick shall court the air,
And every gale a heavenly balm prepare;
To these calm seats serenity retires,
And every passion, but the best, expires;
And they who sigh for self-improving hours,
Will seek these winding walks, these fragrant bowers.

The "fragrant bowers" were those of the pleasure gardens in Lyncombe Vale. What is remarkable about the poem, though, is that it shows how deep an impression the execution of Butler had made upon the collective consciousness of the city. Even three weeks later, it was perfectly natural for it to form the starting point for a poem about an escape to a "cool retreat."

The Butlers were a spectacularly unlucky family, for there is one more footnote to this sorry tale. Eight years later, one of the brothers who had accompanied John Butler on his last journey was unloading a hogshead of cider from a cart in Wells when it slipped and crushed him to death.

The Gordon Riots were about as close as this country ever came to revolution, yet apart from a few, relatively, minor outbursts in Bristol, Birmingham and Hull, Bath was the only place outside London to experience any real trouble. And, whereas London's troubles extended over several days, Bath's were limited to one dreadful night. But it was a night that the city fathers did not forget for many years. They had had a nasty shock and were determined not to let it happen again, even if that meant sending a hot-headed young man to the gallows as a warning to others.

It was in this climate of tension and fear, helped by some vigorous lobbying, that the number of alehouses in Bath fell from 163 to 100 in just a few years. "It is remarked," wrote a correspondent in the *Bath Chronicle* in 1785,

> that the great number of public houses, particularly those in many of the obscure parts, are most of them harbours for the rendezvous of the idle and profligate, who when assembled together generally excite one another to many daring, riotous and illegal acts, to the great dismay and terror of the public in general, as it is too well known by daily experience; therefore I trust this hint will be considered by those Justices, etc., whose province it is to grant licences, and that they will turn it in their thoughts against the next time of licensing alehouses, etc. I have been well informed that our present Mayor has been heard to say, that he is resolved to suppress all those public houses that have any real complaints alleged against them, either by keeping too late hours, allowing gambling, or harbouring or entertaining disorderly or lewd women, or admit of any other riotous proceedings in their houses. I would therefore recommend it to all those inclinable to take public houses in this city to be particularly careful in their enquiries relative to the repute of the houses they may be in treaty for.

The following year another correspondent wrote that, "there are already more [public houses] than are sufficient for the necessary accommodation of the public; and all supernumerary public houses are only receptacles for the labourers and artificers to dissipate their substance in, and thereby burthen the parishes with the maintenance of their families."

In the last 20 years of the eighteenth century, there was a sharp increase in the number of alehouses owned by major brewers, while many independent alehouse keepers were forced out of business. Brewers were part of the establishment, with friends in the right places. Most independent alehouse keepers were not. As far as the establishment was concerned, they were expendable. If alehouses had to close so that Bath's citizens could sleep more soundly in their beds, then it was the independently-owned ones that went. There was, in some cases, the option of doing a deal with one of the brewers and undertaking to sell his beer in exchange for an assurance that renewal of the licence would be looked on favourably. Bath was not unique in this regard. In Canterbury, for example, Thomas Roch wrote in 1776 that "there is scarce a house that is situated for a public house but is either by purchase or lease in the hands of the brewers."

In 1787, William Wilberforce lobbied parliament to secure the issue of a Royal Proclamation Against Vice, which was circulated to all magistrates with an official demand for even tighter controls on licensed premises. In December 1793, the "innkeepers and victuallers" of Bath met at the *Bear Inn* "for the purpose of identifying their loyalty to the King." They unanimously resolved that it was "incumbent on them at this particular juncture to be more than ordinarily vigilant in maintaining regularity and order." In addition, they agreed that they "would suffer no meetings or clubs in which seditious subjects should be agitated, to be held – or language, tending to disturb the public tranquility, to be made use of by any person or persons, in their respective houses, without immediately giving information thereof to the Civil Magistrates." A further resolution was then passed:

> That the thanks of this meeting be respectfully conveyed by the Chairman to the Committee of the Bath Association for the Preservation of Liberty, Property and the Constitution of this Kingdom against Republicans and Levellers, for their loyal exertions, and in particular for their judicious recommendation of a line of conduct which the said innkeepers and victuallers had in some measure in their own minds anticipated, and are happy in this early opportunity of shewing their resolution to adopt in the fullest and most effectual manner ... Taking into account also the violent convulsions, anarchy, and massacres, which have been occasioned in a neighbouring kingdom, by an attempt to reduce into practice the delusive and visionary principles which are laid down and recommended in and by ... seditious publications and persons ... and preferring the quiet and peaceable enjoyment of those inestimable blessings we actually possess to the subversion of the present establishment, in search of imaginary happiness, we are of opinion that it is now become the interest, as well as the duty, of every good and loyal subject, of all ranks and degrees, to unite and publickly avow his attachment to the King and Our Excellent Constitution.

The wording of the resolution, reminiscent of the climate of terror which existed in the Soviet Union under Stalin, is a measure of the feeling of panic that swept through the country as France's revolution spiralled out of control. Woe betide the publican who did not turn up for the meeting or pledge less than total support. The very least he could have expected would have been a stiff interrogation when his licence came up for renewal.

Bath's magistrates also instructed the public to inform on any publicans whose houses were less than reputable, by publishing notices such as this, which appeared in 1800:

> The Mayor and Justices of this City have appointed next [week] for licensing Inns and Alehouses ... All persons having reason to complain of any Inn Keeper or Alehouse Keeper ... for keeping a disorderly house, suffering tippling or gaming therein, harbouring apprentices, or otherwise misbehaving, are desired to give information therein to the Justices.

A few weeks after that notice appeared, a fire destroyed Williams' Brewery on the Quay. Twenty thousand bushels of malt and barley and 1,400 barrels of beer were consumed by the flames. Fires at breweries were not uncommon. Smith's Brewery at Walcot had burnt down in 1794 and Williams' Brewery was once again seriously damaged by fire 38 years later. However, nobody had any doubt that the fire at Williams' Brewery was started deliberately. Only a few days earlier an anonymous letter had been sent to the owners of another brewery, threatening to burnt it down. The following week, there was an attempt to set fire to Stothert's factory. These were not the acts of a casual arsonist but the manifestation of a deep feeling of unrest, anger and despair. Mass unemployment had turned parts of Bath into a virtual famine zone. The breeze that fanned the blaze at Williams' Brewery was not so much one of revolutionary fervour but of long-simmering rage at social injustice and inequality.

Bath never again experienced anything on the scale of the Gordon Riots, yet, in the years following the defeat of Napoleon, the call for reform rumbled on. The Orange Grove was a popular concourse for public assemblies. In 1817, it was the venue for a mass rally which could very easily have had disastrous consequences. Although 37 years had passed since the Gordon Riots, the authorities were still twitchy about large-scale gatherings. After all, they now had the French Revolution as an object lesson in what could happen if they let the lower orders get out of hand. The *Bath Chronicle* described the event:

> On Thursday last Mr Hunt, of political notoriety, presented a requisition to the Mayor, requesting him to call a meeting of the inhabitants, to consider "the propriety of petitioning Parliament for the *immediate* abolition of all sinecure grants, pensions, and emoluments, not merited by public services, as a *temporary measure*; and a Reform in the Commons or People's House of Parliament, as a *permanent means* of relief for the unexampled and complicated distress and misery of the country." The Mayor having declined complying with the request, Mr Hunt and 29 other persons appointed a meeting of the inhabitants, for the aforesaid purpose; and on Monday the meeting took place at twelve o'clock, at Mr Hunt's Yard [now Beehive Yard]. It was shortly after adjourned to the

Grove, where a temporary hustings being erected, next the Abbey Church, Mr Hunt was called to preside. The meeting was then severally addressed by Messrs Hickman, C Young, Crisp, Carpenter and Williams (of Bristol) and the result was the adoption of certain resolutions, attributing the distress of the country to the "unjust" wars in which we have been engaged, and in which we were "involved owing to the corrupt system of representation"; insisting, therefore, upon the necessity of a Reform in Parliament, and of altering the form of election to that "by BALLOT, in order to prevent the influence of the rich powerful"; and urging the abolition of unmerited pensions and sinecure places, particularly noting Marquis Camden's enormous sinecure as Teller of the Exchequer. A petition embracing these topics (to be presented by Lord Cochrane, supported by Sir F Burdett) was agreed to; and the proceedings were concluded by a vote of thanks to the promoters of the meeting and its objects. Mr Carpenter, indeed, proposed a vote of thanks to the Editor of the Independent Whig; but after being twice put by the chairman, it was negatived, with the exception of one hand held up in its favour. The number of persons assembled might have been 500.

So far so good – but the report ended with a chilling codicil:

Precautionary measures had been judiciously taken by the Magistrates, to prevent any breach of the public peace; a great number of the respectable inhabitants came forward, and were sworn as special constables; masters of families, tradesmen, etc. were requested to keep their servants, workmen, etc. *at home* on the day of the meeting; and the publicans were desired to prevent tippling in their houses. Two troops of the 23rd Dragoons, under Major Grove, the Bath, Frome, Shepton, and Batcombe troops of the North Somerset Yeomanry, commanded by Colonel Horner, and the Bath Rifle Corps were also assembled in aid of the civil power, had occasion required; but the day and evening passed off without any occurrence worthy of particular notice.

Such an imposing military turnout seems a trifle excessive for a gathering of 500 people. Except, of course, that it was not a gathering of 500 people. Newspapers in 1817 were even less reliable than they are today when it comes to reporting the number of people attending demonstrations. The *Bath Chronicle* in its role of publishing nothing that might deter potential visitors – a role which some of today's correspondents seem keen to see resurrected – was guilty of a slight understatement. When Henry Hunt wrote his *Memoirs* three years later, he said that he was followed from Walcot Street to the Orange Grove by an "immense multitude of from twelve to fifteen thousand people." He may have been exaggerating, of course, but, in the absence of an impartial observer, we can only point to the number of signatures he collected on a petition calling for reform in Bath – 20,000. With that level of support, it seems unlikely that only around 500 people turned up to hear him speak.

Two years later, Henry Hunt addressed a similar meeting at St Peter's Fields in Manchester, when around 80,000 people turned up. Despite, once again, there being no threat of serious civil disturbance, the magistrates ordered the meeting to be broken up, and the military charged the crowd, killing eleven people and wounding around 400. The massacre was christened Peterloo, an ironic echo of the British victory at Waterloo four years earlier. Bathonians can be thankful that the authorities in Bath managed, unlike their counterparts in Manchester, to keep their heads.

In 1831 it was Bristol's turn to suffer the full fury of the mob. Although the Bristol Riots were nominally about parliamentary reform, they were also fuelled by hatred of the Corporation. Although the trouble threatened to spread to Bath, a combination of quick thinking and good luck ensured that there was nothing more than a little local disturbance in the vicinity of the *White Hart* in Stall Street. Captain Mainwaring, who was present at the time, takes up the story:

> The tides of destruction attending [the Bristol] riot, as they followed each other with appalling rapidity, were hourly communicated here; and groups of the lowest rabble, ripe for plunder, consisting chiefly of grown-up boys, were collected at the *White Hart*, on Sunday evening, listening, with savage satisfaction, to the detailed accounts of their victorious brethren. As the evening closed, the crowd increased; and with them, their noisy tumultuous proceedings. This they considered the 'opening scene' of a tragedy to be enacted here, similar to the fatally successful one at Bristol; and they were not without hopes of assistance from the belligerents of that city.
>
> About seven o'clock, Captain Wilkins [the Twerton industrialist], of the Bath troop of Yeomanry Cavalry, who had been applied to by the Bristol magistrates for assistance, arrived in Bath to collect his men, and rested at the *White Hart*. – Thither he was followed by an increasing mob, who greeted him with the most opprobrious epithets; and expressed, in very significant terms, their decided intention of opposing his progress. In vain, he pointed out, that he was compelled, as a matter of duty, to repair to Bristol with his troop. They insisted he should not go; while the gallant Captain expressed his determination to do so. Symptoms of serious mischief then began to shew themselves; and some of the most daring of the mob endeavoured to follow him into the *White Hart*, the doors of which were immediately closed. Then commenced an attack on the windows, which were demolished without mercy; and, in many instances, the frames shared the fate of the glass. Not satisfied with this they proceeded to a faggot-pile in the neighbourhood; and, returning to the scene of action, commenced demolishing the shutters of the lower windows; and some of the mob effected an entrance into the premises. There, however, they met with a warmer reception than they calculated on, a charge being made by the inmates, not with the bayonet, but with a part of the "batterie de cuisine," red-hot kitchen pokers, previously prepared, which had an admirable effect in causing the assailing party to turn quickly round, and beat a precipitate retreat; in effecting which, some few were partially singed on that part where the "seat of honour" is supposed to be situated.
>
> By this time the magistrates had sworn in about three hundred special constables, who immediately dispersed the mob, and took several into custody.

AWASH WITH ALE

> Tranquillity was restored; and, at two o'clock in the morning, the streets were entirely cleared.

Despite the city being spared, two of the Bath rioters were sentenced to death the following year, although the sentences were later commuted to transportation for life.

The passing of the Great Reform Act the following year was a triumph of sorts for the Bristol rioters, but, although it extended the franchise and got rid of certain other abuses like the election of members for "rotten boroughs," its scope was very limited. The vast majority still did not have the vote. For the Chartists, who now took up the banner of reform, nothing less than universal manhood suffrage would do. The *Bath Chronicle*, not surprisingly, hated them. In 1838, for example, when one of the movement's national leaders addressed a meeting in the Orange Grove, his listeners were dismissed as "rabble," while a "grand demonstration" at Combe Down was described as a "contemptible concern." When a group of Chartist women met at the *Larkhall Inn*, the *Chronicle* reported that "a chairmanness called Bolwell delivered a she-speech."

Although the *Bath Chronicle* sought to belittle Chartism, the authorities had good reason to fear the movement. Armed Chartists arrived in Radstock in April 1839, although they were driven out before they could rouse the mob to action. This, however, served as the prelude to a march on Newport, Monmouthshire, later that year, when a mob, several thousand strong, were beaten off by a small contingent of soldiers holed up, like Captain Wilkins, in one of the town's principal inns. Around a dozen of the marchers were killed as they fled the soldiers' bullets, but initial reports received in Bath indicated either that Newport had been taken or that the Chartists were regrouping for a renewed attack after dark. The mass rising in Monmouthshire, although it was a shambles, was a profound shock to the establishment. The authorities in Bath responded a few days later by arresting two prominent Chartists, Anthony Phillips and Charles Bolwell, at their meeting room in Monmouth Street.

Despite the failure of the Newport rising, Chartism continued to be a potent force in British politics. In the 1840s, Bath's Chartists allied themselves with Anti-Corn Law campaigners and a mass meeting were held at the Corn Market in Walcot Street. At a rally in 1842, an effigy of Robert Peel, the Conservative Prime Minister, was paraded through the streets before being carried up to Beacon Hill and "demolished." Ironically, it was Peel who, four years later, repealed the corn laws, causing a major rift within his party.

1847 saw food riots again flare up across the country. Troops were called out to quell disturbances at towns such as Radstock and Taunton. Not all rioters in that year of dearth, however, had a political or social agenda. Some, like this rabble down by the riverside in Bath, had simply had too much to drink:

> On Friday afternoon, several drunken men created a disturbance in Avon Street. PC Brooks happened to be there, and endeavoured to quell the affair, but finding his efforts ineffectual, he went to the station house to procure aid. On the arrival of the police in the street, one of the men, named James Bollen, who had a knife

in his hand, stabbed Brooks severely in the arm. Brooks was immediately led to the hospital and had the wound dressed. Bollen escaped down Avon Street, and eventually jumped into the water and swam to the opposite side. Finding that he was pursued, he again plunged in, and afterwards swam up a common sewer which debouches near the Quay, where he remained for some time, till a lad named Michael Greenman, tempted by a gratuity that was offered him, swam up the sewer in order to bring the man down, which he did. Bollen, on reaching the mouth of the sewer, was nearly lifeless. He was conveyed into a boat that Mr Hall and some officers were in, in order to secure him, and afterwards taken by them into the *Duke of York* public house on the Quay. This circumstance caused between two and three thousand people to congregate. He was removed from the *Duke of York* public house to the United Hospital. He was immediately bled, and other means were taken for his recovery.

Michael Greenman, the hero of the hour soon turned villain, however. A month later, the *Bath Chronicle* reported that he had been hauled before the bench charged with picking the pocket of a man who had fallen asleep in the tap room of the *Fountain* in Avon Street. The magistrate expressed the opinion that the sovereign he had received as a reward for his bravery "had done more harm than good, by encouraging idle and intemperate habits."

AWASH WITH ALE

CHAPTER NINE

SOLDIERS

I went into a public 'ouse to get a pint o' beer,
The publican 'e up an' sez, "We serve no redcoats here."
The girls be'ind the bar they laughed and giggled fit to die,
I out into the street again an' to myself sez I:
O, it's Tommy this an' Tommy that, an' Tommy, go away,
But it's, Thank you, Mr Atkins, when the band begins to play.
Rudyard Kipling, Tommy, 1892

Soldiers have had a long and not always amicable relationship with Bath's pubs. First of all there was the problem of billeting. This was a long-standing cause of friction, as innkeepers had, by law, to accommodate soldiers when requested. The Civil War saw many of Bath's inns wrecked by the troops who abused their hospitality. Soldiers from each side were quick to show their displeasure if they suspected their hosts were less than sympathetic to their cause.

It was not only innkeepers who were forced to accommodate soldiers. Private individuals such as John Turbeville, a Somerset landowner, were also likely to find themselves with a houseful of unwanted guests. He complained to a friend that:

> My house is, and hath been, full of soldiers for a fortnight: such uncivil drinkers
> and thirsty souls that a barrel of good beer trembles at the sight of them; and the
> whole house nothing but a rendezvous of tobacco and spitting.

In the late eighteenth century, the American and French wars and widespread fear of civil unrest led to unprecedented numbers of troops moving around the country. Innkeepers in Bath, as in other towns, were called upon to accommodate them. Naturally, the more soldiers there were, the less room there was for other visitors. Eventually, in 1795, the innkeepers of Bath clubbed together and placed a notice in the *Bath Chronicle*:

> The burthen sustained by the innkeepers of Bath, in consequence of the numerous
> soldiers and horses quartered upon them, is immense. – So astonised were a number
> of respectable tradesmen a few days since at seeing the particulars of the expenses
> incurred within this twelvemonth, by one of our innkeepers, that they immediately
> resolved on a voluntary subscription for the general benefit of one shilling a week,

in order to alleviate those burthens, and which they intend to continue during the
war. An example which we hope will be followed throughout the city.

In many other towns and cities, the problem was solved by the building of barracks. Although this solution was not adopted in Bath, the late eighteenth century marked a high point as far as the numbers of troops billeted on innkeepers was concerned.

Nevertheless, problems still continued to occur from time to time. As late as 1917, when Britain had been at war for almost three years, some of Bath's landlords were only too willing to express their resentment at having soldiers billeted on them. Alfred Tanner, of the *Full Moon* at the bottom of Southgate Street, for instance, was fined £5 for preventing soldiers staying at his inn from using fire and utensils "for dressing their meat." The hostility of innkeepers towards soldiers did have some historical justification, however. In 1805, for example, "a party of Irish recruits, belonging to the 43rd Regiment, passing … through Kelston, most inhumanly beat and cut Mr Bence of the *Crown Inn*."

Throughout history, pubs have been used as recruiting centres, a glass or two of ale often being used to bolster arguments for taking the King's Shilling. In 1758, for example, "the militia for this division were sworn at the *Three Tuns Inn* by the Deputy Lieutenant; several volunteers offered, and they all had money given them to drink his Majesty's health." In January 1900, as the Boer War got under way, 46 volunteers joined the North Somerset Yeomanry at the *King's Arms* on Monmouth Street.

Recruitment was often accompanied by coercion. In the eighteenth century, some petty criminals were offered enlistment as an alternative to prison or transportation. In 1771, for example, "Arnold, a mason, for stealing a loin of pork from the *Saracen's Head* in this city, was sentenced either to seven years transportation, or to enlist as a soldier, the latter of which he accepted." Needless to say, enlistment was no soft option. It was not just the enemy you had to be worried about. In 1793, the Mayor of Bath called for an investigation after a soldier billeted in the city died after being flogged for a minor misdemeanour.

Recruiting soldiers in pubs was often a successful way of making the numbers up, although some of those who took the King's Shilling woke up regretting it the next morning. Take John Bray, for example, who got more than he bargained for when he took up a trip up to Holloway Fair in 1846:

> George Knight, a sergeant of the 6th Royal Warwickshire Regiment, brought two recruits to be sworn before the magistrates. The men objected to their enlistment as illegal, because they were drunk at the time. The sergeant maintained that they were quite sober. John Bray, one of the recruits, a stripling in a smock coat, was the first who pleaded the objection. The sergeant, being sworn, stated that, on Friday evening, he was at the *Young Fox* public house in Holloway, when Bray came to him and asked to be enlisted, telling him he was "free, willing and able." The sergeant said he would take him, and he asked for half a crown, but the sergeant told him he should only give him the customary shilling. Bray was sober when he enlisted. This was confirmed by a private of the regiment, who saw him enlist and also by William Dick, the landlord of the *Smith's Arms*, Avon Street, at

His Lordship was in great peril of losing the prop from under him

whose house Bray was billeted for the night, with two others. The recruit called several witnesses to prove the contrary, but they did not agree in their statements of some of the facts connected with his intoxicated state. They all concurred, however, in representing the occasion of his potations to be the annual fair held at Holloway, and the usual mockery of electing a Lord Mayor, which functionary they described as being carried in a procession on the shoulders of Bray and another man, who were so drunk that his Lordship was in great peril of losing the prop from under him, and exchanging his dignified elevation for an ignominious prostration on the stones. After a patient hearing of the evidence, the magistrates expressed themselves satisfied that the sobriety of Bray when he enlisted had been proved and ordered him to be sworn or pay the smart. He was not prepared for the latter, but his friends asked for time before he was sworn. It was agreed to give him till four o'clock.

No prizes for guessing what they did till four o'clock.

A few years earlier, in 1841, a melancholy story appeared in the *Bath Chronicle* concerning a soldier who was billeted at the *Shakespeare* in Old Orchard Street. George Walton, of the 21st Fusiliers, decided he had had enough of army life and deserted. He made his way to Wells, but, after a while, returned to Bath and took a job in a stone yard on the Lower Bristol Road. When the recruiting sergeant heard of this he went down to the yard with a police inspector. "They found him," the report continued,

> breaking stones there and the recruiting sergeant beckoned to him and called him by a nickname that he had – 'Scruffy.' As soon as he heard him he jumped over the yard wall to the next buildings. Witness then went round and found that he had jumped into the river. He was swimming and had got about 20 yards across when he appeared to be suddenly seized with the cramp and brought forward his right shoulder and went with the stream.

A verdict of accidental death was recorded.

To end this section on a more cheerful note, the following story, from August 1856, shows that, even when pitted against almost insuperable odds, soldiers were still prepared to give a good account of themselves:

> William Maggs, William Bishop and Frederick Watkins, three young men, all of whom are "Crimean heroes," and two of whom have lost a leg each in the late war, were charged with being drunk, riotous and assaulting PCs 30, 55, 52, 61 and 62.

The soldiers were in the company of certain ladies of easy virtue near that den of vice, the *Bell Inn* in Lower Borough Walls (now the Fairie Shop), between one and two o'clock in the morning, and laid into the police when asked to move on. Given that the soldiers only had four legs between the three of them, and still managed to put up a good fight against five fit and fully-equipped constables, you do wonder what they had been drinking.

CHAPTER TEN

CRIME AND PUNISHMENT

If a man indulges himself in murder, very soon he comes to think little of robbing; and from robbing he next comes to drinking and Sabbath-breaking, and from that to incivility and procrastination.
Thomas de Quincey

As far back as you care to go, people have been blaming alcohol for just about everything. James I, for example, declared in 1606 that:

> the loathsome sin of drunkenness is of late grown into common use within this realm, being the root and foundation of many other enormous sins, as bloodshed, stabbing, murder, swearing, fornication, adultery, and such like, to the great dishonour of God, and of our nation, the overthrow of many good arts and manual trades, the disabling of divers workmen, and the general impoverishing of many good subjects, abusively wasting the good creatures of God.

So he passed a law imposing a five shilling fine for drunkenness – or, indeed, for spending too long in an alehouse. If the money was not forthcoming – and five shillings back then was equivalent to around £30 today – the culprit ended up in the stocks for six hours. That was if they were found drunk away from home. If they were found drunk in their own neighbourhood, the fine rose to eight shillings and fourpence or ten hours in the stocks. The reasoning behind this was that "the ancient, true and proper use of inns and ale houses is for the receipt, relief and lodging of wayfaring people [and not] for the entertainment and harbouring of lewd and idle people to spend their time and money in a lewd and drunken manner."

If you think that was a bit stiff, things were even worse across the Channel. A sixteenth-century French edict laid down that

> any man found guilty of being drunk will be condemned: on the first offence, to detention in prison on bread and water; on the second offence, to be whipped in the inner court of the prison; on the third offence, to be whipped publicly; and on the fourth offence, he shall have both his ears cut off and be banished from the Kingdom of France.

Which, if nothing else, is an interesting spin on the concept of "Three Strikes and You're Out." It is not recorded, however, whether the English Government of the day was concerned about a growing tide of earless, drunken French asylum seekers clogging up the Channel ports.

Another instrument of punishment for drunkenness, popular during the reign of Cromwell, was the Drunkard's Cloak. In 1655, Ralph Gardner wrote that he had:

> seen men drove up and down the streets, with a great tub or barrel open in the sides, with a hole in one end to put through their heads, and so cover their shoulders and bodies, down to the small of their legs, and then close the same; called the new-fashion cloak, and so make them march to the view of all beholders, and this is their punishment for drunkards and the like.

Although the drunkard's cloak soon fell out of favour, the stocks survived, as a method of teaching Bath's impoverished drunkards a lesson, until the mid-nineteenth century. In September, 1816, for example,

> an old woman was confined in the stocks in the Market Place for acts of repeated intoxication. Saturday a man was placed in the stocks near St James's church for a similar offence and was also ordered to be imprisoned for three weeks.

Just before Christmas 1829,

> Sarah Jane Manley was fined five shillings and costs for being in a state of intoxication and for improper conduct in the streets of this city; and in default of payment, she was confined in the stocks for two hours.

As a form of punishment, the stocks was not far removed from lynch law. If you were regarded as a good sort of chap, or had a band of strong-armed relatives ready to defend you, then a few hours in the stocks would be little more than a minor – if uncomfortable – inconvenience. If, on the other hand, you were friendless and unpopular, a stint in the stocks was no laughing matter. It was also a question of the type of crime you were put in them for. If you had been cocking a snook at authority, the chances are you would be hailed as a hero. If you were a market trader and had been caught giving short measures – or short change – then the chances are you would not get off so lightly. Drunkards did not generally get much hassle – although it cannot have been too pleasant sobering up in the stocks, especially as the sort of facilities you would be likely to need after downing copious amounts of alcohol were unavailable.

Ironically, the last man to sit in the stocks in Bath was not put there for drunkenness, but ended up drunk anyway:

> The last man that appeared in the public stocks in Bath [in 1839] ... was the bibulous old newsagent Bobby Crocker, not for his usual habit of imbibing unwisely or too freely, but for the heinous offence of selling the abusive and offensive *Bath Figaro* on a Sunday ... Robert was not the only one that vended this opprobrious and ribald publication on the Sabbath, but through his indigence he was the most powerless to defend himself for the offence. The scene of poor old Bobby's appearance, with his legs locked in the implement of punishment, was in the green of the Orange Grove, before it was laid out in flower beds. The poor old offender, who was between 50 and 60 years of age, perhaps nearer the latter, sat facing the *Cross Keys* and what is now the Police Station, with his back to the obelisk. A policeman was there on sentry, and promenaded in front of the

delinquent, inside the railing, during the two or three hours the unhappy man was padlocked in his unenviable position. Whilst Robert was thus situated, thousands of the populace flocked to the Grove to witness the spectacle, and hundreds cast into the enclosure coppers for the unfortunate man's benefit. Besides which, kind friends, who were patrons of the *Cross Keys* tavern, chief among them being a well-known official at the Guildhall, a rollicking, good-natured fellow, up to any bit of fun, frequently handed to the policeman an orange for Bobby to moisten his parched tongue with and these he sucked with great relish. Luckily for him the sentry was a man with pity and sympathy for his miserable position, and every copper thrown into the green was immediately recovered and put into the culprit's hat. By the time the period of incarceration had expired, Bobby's hat was half full of current coins of the realm, and how many half-pints it furnished him with after he gained his liberty I am utterly at a loss to guess. But I must here inform my readers that the oranges passed on to Robert had been cleverly doctored and each contained a quantity of neat brandy, so that when the time arrived for his release he was quite fuddled. The policeman and the public were fairly puzzled at Robert's droll condition, none but he and his kind friends at the hotel possessing the secret. Bobby's friends were on hand to take care of him when released.

Bath's stocks now reside in the Guildhall as a reminder of the good old days. Each parish had its own set. Twerton's was opposite the *White Hart* in the High Street. Walcot's was at the junction of London Street and the Paragon. REM Peach, writing in 1890, recalled the stocks at Swainswick:

In the centre of the open space was a green where the maypole was erected and against Pickwick's stabling (which opened onto the barton) were the stocks. They have disappeared, but I well remember Brain, the constable, placing a drunken man there, and my amusement at seeing him from my nursery window.

For more serious crimes there was the pillory. In effect, this meant handing criminals over to the mob. In 1698, a foreign visitor described the pillory as follows:

Offenders are exposed in a high place, with their heads put through two pieces of notched wood; the uppermost whereof being made to slide down, shuts the neck into the notch. The criminal's hands are confined on each side of his head in the same manner; and thus he stands in this ridiculous posture for more or less time, or with more or fewer repetitions, according to his sentence.

Looking ridiculous was the least of the culprit's problems, for, no sooner had his head been secured, than he found it was serving the same function as that served by a coconut in a shy. Mud, rotten fruit, excrement, dead cats, offal, bad eggs and stones were among the weapons employed, their variety limited only by the imagination of the mob. It was not unknown for victims to be pelted so severely that they died. The crimes for which the mob reserved particular opprobrium were sexual – rape and child abuse, in particular. In Bath in 1763, for example, Thomas Newman, aged 20, was sentenced to stand in the pillory for assaulting two children. The sentence was later commuted to 18 months imprisonment because feelings against him ran so high that the magistrates thought he would be killed if placed in the pillory.

She has danc'd naked before a number of gentlemen

Newman's was a sad case. At his trial it was revealed that, prior to his arrest, he had slept in the same bed as his mother every night since he was a child. There were, unfortunately, no social workers in the eighteenth century.

Brothel-house keeping also roused the mob to anger. In 1727, *Farley's Bristol Newspaper* reported that:

> we hear … from Bath that one Lewes and his wife stood in the pillory there on Saturday last, being convicted of keeping a bad house of repute, and procuring young women to be debauch'd, and forcing them so to do; for which they were severely pelted; when his wife was mounting the scaffold, she had the arrogance to make the following blasphemous comparison, saying that she was now going to imitate the sufferings of our Saviour, being as innocent of the fact she was going to suffer for, as he was when crucified; the chief evidence against her, it seems, was one of her female servants, who having some words with her said mistress, would live no longer with her; and therefore demanded her wages and clothes; but she refusing to comply with her demands, the servant went immediately to a magistrate, and blow'd up the whole scene of her mistress's way of life; particularly that she has danc'd naked before a number of gentlemen, and for her agility, had half a crown of each.

Mr and Mrs Lewes were luckier than Mother Needham, a notorious London

AWASH WITH ALE

procuress, who died after being pelted in the stocks four years later.

Mob fury was also reserved for homosexuals. Sodomy was made a capital offence in 1533, although the first execution was not carried out until over 100 years later. In the eighteenth century, however, the Society for the Reformation of Morals started a crusade against homosexuality, and the number of executions started to rise, reaching an average of two a year by the early nineteenth century. It was a difficult thing to prove, however, and many prosecutors went for the easier option of attempted sodomy. For this the punishment was generally a spell in the pillory. Many of those sentenced died of the injuries they received. In 1810, a number of men were caught in a gay bar in Vere Street, London. When they were dragged to the pillory, a crowd of between 30,000 and 50,000 people were there to greet them:

> Before any of them reached the place of punishment, their faces were completely disfigured by blows and mud … Upwards of 50 women were permitted to stand in the ring, who assailed them incessantly with mud, dead cats, rotten eggs, potatoes, and buckets filled with blood, offal and dung, which were brought by a number of butchers' men from St James's Market.

Incredibly, they all survived, a circumstance which the newspapers regarded as regrettable. There are no records of a similar outrage in Bath. When an Alderman called John Ford was excluded from office in 1741 for making a "sodomitical attempt," his family and business connections meant that no further action was taken.

Other forms of punishment did not leave the severity of the sentence to the whim of the mob. Crimes against property were often viewed more seriously than crimes against people. From the late seventeenth century onwards, the number of offences for which you could be hanged rose dramatically. Some of them were bizarre – if you maliciously cut down hops, consorted with gypsies, chopped down a tree, stole a fish out of a pond or impersonated an out-pensioner of Greenwich Hospital, you could end up at the end of a rope. Grand larceny – also punishable by death – was defined as the theft of articles worth a shilling or more. Trials seem designed to produce travesties of justice. Prisoners were not allowed to give evidence on their own behalf or defend themselves except on a point of law – and they could only do that without prompting. The judge generally doubled as Counsel for the Defence. The arbitrariness of the legal process was not the only thing prisoners had to contend with. Conditions in prison were so bad that many of those awaiting trial died through ill-treatment, malnourishment or disease before they got to court.

One execution among thousands will serve to highlight the soulless brutality of the justice system in the late eighteenth century. In 1770, Mary Jones was turned out onto the streets of London after her husband was press-ganged "on the alarm about the Falkland Islands." She was 18 years old. Reduced to poverty, with two near-naked and starving children to look after, she picked up some coarse material in a shop in Ludgate Street and slipped it under her cloak. When she realised she had been spotted, she put it back, but it was too late. Brought to trial, she was sentenced to be hanged, despite assurances of previous good behaviour from the parish officers. There had, it was pointed out, been a lot of shoplifting in the Ludgate Street area, and it was necessary to make an example of her to discourage others. She was

> hanged for the comfort and satisfaction of shopkeepers in Ludgate Street. When
> brought to receive sentence, she behaved in such a frantic manner, as proved her
> mind to be in a distracted and desponding state; and the child was sucking at her
> breast when she set out for Tyburn.

Over two centuries later, the echoes of her cries still call to heaven for retribution. It is no wonder that the vast majority of people – those who did not swan around in gilded carriages and gulp fine wines – were angry. No wonder, too, that the establishment walked in such fear and trepidation of the mob.

Executions were carried out in public until well into the nineteenth century. Public hangings were the occasion for the worst type of mob frenzy. In 1822, for example, the *Bath Chronicle* reported the case of George and Benjamin Day, found guilty of burglary at Wincanton, and sentenced to be hanged at Ilminster:

> The spectators were unusually numerous, and consisted of three females to one
> man; their behaviour is reported as being disgraceful in the extreme, their brutal
> shouts and mirth even disturbing the administration of the last Holy Sacrament.

The majority of people lived closer to ending up at the end of a rope than we may like to think. Suddenly finding yourself without the means to support yourself or your family was an ever-present threat, whether through illness or lack of work. A spot of petty pilfering or poaching to stave off gnawing, chronic hunger or to clothe sick, shivering infants could easily end in a one-way trip to the gallows. The powers that be accepted this state of affairs as perfectly normal. After all, this sort of punishment was only meted out to the poor. If you belonged to the middle or upper classes, you could afford to buy your way out of trouble – at least that was the theory. It did not always work like that, however. Take the case of Mrs Leigh Perrott, Jane Austen's aunt, who lived on the Paragon in Bath. Accused, like Mary Jones, of stealing material from a shop, the allegedly purloined item was found wrapped up with some other material she had paid for. It seems fairly clear, from the evidence, that she was set up, and that the shop was running a scam to extort money from wealthy Bathonians. Others had coughed up without a murmur, fearing the consequences if they did not. Mrs Leigh Perrott, however, refused to pay the hush money demanded and was carted off to gaol to await trial. It was a dangerous gamble. If found guilty, the very least she could have looked forward to would have been transportation. Her gamble paid off, however, and her innocence was vindicated.

William Dodd, Doctor of Divinity, Prebendary of Brecon, Chaplain in Ordinary to His Majesty, Minister to the Magdalen Hospital and Brock Street Chapel, Bath, was not so lucky. He was a benevolent man who founded a number of charitable bodies, such as the Magdalen Society for Reclaiming Young Women who have Swerved from the Path of Virtue, the Society for the Relief of Poor Debtors, and the Humane Society for the Recovery of Persons Apparently Drowned. He also had a fairly extravagant lifestyle, and, finding himself financially embarrassed, forged a cheque for £300 in the name of his patron, Lord Chesterfield. When the fraud was discovered, Lord Chesterfield offered to overlook the matter, but despite this, and the intervention of a gallery of influential friends, including Dr Johnson, Dr Dodd was tried, found guilty of fraud and hanged at Tyburn in 1777. The ensuing outcry did much to bring public opinion around to the view that the laws relating to capital punishment needed a major overhaul. While it is impossible to argue with those who saw Dr Dodd's execution as the breaking of a butterfly on a wheel, why did they not raise their voices when Mary Jones, and thousands like her, met their untimely end? The sad thing is that they would not have seen themselves as hypocrites. Dr Dodd was a member of polite society; Mary Jones was not. Even people as supposedly wise as Dr Johnson hardly questioned assumptions which, today, would not be entertained by even the most rabid reactionaries.

Even when the ultimate deterrent was not applied, punishment was draconian. In Bath in 1754, for example, "Martin Dibble was publicly whipped from Northgate to the bridge for stealing two kilderkins from the brewhouse of Mr Benjamin Wingrove of this City." In 1758 a twelve-year-old Bathonian called Thomas Barber was sentenced to seven years transportation "for stealing a sixpenny loaf, a pound of bacon and a knife value sixpence." In February 1773, Thomas Fuller was caught with "a silver tankard from Mr Fuller at the *White Hart Inn* in Avon Street in this city." He was sent to the Bridewell at Shepton Mallet where he languished until April. Then, at the Wells Assizes, he was condemned to death, along with twelve other miscreants, but was later reprieved and sentenced to transportation.

The severity of the sentences meted out does not seem to have deterred the light-fingered fraternity, however. At times, the theft of tankards from pubs reached crisis level, as this announcement from the *Bath Chronicle* for 21 April 1774 indicates:

> Joseph Thwaites at the *Queen's Head* [in Cheap Street] returns his sincere thanks for the many favours he daily receives; and is extremely sorry that many of his customers should be offended and leave his house, owing to a want of measures to serve them: The real cause of which proceeds from the great number sent out of doors, and the difficulty to get them returned. He therefore hopes that those who have any of his measures will be kind enough to return them or let him know where he may send for them, as he doubts not but there are many in the houses of those who are not his constant customers, he having lost six dozen within the last six months … Joseph Thwaites having been informed that several of his measures have been wilfully melted, and otherwise destroyed, and sold for old metal, or concealed for that purpose, offers a reward of one guinea to anyone who will give information of the persons guilty of the said offence, so that they may be brought to justice.

Transportation was not the only alternative to execution. In 1763 the *Bath Journal* reported the case of a condemned prisoner who agreed to have his leg amputated, as a medical experiment in staunching the flow of blood, in exchange for his life.

Well into the nineteenth century, whipping and transportation were commonplace. In 1839, for example, "William Barnes, tailor, pleaded guilty to [stealing] a beer warmer, value one shilling and sixpence, the property of George

Kelly. The prisoner had been in prison before, and was told by the Recorder in passing sentence, that if brought before him again he would be transported." He was sentenced to "one month's imprisonment, and during that time to be twice privately whipped." This hardened criminal was just 14 years old. At the same time, William Rawlings, an eighteen-year-old labourer, was sentenced to ten years transportation for stealing four pounds of potatoes, value fourpence, as it was his second offence. Such sentences were not particularly uncommon. At the Bath Quarter Sessions in January 1853, for example, three people were sentenced to transportation – John Wheeler (27) for stealing a turkey, Henry Brown (23) for stealing a hammer, and Harriet Hill (22) for stealing a pair of trousers.

As Fred Wedlock has pointed out, the only difference between us and the Australians is that their ancestors got caught. The government had decided that enforced settlement of people from the lower classes was the best way to develop the colonies and relieve overcrowding at home. Instead of conscripting them, they let candidates for transportation select themselves by breaking the law. Between 1788 and 1868, 160,000 convicts were transported to Australia. Somerset, naturally, contributed its share. To take just one year – 1835 – as an example: of the 684 people tried at the Assize or Quarter Session Courts in Somerset, 50 were sentenced to transportation for life, 21 to transportation for 14 years, and 70 to transportation for 7 years. Fifteen were sentenced to death, although in all but three cases, the sentence was commuted to transportation for life.

Many of the crimes which carried heavy sentences in the eighteenth and nineteenth centuries, such as stealing a loaf of bread or a handkerchief, would be likely to lead to accusations of wasting police time if reported today. It really was a case of zero tolerance. In 1835, for example, "James Whalley and Moses Flower, two notorious juvenile thieves, were committed for three months hard labour for stealing apples, the property of TM Crutwell Esq."

Transportation was as brutal a piece of social policy as can be imagined, tearing what were regarded as the less desirable elements in society away from their loved ones, shipping them off to the other side of the world and forcing them to work as slaves in atrocious conditions. The journey out was pretty appalling as well. You had to be tough to make it. Many did not. Take the case of another Mary Jones in 1764, for example:

On Monday last Mary Jones, one of the convicts lately transported from Bristol for stealing a silver pint was taken out of the river and landed at Gibb. The cause of her death is said to proceed from the ship, *Albion*, giving sudden motion, which threw them confusedly together, and she being undermost was smothered.

That was not the end of the troubles of the *Albion*, as the *Bath Chronicle* reported a week later:

We hear from Bristol that on Saturday morning put back again into King Road the *Albion* transportation ship. The convicts on board had formed a scheme to make themselves masters of the vessel, and after destroying the crew, to carry her to Spain. For this purpose they had got their irons off through the help of a blacksmith (one of their number) and everything was ready to carry their bloody design into execution the Wednesday before the vessel returned; when one of the persons concerned informed the Captain of the whole affair. The crew being alarmed, they were all properly secured, after they had fired on them through the deck; happily no lives were lost, but one of the transports was shot through the leg, and another through the arm, who were brought up and sent to the infirmary Sunday last.

Drunkenness was at the root of much of the petty crime which came before the magistrates. So accustomed was the *Bath Chronicle* to publishing long lists of convicted drunkards that, when the numbers dropped, it was reported with some surprise. On 29 May 1851, for example,

there was only one drunken case and a man charged with deserting his wife and children. Both prisoners were discharged.

Earlier that month, however, there had been more than enough to keep the magistrates busy. The previous week,

Jacob Simmons, well known as 'Drop-me-down,' was charged with being drunk and incapable. Having been previously fined for the same offence, he was required to find bail in £10, to be of good behaviour for one month, or to go to gaol for that time.

A couple of weeks earlier there was the sort of case that makes a journalist's day:

Three working men named William Stone, Henry Baker and John Pullen were placed at the bar, Stone charged with being drunk, and all three with being disorderly ... Police constables Matthews and Worthing stated that, at a late hour on Saturday night, they met the prisoners coming from Monmouth Street shouting and making a noise. They ordered the prisoners to desist, but they went on through Westgate Buildings continuing noisy, when Stone and Baker were taken into custody. Baker resisted, and Pullen attempted to rescue him, and having followed them to the station house, he was locked up, but, with Baker, subsequently bailed out. Stone, being, as was alleged, in a state of intoxication, was detained. On the prisoners being asked what they had to say to the charge, Stone, as spokesman for them, first denied that he was drunk, and then stated that, instead of being noisy or disorderly, they were returning home gravely discoursing on the pendulum experiment recently made in illustration of the earth's diurnal motion, and he (Stone) was proposing to convince his rather incredulous companions of the truth of the theory, by employing his own apparatus, when the constable interfered.

Pullen was discharged, the other two were fined two shillings and sixpence with costs.

It was not only in the rougher parts of town, nor in the small hours, that drunken outrages occurred. Mid-afternoon in mid-Victorian Milsom Street might have seemed a safe haven from the delirious depredations of the drinking classes. It was not:

Henry Huntley, a cooper by trade, was charged with insulting several ladies in

Milsom Street yesterday afternoon. Inspector Dunn said he found the prisoner grossly insulting several ladies by hitting them and pulling their dresses with a stick. The officer remonstrated with him for his indecorous conduct, upon which the prisoner abused him and he took him into custody. His conduct on being taken to the station house was extremely violent and he made a furious assault upon the officer whom he threw down several times and kicked him. The prisoner in his defence said he was very drunk indeed, and his senses really gone through some persons having put something into his beer, which they forced him to drink.

A plea of involuntary intoxication still crops up in criminal trials, and the danger of Mickey Finns has now been augmented by that of date-rape drugs. Huntley's defence, however, cut no ice with the magistrates, and he was sent down.

The editor of the *Bath Herald* had first-hand experience of the evils of drink when he accused a news vendor of stealing newspapers in 1850. The vendor went on a bender and, when he returned to the newspaper office, put a pistol to the editor's head, demanding an apology.

Some drunken outrages were comic rather than threatening. The following disturbance led a budding Dickens from the *Bath Chronicle* to burst into panegyrical effluence:

William Fenwick, a well-known peripatetic in gastronomic philosophy, vulgarly called a pieman, was charged with being drunk and riotous. It appears that the defendant is accustomed to traverse the streets at night with his portable bakehouse, the produce of which he announces in certain vocal modulations, calculated to catch the ears of his customers and extract the pence from their pockets. He was following his vocation in this way beyond the midnight hour on Saturday, and was found by a policeman between twelve and one o'clock on Sunday morning in Southgate Street, more vociferous and elated than was compatible with the quiet of the inhabitants; and, on being requested to desist, refused to do so, and became abusive.

And then there was the case of the Phantom Potato Thrower of Great Pulteney Street:

A young man named John Fowler was brought before the magistrates on Monday, charged with being drunk on the preceding evening. Whilst in this condition he had been amusing himself by throwing potatoes, stones and other missiles through the windows of the houses at the back of Pulteney Street, much to the annoyance of the inhabitants. After a suitable admonition, he was bound over to keep the peace for three months.

The leniency of the sentence suggests that Mr Fowler was not a member of the working classes. In the nineteenth century, what counted as a crime if you were working class often became a misdemeanour if you were middle class and an amusing foible if you belonged to the gentry. There seems little doubt which class the unfortunate character in the following story belonged to:

On Tuesday evening one of the policemen on duty near the Old Bridge met a man, named Thomas Clarkson, to whom his attention was more than particularly drawn from observing the end of a tea spoon sticking out beneath his hat. On taking off the *chapeau* he found it also contained a rummer glass; from the appearance of which it would seem that he had been treating himself to a glass of grog and had brought away the articles which accompanied it by way of a set-off against payment. The prisoner had been seen coming from the neighbourhood of the *Full Moon*, and on enquiry being made it was discovered that the articles had been taken from there.

There were some bizarre notions of what constituted a crime in the nineteenth century. In 1851, for example, Christopher Doyle, "an Irish wise man, was sentenced to 21 days with hard labour for pretending to be a fortune teller." As late as 1900, George Davis, aged 32, of Oxford Cottage, Camden Row was charged with "practising palmistry with an intent to deceive."

Simply spending too much time in the pub was enough you get you locked away. In 1814,

John Parker of Bathwick was sentenced to one months hard labour for not using proper means to get employment, but spending his money in alehouses and places of bad repute, and suffering his wife and family to become chargeable to the said parish.

In October 1835, "William Roberts and Robert Hook were committed for three months imprisonment with hard labour for playing on the roadside the game of Pricking the Garter near Twerton." Pricking the garter was a con trick which dated back to the middle ages. Even so, people were still being taken in by it in 1835. A fast-talking conman gathered a crowd around him, took a garter or thin strip of leather and folded it in half. He then wound it into a coil, making two loops in the centre of the coil, and invited a gullible bystander to put a stick in the centre, betting that it would not hold fast when both ends of the coil were pulled. If the conman was nimble-fingered enough, he would win the bet every time. It was also known as "Fast and Loose," under which guise it was mentioned by Shakespeare, and has, of course, given rise to the phrase, "don't play fast and loose with me."

No survey of petty crime in bygone Bath would be complete without mentioning that noble group of chaps – drinkers to a man – the sedan chairmen. They were already carrying "the better sort of people" around the city when Celia Fiennes visited the city around 1700. Possibly the most inefficient form of transport ever invented, with two people carrying one, the sedan chair epitomised the social inequalities of eighteenth-century Bath. But the sedan chairmen had one advantage over their customers. When it came to arguing about the fare, the customer was always outnumbered two to one. Initially, there was no control over the sedan chairmen and they charged what they thought they could get away with. If there was a dispute,

they would not let their customer out of the chair, though if it was raining they would open the top and let him or her – often an invalid – be exposed to the wet, until in despair the charge was met. This state of affairs was much improved under Nash's reign, but the men were independent; and misbehaved upon occasion. Even so late as 1743 they came into conflict with the authorities on a night when a certain duke and his friends, staying at one of the Assembly Houses after the ball, instead of availing themselves of the services of the expectant chairmen, as was customary, the night being fine, decided to walk home. The sequel appeared in a proclamation:

Bath, May 18th, 1743.

Whereas on the 12th instant, between hours of twelve and one o'clock several gentlemen and ladies were greatly insulted, by having dirt thrown upon them, by some persons unknown, in, and near the churchyard, and Mr Nash having promised a reward of two guineas for the discovery of such person or persons, so as he or they may be thereof convicted.

Just because the eighteenth- and nineteenth-century authorities spent large amounts of their time pursuing what would today not even be regarded as petty criminals, does not mean there was no serious crime to worry about. Theft and violent crime were endemic and many pubs were little more than thieves' dens. In a report sent to the Watch Committee in 1869, 15 pubs were described as "the haunts of thieves and prostitutes."

By the mid-nineteenth century, armed robbery was rare, but 100 years earlier, reports like the following were commonplace:

Last Monday night, about ten o'clock, Mr Philip Brown, Nursery Man, was attack'd near the end of the Terrace Walk in Kingsmead by two footpads, one of whom presented a pistol to his breast, and bid him stand; upon which he catch'd hold of the pistol and wrench'd it from the fellow's hand; and then they made off. The pistol was loaded with a ball and coarse cannon powder; it has a screw barrel and on it is engraved J Jenkins.

If you were incautious enough to wander outside the city, the risk of being attacked was much higher. The monument on Lansdown, where travellers had to negotiate the steep hill down towards Hamswell, was a favourite spot for footpads and highwaymen. Here is a typical report from 1772:

Wednesday last as Samuel Evans, butcher, of Bridget, in the Parish of Wick, was returning from Bath Market, he was attack'd near the monument on Lansdown by two footpads who demanded his money, and on his refusing to deliver it, one of them put a pistol to his head and discharged it. They then pulled him off his horse and robbed him of about £20. When he got home he found in his breeches part of a pewter spoon, with which the villains had loaded the pistol.

Messrs Brown and Evans were lucky. Unreliable guns meant that many who resisted highway robbery lived to tell the tale. Although death at the hands of a footpad or highwayman was an ever-present possibility in the eighteenth century, death during an alehouse brawl was more common still. Here it was knives rather than guns that were used. Most men carried some sort of knife, and the temptation to reach for it in a moment of drunken fury, especially if they were getting a drubbing at the hands of an opponent, sometimes proved too much. Here, for example, is the report of a

Friday night drinking session in Walcot Street in 1793 which ended in tragedy:

> A very unfortunate instance of human ferocity occurred in this city last week. Some tradesmen of character were sitting in the publick room of a house in Walcot Street on Friday evening, when one Peter Cottel, a follower of sheriff's officers, came in, and during the course of conversation used language exceedingly opprobrious and insulting, which exasperated several of the company, but particularly Francis Morley, a plasterer. On Morley's first remonstrating with, and afterwards threatening to chastise Cottel for his insolence, he increased his abuse, and invited Morley to strike him. This Morley did, and some blows ensued, in which Cottel was knocked down. After a second round, whilst lying on his face, he secretly took a small penknife from his pocket; and on getting up, after an interval, he invited Morley to a renewal of the attack. In the course of this scuffle, Cottel gave Morley a severe stab in the chest, and attempted another on the thigh, which was averted by money in his pocket. Morley stood a few seconds, and exclaimed he was stabbed, the blood gathering from the wound. Mr Creaser, surgeon, was sent for, who discovered that the heart was penetrated, in consequence of which he died in a few minutes. Cottel was immediately secured, and the Coroner's Jury, without hesitation, gave a verdict of wilful murder. The deceased was a man of industrious and peaceable character. The behaviour and expressions of Cottel after his apprehension were an aggravation of his crime. The wound was inflicted with peculiar violence, as part of the knife was found on Cottel, and another portion broken on the floor

Almost fifty years later, in January 1842, the old *Weymouth Arms* on Julian Road was the venue for a similar affray:

> On Tuesday night, two men named Edward Cains, a clipper of horses, and William Bushell, a plumber, were drinking together when a quarrel arose between them and blows followed. After beating each other for some time Cains went out and returned with a large clasp knife with which he inflicted a fearful wound on the side of Bushell's neck, from which the blood flowed copiously. Surgical assistance was procured and the wounded man was taken to the hospital, where he lies in a precarious state.

Less than three months earlier another man had died as a result of a fight that broke out in the tap room of the *Carriage Inn* at Combe Down. These three examples were not isolated incidents, but ones taken at random from eighteenth- and nineteenth-century newspaper reports.

Outrages of this kind were not confined to alehouses, although overindulgence in alcohol was almost invariably a contributory factor. Most murder – certainly most unpremeditated murder – was alcohol related. A common defence, throughout the ages, has been that a murderer cannot be held responsible for actions carried out under the influence of alcohol. Waking up the morning after with no knowledge of what happened the night should absolve the murderer of responsibility, in the same way that they would be absolved if they were insane – or so the argument goes. It was, however, thrown out of court as long ago as 1551. The judgement made then still holds good today:

> If a person that is drunk kills another, this shall be felony, and he shall be hanged
> for it, and yet he did it through ignorance, for when he was drunk he had no
> understanding nor memory; but inasmuch as that ignorance was occasioned by
> his own act and folly, and he might have avoided it, he shall not be privileged
> thereby.

Drink also figured in many suicides. It was not just a question of Dutch Courage. Frequently, coroners recorded that the deceased had been drunk for weeks before taking his or her life. Despite – bizarrely – being a capital offence, suicide was far higher in the eighteenth and nineteenth centuries than it is today, a reflection of the lives of unrelieved misery many people had to endure.

Until the 1840s, there were three favoured methods of doing away with yourself – hanging, cutting your throat or jumping into the river. To this unholy trinity was added, in the 1840s, poisoning. Poisoning also became a popular way of getting rid of other people. Although poison had been around for centuries – in 1753, for example, a woman had been burned at the stake in Wells for poisoning her husband – it was a minority pursuit. A century later, however, it was so popular that, when a woman in Dolemeads died suddenly of natural causes in 1853, the neighbours immediately jumped to the erroneous conclusion that her husband had poisoned her.

The saddest eighteenth- and nineteenth-century murder stories are those concerning infants. Infanticide was a regular occurrence until after the First World War. On 26 May 1853, for example, the *Bath Chronicle* reported the "shocking depravity" of two murdered infants found within a few days of each other in Bathwick – one in a ditch and one in the river. Such acts were the natural consequence of casual prostitution or of servant girls falling for the wiles of their masters (or of servants higher up the ladder). Sometimes babies were left outside the doors of large houses or churches in the hope that they would be taken in, but just as often they were drowned in the river or left to the mercy of the elements. The unimaginable desperation of the girls who were driven to murder their own babies is a measure of the certain destitution which faced them if they kept them, and the barbarity of a system which forced them to this terrible choice.

We have a tendency to think that people in the past were fundamentally different to us, immune to tragedy and suffering because they suffered so much. They were not. Superficially, they differed from us in myriad ways. Essentially, they did not differ at all. Girls driven to kill their babies were haunted by their guilty secret until their death. Some were so overwhelmed by remorse that they took their own lives, following their unfortunate offspring into the unforgiving river. In the dim, distant past, a girl who became pregnant had little choice but to have the baby. Taking more desperate measures, as this newspaper report from 1800 indicates, often had fatal consequences:

> Saturday an inquisition was taken of the body of Doneslayte (or Daws), whose
> death was occasioned by a medicine taken to cause abortion. She was a native

of Keynsham, and lived as a servant at a public house in the Upper Bristol Road, where she became pregnant. By the evidence given before the jury, it appeared that the dose had been administered by Mary, the wife of Stephen Longford. A verdict of wilful murder was returned against her, and she has in consequence been committed to Shepton Mallet Gaol.

To end this chapter on crime and punishment on a more upbeat note, it is salutary to remind ourselves that some criminals lived to reap the benefit of their crimes. Although his crimes were not alcohol related, the Duke of Chandos – possibly the biggest criminal in Bath's history – has an indirect connection with alcohol, as the house built for him by John Wood later became a pub.[*] Here is Professor Park Honan's assessment of the Dubious Duke:

> Nobody else before the eighteenth century had robbed England on such a scale. At 29, James Brydges was an Admiralty Commissioner ... and at 30 Paymaster General to the Forces Abroad. Secretly pocketing money on nearly every payment he made to Marlborough's troops, Brydges had exploited the difference between market and official rates of exchange and skimmed the top off £15,374,689 in public funds that were under his control between 1705 and 1711. Supplying inferior equipment to troops who were later defeated in Spain, he made such a fortune that his private turnover with Antwerp and London brokers equalled in a short time one-fiftieth of the national debt, or later what would be one-thirty-seventh of the whole state debt of the kingdom. [He] was created first Duke of Chandos in 1719.

Perhaps, after that, it is perhaps best to end with a song – the one sung by the condemned highwayman Macheath at the end of John Gay's *Beggar's Opera*, written in 1728:

> *Since laws were made for every degree,*
> *To curb vice in others as well as me,*
> *I wonder we han't better company*
> *Upon Tyburn tree!*
>
> *But gold from law can take out the sting;*
> *And if rich men like us were to swing,*
> *'Twould thin the land, such numbers to string*
> *Upon Tyburn tree!*

---

* Chandos House was built by John Wood for the Duke of Chandos in the late 1720s. By 1848, part of it had become a pub called the *Chandos Arms*. It closed in 1914 and today forms part of St John's Hospital.

CHAPTER ELEVEN

SEX AND LOATHING IN SODOM CITY

I always esteemed drunkenness the most odious of vices. There is something to be said for whoring: whoring is according to nature.
John Dennis, The Impartial Critic, 1693

There was one crime which was inextricably bound up with Bath's pubs in the eighteenth and nineteenth centuries – at least the ones at the lower end of the scale – prostitution. At its root lay economic – and sexual – inequality. There was probably no town in England with such a glaring contrast between rich and poor as Bath. Prostitution in eighteenth- and nineteenth-century London is well documented, but the seamy side of Bath's history is hardly acknowledged. Yet visitors from John Wesley to George Sanger tell us that Bath was just about the most sinful and depraved place in the country.

John Wesley called Bath "that Sodom of our land," thereby setting the seal on its success as England's top pleasure resort. It was indeed a town of easy virtue. Jeremy Melford, in Smollett's *Humphrey Clinker*, describes how an acquaintance of his was frittering away his inheritance:

> Jack Holder, who was intended for a parson, has succeeded to an estate of two thousand a year, by the death of his elder brother. He is now at the Bath, driving about in a phaeton and four, with French horns. He has treated with turtle and claret at all the taverns in Bath and Bristol, till his guests are gorged with good cheer: he has bought a dozen suits of fine clothes, by the advice of the master of the ceremonies, under whose tuition he has entered himself; he has lost some hundreds at billiards to sharpers, and taken one of the nymphs of Avon Street into keeping.

Bath was also notorious as a marriage market. As late as 1803, Robert Southey wrote that:

> it is a fine place for gamblers, and for that species of men called fortune hunters, a race of swindlers of the worst kind ... They make it their business to get a wife of fortune, having none themselves; age, ugliness and idiocy being no objections.

Those who did not manage to make their own arrangements could use the services of a dating agency, like the one advertised in the *Bath Journal* in 1752:

The New BATH REGISTER for Marriages;
Where all persons of either sex may,
By registering by letter their names, fortunes, etc.,
Receive information of parties suitable to their own condition.
Letters left for AB at the Bath Ring Shop in Wade's Passage
will be punctually answered
According to the direction they shall give.

For men who did not want to bother with the rigmarole of courtship, however, there were prostitutes. The hub of Bath's red-light district from the mid-eighteenth century onwards was Avon Street. Its presiding deities were known as the Nymphs of Avon Street. And, of course, where you find nymphs, you also find shepherds. To blame the prostitutes for dragging Avon Street downmarket is like blaming someone for falling over once you've pushed them. But, of course, that was exactly what the (all male) establishment did. They pilloried the prostitutes – sometimes literally – and let their customers get away scot free. The aggrieved punters who resorted to the rule of law when the women they picked up repaid them by picking their pockets were rarely prosecuted. The following story, from 1850, is typical of hundreds which graced the pages of Bath's newspapers in the eighteenth and nineteenth centuries:

> Fanny Hooper, a woman of the town, was charged with having robbed Henry Silver of a purse and money. The prosecutor said that he met the prisoner in Westgate Street at 8.30 on the evening of Saturday last, and they went into the *Westgate House* [in Westgate Buildings] to have something to drink together. Shortly afterwards they went to her lodgings at 1 Peter Street and thence to the *King's Head* [in Lilliput Alley], where they procured a bed. He there changed half a sovereign for something to drink and to pay for the bed with, putting the change into his purse, which contained eleven shillings more. When they had been in bed about an hour the prisoner got up, dressed herself and left the room. Finding that she did not return, he examined his trouser pockets and found that she had taken all his money out of the purse, excepting half a crown.

This case, like most similar cases, was dismissed for lack of evidence, leaving Mr Silver out of pocket, out of sorts and looking a proper charley. There was no question, however, of him being prosecuted. It is likely, however, that Fanny Hooper, and the landlords of the *Westgate House* and the *King's Arms*, were watched more closely by the police and magistrates in the future.

Bath was awash with money in the eighteenth century. In 1787, for example, two men caught operating an illegal gambling den – a faro table – in Alfred Street were fined £1,800, equivalent to around £130,000 today. The ease with which they paid up indicates how much could be made from wealthy visitors. The only way most working-class women could hope to get their hands on some of this wealth, however, was by putting their bodies up for sale on a casual or regular basis. Middle- and upper-class moralists might have denounced their actions as disgraceful, but the conditions the women had to put up with were, by any objective standard, disgraceful to start off with. To provide food for themselves or their children – or to pay the rent

– they sacrificed what little dignity was left to them. No doubt some were the hard-bitten harridans familiar from newspaper reports, but many were just desperately poor and desperately hungry. Casual prostitution was a fact of life. Many women were faced with a stark choice between submitting to a brief, undesirable liaison or being thrown out onto the street, with all that entailed in the pre-welfare state. As Peter Fryer says in his study of nineteenth-century sexuality, "where libertinism flourished among the rich, it did so because thousands of women were so poor that selling themselves in occasional or professional prostitution was less disgusting than the ill-clad, ill-fed existence they would otherwise have led."

There were regular attempts to control the problem of prostitution in Bath. In 1795, for example, "sixty of the frail sisterhood were … apprehended at their lodgings, etc., in this city and confined in the several watch-houses. They were liberated the following morning, on promising amended conduct, and to return to their families." In 1805 a meeting was called to establish an "Asylum for Penitent Prostitutes," the name of which was later changed to the Bath Penitentiary.

Locking prostitutes up in a penitentiary was one way of dealing with them. The ones thought to be beyond redemption were ordered to leave town. In 1823, for example, Eliza Clark was charged with stealing £3 from a farmer. Although it could not be proved, she was only discharged on condition that she left Bath. However, John Harris, "one of the tythingmen of the city," saw her on the night after she was discharged asking a man for a drink near Walcot Burial Ground. As he "verily believed from the general conduct of the said Eliza Clark" that she was "a common prostitute and street walker," he prayed that she may be dealt with "according to law."

Even some very young girls seem to have been regarded as beyond redemption, and locked up simply because they had no fixed abode. In 1842, for example, Sarah Richards, "a girl apparently not more than 14, was charged with being drunk and assaulting a young woman, named Eliza King, who had never seen her before the night of the offence. Having been wandering about the streets late at night she was committed for one month." When John Skinner, the Rector of Camerton, visited Bath, he recorded his astonishment at observing "the streets so crowded with prostitutes, some of them apparently not above 14 or 15 years of age." Back home in Camerton, he tried to prevent girls going to work in Bath, aware of how easily they could find themselves on the slippery slope to prostitution. Present-day moralists may drone on about Victorian values, but the brutal fact is that, for much of the nineteenth century, sex with under-age girls was readily available on the streets of Bath.

Bygone Bath was, undoubtedly, a very sinful place. Sometimes, however, those who sought to reform its morals went rather over the top. In September 1766, for example, a young man who had sedulously avoided the company of ladies of the night, never strolled down Avon Street, and never bought a drink for one of the nymphs who tugged his sleeve as he hurried along the High Street, may have felt the colour drain from his cheeks and a knot form in his stomach as he picked up his copy of the *Bath Journal* and read an advertisement for the latest bestseller to hit the bookshops:

This day is published the second edition of *Onanism; or a Treatise Upon the Disorders Produced by Masturbation, or the Dangerous Effects of Excessive Venery*, by M Tissot MD.

Sometimes, he must have thought, you just cannot win.

The arm of the law may have been long, but the hand at the end of it was often to be found wrapped round a pint

CHAPTER TWELVE

'ELLO, 'ELLO, 'ELLO

Dogberry: You are thought to be the most senseless and fit man for the constable
of the watch, therefore bear you the lantern. This is your charge: you shall
comprehend all vagrant men; you are to bid any man stand, in the prince's name.
Watchman: How if he will not stand?
Dogberry: Why them, take no note of him, but let him go; and presently call the
rest of the watch together, and thank God you are rid of a knave.
Shakespeare, Much Ado About Nothing

The lawlessness of Bath's streets in the eighteenth and nineteenth centuries may
have had something to do with those who were supposed to be patrolling them. In
1799, for example, the *Bath Chronicle* reported the case of "a watchman, stationed
in Gay Street, on Sunday evening last," who, it alleged, "was seated in a public
house for an hour from half past ten. From such nightly guardians," it fulminated,
"what are the public to expect?"

It was a cry which was repeated throughout the nineteenth century. The arm
of the law may have been long, but the hand at the end of it was often to be found
wrapped round a pint. The affinity of the upholders of the law with pubs was a strong
one. The Bath City Police Force was set up in 1836, replacing a system which had
developed, in a fairly ramshackle way, over the centuries. There were separate forces
for Bathwick and Walcot, as well as for the city, and there was little co-operation
between them. Lyncombe & Widcombe had no police force at all. For anything more
than a minor disturbance, the troops were likely to be called out. The creation of the
Bath City Police Force, with 132 officers, was an attempt to change all that.

It did not get off to a good start. On the first day, Constable James Connolly
celebrated his appointment by having a few drinks, thereby achieving the distinction
of being the first policeman in Bath to be dismissed for drunkenness. He was not
the last. In one fairly typical month – March 1836 – four policemen were found
drunk on duty. Another was found on his stand near the *Talbot* in St James's Street
at one o'clock in the morning with a half-gallon can of beer in his possession. All
were discharged. Later that year, on 12 October, "William Lewis was dismissed for
neglect of duty and being found in a public house asleep." In the previous year, when

Inspector Withers reported Joseph England "for returning to his office at twelve o'clock at night drunk," he referred to it as "a common misdemeanour."

Bath has a tradition of disorderly guardians of the peace. In 1689, John Robins, a night watchman, partook too freely of the Christmas spirit, and was "dismissed from his post ... for insulting Alderman Baber." Six weeks later, he was "restored to his place as nightwatchman, having apologised to Alderman Baber."

The incidence of drunkenness among nineteenth-century policemen might lead one to assume that they were a particularly bibulous section of the community. But this was almost certainly not the case. They were certainly more open to temptation than most people, walking around the streets at unsocial hours and mixing with the roughest elements of society. But they had to be of good character to get into the force in the first place and the majority of them carried out their duties diligently. A policeman's lot in early nineteenth-century Bath was not a happy one. Violence, generally fuelled by alcohol, was rife, and a disturbance could easily turn into a riot if the police intervened and tried to arrest the ringleaders.

Taken as a whole, Bath's early police force would have been, by the standards of the time, a remarkably sober body of men. The incidence of drunkenness among them is a measure of how endemic drinking was in the early nineteenth century. Nevertheless, the Corporation was determined to stop policemen drinking on duty, and in 1835, all other efforts having failed, they took the bizarre step of placing a notice in the *Bath Chronicle* threatening publicans with prosecution if they served them:

> To Victuallers, and Others.
>
> Guildhall, 2 July 1835
>
> It being strongly suspected that watchmen are supplied with spiritous and other liquors when on duty, thereby rendering them incapable of affording that nightly protection to the public to which they are entitled, and in direct violation of the statute; the commissioners acting under and by virtue of the statute passed in the 54th year of the Reign of George III for ... watching the City of Bath ... resolve that publicity be given to the following clauses in the aforementioned statute, viz: ... That if any victualler, publican or other person selling spiritous or other liquors shall entertain without sufficient cause assigned, or harbour in their house, habitation or other place, any watchman or constable during any of the hours or times appointed for such watchman or constable to be on duty ... then every victualler, publican or other person shall for every such offence forfeit and pay any sum not exceeding £5.
>
> By Order of the Commissioners,
>
> Thomas M Cruttwell, Clerk

It must have placed publicans in a cleft stick. Refusing to serve a thirsty policeman was not the best way of ensuring that lock-ins or other minor infringements of the law went unpunished – or that assistance would be forthcoming if a customer turned nasty. Not surprisingly, most of them seem to have ignored Mr Crutwell's instructions, and life went on much as before.

Over-indulgence sometimes had bizarre consequences. On one occasion, three policemen absent from duty were found drunk at the Grove Street police station, two of them in bed together "contrary to regulations." On another, the Watch Committee heard how policemen had been seen consorting with prostitutes in a pub:

> Mr Sainsbury, auctioneer, having complained to the committee of the conduct of Police Constables Fitzgerald and Snook for having on the night of the 20th June last improperly conducted themselves, by encouraging two prostitutes to go into the *Victoria Tavern* in Bridewell Lane and persuading Pullen, the landlord, to draw them gin and peppermint, which they drank at the bar, partaking of it themselves. They denied the charge, Fitzgerald alleging that they went in for the purpose of getting evidence against Pullen for selling without a licence, but the committee disapproving the defence and considering the charge proved, it was moved by Mr Orchard, seconded by Mr Edwards, "that the committee being of opinion that the police constables had on the occasion exceeded their duty, the chairman be requested to admonish them," which motion being put there were three for, two against it, the motion being carried, they were then called in and admonished accordingly.

What the minutes do not explain, of course, is what Mr Sainsbury was doing in the pub in the first place.

The *Devonshire Arms* (now the *Bath Tap*) in St James's Parade also deserves a special place in the annals of police history for having pioneered the sleeping policeman, this auspicious event being recorded in the minutes of the Bath Watch Committee for 1852:

> PC Cox is charged with being found asleep in a cart in a yard belonging to the *Devonshire Arms* Public House on the morning of the 20th instant at half past four instead of being on his beat, and the same being proved by Superintendent Frost, resolved that he be permitted to resign.

But, of course, the majority of policemen – and the night watchmen who preceded them – took their job very seriously, even if they did sometimes fail to get their man. This reminiscence, from the *Bath Journal* of 7 February 1903 shows that smugglers were as ingenious two centuries ago as they are today:

> Although Bath was an inland town, there was contraband business and some amount of smuggling carried on within its precincts, and the old chairmen, whose avocation, of course, called them out at all hours of the night, were the chief offenders in this illicit traffic. Peter Glass was one of the greatest, if not the greatest, wag of the whole confraternity, who then numbered . . . some 400, and was licensed to the "stand" connected with the *Darby & Joan* [at 16 Guinea Lane]. The kegs of spirits were in the town, but the difficulty was to get them to their destination in the upper part of the city, and the hero of my narrative was deputed to use his own stratagem. He started from a given point late at night, when the old night watchmen were on duty – under the cover of the dim light emitted from the oil lamps – with a keg on his shoulders uncovered and exposed. Near the bottom of Lansdown Road, between Mr Gould's stables

and Mr Stuckey's back entrance is ... what was once a doorway, but is now filled in with stone. This was a watchman's box, and when Peter reached here he was challenged and brought to bay by the "Charley" in occupation ... Peter cautiously feigned obstreperousness when the watchman vehemently sprung his rattle. This, of course, brought other "Charleys" on the scene and the prisoner was taken in triumph to the watch-house, the "Charleys" carrying the keg, which Peter put on the ground when challenged and resolutely refused to carry. The prisoner was placed in a cell, which, in those days, was not like the cells in modern police stations, for he could hear distinctly the conversation taking place between his captors. A proposition was made to spile-hole the keg, with a view to tasting the contents, which was immediately agreed to. One tasted and pronounced the liquor tasteless, a second expressed a similar opinion, and after all the "Charleys," who had been summoned together from off their several beats by the vigorous springing of the rattle, had held consultation, they came to the conclusion that they had wrongly apprehended Peter as the keg contained nothing but water. The prisoner was summoned from his cell, and after expostulating with his captors for apprehending him and locking him up for carrying a keg of water, threatened them with all kinds of proceedings, and parleyed with them as long as suited his purpose. Whilst this little episode was being enacted the blockade was safely run by Peter's accomplices and the cargo of real Cognac safely and securely landed at its destination. There were high jinks at the *Darby & Joan* for several evenings after the occurrence. Peter lived many years after to tell the amusing tale, "how he tricked the Charleys."

CHAPTER THIRTEEN

POLITICAL PANDEMONIUM

Politics is not an exact science.
Prince Otto von Bismarck

Until the mid-nineteenth century, elections were synonymous with drinking. The weeks leading up to the poll were protracted communal binges, with rival candidates plying voters – and the mobs who influenced them – with as much beer as they could get down their necks. Nor did the drinking stop once the results were announced. After the 1830 election, as Bath's two newly elected MPs, General Palmer (Liberal) and Lord John Thynne (Tory), were carried aloft in procession through central Bath, "both MPs sought the goodwill of the unenfranchised, by distributing, as they passed, silver coins and 'tickets' for some 600 gallons of beer." A year later, with pressure for reform growing, there was another election. General Palmer was once again carried through the streets, but Lord Thynne was pelted with rotten fruit by the drunken mob and sought refuge in the *White Hart*. When the Reform Bill was passed in 1832, there was yet another election. This time the Liberal candidate, JA Roebuck, pre-empted the mob by laying into his Tory opponent when he came across him at the polling station in Sydney Gardens.

Political meetings took place either in the open air or in pubs. In the run-up to the 1837 election, Roebuck addressed meetings at the *Lamb Inn* in Stall Street, the *Crown* at Bathwick, the *Weymouth Arms* in Julian Road, the *King William* in Thomas Street and the *Garrick's Head* in the Sawclose. Despite all this campaigning, Roebuck and Palmer, the two Liberal candidates, lost their seats because of what Roebuck described as "Tory gold, Tory intimidation and Whig duplicity."

Bath was not alone in the corruption of its politics. Secret ballots were not introduced until 1872; widespread "treating" and the opportunities for coercion afforded by an open voting system were a volatile combination. In the 1844 election at Horsham in Sussex, for example,

> every public house and beershop in the Parish was secured by one side or other as an electioneering stronghold ... If a voter wanted a drink he could go into any public house and obtain any kind of refreshment without being asked for payment. The labourer whose taste was usually satisfied with small beer was now

in a position to discover and indulge his taste for more aristocratic beverages … It is not too much to say that most of the male population of Horsham were frequently drunk, many were continually drunk and some were continuously drunk for the whole six weeks preceding election day.

Leaving aside the question of how being continually drunk differs from being continuously drunk, one thing is clear. Until the mid-nineteenth century, election campaigns were marked by appalling levels of drunkenness. Rival candidates showered the populace with free beer, heedless of the breakdown in public order which inevitably resulted. They were, in effect, unleashing the power of the mob, albeit on a limited scale. Whereas today's politicians boast about the number of points they are ahead in the opinion polls, 200 years ago they boasted about the number of drunken louts prepared to duff up the opposition on their behalf. As an alternative to spin-doctoring, it lacked a certain subtlety, but at least its message was unambiguous.

There was one election, however, where things really got out of hand. The Bath election of 1841 has gone down in history as the "Drunken Election." Given the level of competition it had from all the other drunken elections, this one had to be pretty bad to warrant such a distinction, and, by all accounts, it was.

In the weeks leading up to it, bill stickers were busy all over town with an intensive poster campaign. The names of the two Liberal candidates, Roebuck and Duncan, were stencilled in yellow on shops and houses belonging to prominent Tory supporters. As the election grew nearer, the Bath Chronicle reported the rising tide of violence with alarm:

The attention of the city magistrates [has been] considerably taken up in the hearing of cases of drunkenness and assault arising out of the electioneering excitement. Numerous charges of assault have been made good against the Liberals, who have, throughout the election, behaved most outrageous. At the Britannia Inn, Walcot [now the Piccadilly], an almost complete demolition of the glass has been effected by the friends of Roebuck and Duncan … The Hand & Shears, Walcot Street, the Crown & Thistle, Avon Street, Messrs Vezey's coach factory [near the Long Acre Tavern] and the White Horse Cellar have also shared the "Liberal" furies.

Further details appeared the following week. A Liberal band, marching down Walcot Street, lost two of its members when they decided to rush into the Hand & Shears to break the windows "and otherwise damage the property." In Avon Street, 13 people were:

charged with bursting open the door of the … private residence of Mr Burrell, a Conservative, the landlord of the Crown & Thistle in the same street. Among the leaders of the outrageous set were Bollin and Collins, who with their party next besieged the public house itself. Finding that the affair was likely to prove somewhat serious, Burrell ran to the police office for assistance, and on his return with a body of the police force, he found that the house had been forcibly entered, and, besides the breaking of the windows, doors, etc., he found the

The language used by the mob was of the most disgusting and outrageous description

spirits running to waste, and a dozen spoons missing. The language used by the mob was of the most disgusting and outrageous description, and their violence for a time knew no bounds. It was stated that an old man who was standing near to No 8 with a blue favour attached to his coat, was struck by Hughes, who, it was alleged, having first thrown his yellow colours into his face, knocked him into the passage.

Duncan and Roebuck were duly elected, much to the disgust of the *Bath Chronicle*, who commented on their victory as follows:

> Bath is a dark blot of the present general election. At a time when other places are, to their high honour, throwing off the trammels of modern liberalism, Bath has put them in their worst shape. It has returned not merely radicals or ultra-radicals, but persons who are "something more." We are taunted throughout the country with having sent to Parliament two disciples of revolution ... Mr Roebuck is the open advocate of republicanism; and, in a city which is mainly supported by the aristocrat, he is cheered and applauded to the echo when he makes a speech in which he lays it down as part of his political creed that the people ought not to rest satisfied until "all aristocratic distinctions are done away with." ... How can it be expected that the classes upon which Bath leans for its very existence will choose to uphold a place in which they are loaded with foul-mouthed abuse, and their very existence as classes is pronounced to be a nuisance, by the men whom the electors choose as their Parliamentary representatives?

Six years later, Roebuck lost his seat to the Conservative Lord Ashley, who proudly claimed, after his election, that "not a penny during six months was expended on beer." This was like a red rag to a bull. The mob expected free beer. For a candidate to announce that he had won without putting his hand in his pocket was a disgrace. They decided to teach him a lesson:

> Mr Roebuck's supporters formed themselves into mobs, one attacking the houses of the North and South Parades, whilst another marched up Union Street and Milsom Street, making for the premises occupied by [Lord Ashley's election agent]. This contingent of the rioters demolished all the windows in the front of these premises, after which they marched along the Paragon until they arrived at 7 or 9 Somerset Buildings, occupied by a baker and confectioner, who was a conspicuous supporter of Lord Ashley, and here they left one or two whole panes of glass in the front of this free and independent elector's premises, to mark their respect for the rights of political opponents. Passing on they made a halt at the Radical headquarters of Walcot – viz, the *Gloucester Inn* [where Hayes' Carpet Store now stands] – and here they regaled themselves with sundry gallons of the potent treble X of this well-known hostelry.

Thus fortified, they proceeded across Cleveland Bridge, forced the gatekeeper to unlock the tollgate and let them through, before smashing all the windows in 11 Bathwick Street, which they mistakenly believed to be the home of Sir Robert Preston, another supporter of Lord Ashley. They carried on along Bathwick Street and up Bathwick Hill, smashing windows as they went:

> When they arrived at the residence of Mr WT Blair [Bathwick Hill House], a town councillor and Mayor in 1836, their fury appeared to reach its height and the havoc wrought here was very great indeed. The thirst of the mob for revenge at defeat being thus apparently satiated, they retraced their footsteps down Bathwick Hill.

Even though many of those who took part in such demonstrations did not have the vote, they certainly knew how to make their views known. The extension of the franchise, more effective policing, an end to the practice of treating voters, and the introduction of secret ballots led to a gradual reduction in electioneering rowdiness. By the late nineteenth century, drink itself became a political issue, with the Tories espousing the drink lobby and the Liberals that of temperance. Some temperance campaigners, however, let reforming zeal get the better of political acumen. In 1870, for example, Mr Dallaway damaged his chances of getting re-elected as a councillor for Lyncombe & Widcombe when he announced in a council meeting that many of the residents in his ward were drunk for much of the day. His opponents seized on this gaffe and printed the following poster:

LYNCOMBE & WIDCOMBE ELECTION

Those electors of Lyncombe & Widcombe who are stated by Mr Dallaway to be always "DRUNK" after a certain hour of the day, are requested to vote for that Gentleman as *early as possible* on Tuesday morning.

The Taxidermist's Arms … ?

CHAPTER FOURTEEN

NINETEENTH-CENTURY VALUES

It's the same the whole world over,
It's the poor what gets the blame,
It's the rich what get the pleasure,
Ain't it all a bleedin' shame?

Anon

However much we may cherish the idea of the Victorian pub, a time-machine trip back to a nineteenth-century hostelry would almost certainly induce profound culture shock. For a start, there is a fair chance that several of the customers would be children. Not until 1886 was the sale of beer to children under the age of 13 outlawed, although they had been banned from buying spirits since 1872. Even after 1886, it was standard practice for children to call at a pub to take beer home, although respectable publicans made them use the jug and bottle department rather than the main bar.

Many nineteenth-century publicans had other jobs, which they often carried out on the premises. Brewing came top of the list, but shoemakers, coopers, carpenters, woodturners, bakers, painters, grocers, farmers, coal dealers, masons, blacksmiths, wheelchairmen and tobacconists could all be found running pubs in Bath in the nineteenth century. There was even a taxidermist. Between 10% and 20% of pubs were run by women, generally the widows or daughters of previous landlords. Despite an increase in restrictions on women's employment, and the buying up of pubs by large breweries, this percentage remained fairly constant throughout the nineteenth century.

A list of the 27 licences transferred in Bath between 1829 and 1832 sheds some light on the occupations of the people who went into the licensed trade. The occupations of six of the new licensees were not recorded. Of those that were, three were already beer retailers or victuallers. One was a maltster. Those coming from outside the trade included six yeomen, an auctioneer, a cooper, a carpenter, a haulier, a waiter and a servant. Only one was a woman, a widow taking over from her husband.

At the beginning of the nineteenth century, the average town pub looked, from the outside, much like the houses which surrounded it. Most small pubs had two bars. The tap room, used by labourers or factory workers, would be simply furnished, with benches fixed round the walls and a few tables. The parlour, reserved for tradesmen, shopkeepers and other guests, would be more elegant, with pictures on the wall, chairs instead of benches, a few ornaments and something to cover the bare boards of the floor. This layout has survived to the present day in those pubs which retain public and lounge bars. The big difference between then and now is that, in the early nineteenth century, many pubs did not have counters. Barrels and bottles were either kept in the cellar or in the tap room. Waiters, pot boys or serving maids scuttled to and fro carrying drinks to customers. This custom survived in some pubs until the mid-twentieth century, and disconnected bell-pushes to call for service can still be seen in a few unrestored pubs. It still survives in North America, where licensing authorities take the view that groups of men sitting at tables are less likely to cause trouble than a crowd jostling round a bar. It was a view shared by temperance campaigners in this country, who pressed for similar legislation when bars started to become standard later in the nineteenth century. Fortunately for those for whom standing at a bar is one of life's principal delights, their campaign was unsuccessful.

However natural it seems today that a pub should have a bar, it was a revolutionary concept in the early nineteenth century. When a bar was installed it changed a pub from a house, where the landlord welcomed guests to sit and quaff at their leisure, to a shop, where they queued up at a counter and bought goods, as they would in a grocer's or a butcher's.

The frontages of pubs began to change as well. The old ground-floor windows were ripped out and replaced by shop-type windows. Instead of goods being displayed, however, panes of frosted glass, blinds or curtains maintained the privacy of those inside while glimmering with the prospect of the hidden pleasures within. To support the wall, pilasters were installed at intervals along the frontage. Above the windows, the name of the hostelry was emblazoned in large letters and illuminated by elaborate gas lamps.

These momentous changes in pub design have generally been seen as the result of a conscious attempt to change the nation's drinking habits, but they probably came about in a more roundabout way. In the late eighteenth century, there was a significant increase in the number of wine merchants. These catered for the gentry, or at least the well-to-do, and were located in the better parts of town, alongside shops selling other luxury items. Naturally, their design followed that of the shops around them and was aimed at encouraging well-heeled customers to sample their wares. By the early nineteenth century, many of these wine merchants had started to sell drinks for consumption on the premises. Beer as well as wine was generally on offer and, while the clientele at the front of the house would be eminently respectable, many licensees also had a room at the back where servants, sent into town to collect their master's or mistress's orders, could whet their whistle. Some of the wine merchants found this new business so good that they decided to concentrate on it at the expense of selling wine. And so it was that new pubs were born – but pubs very different from the traditional alehouse or tavern. Not only did they have counters, like shops – they had large windows, fancy decorations, and were much more comfortable and upmarket than the old-style boozers. And, naturally, they were much more popular. When other landlords saw their customers drifting away to these new-style pubs – or gin-palaces as they were sometimes known – they realised that the only way to beat them was to stick in a counter, fix up a few partitions, slap in some fancy windows, and join them.

These changes were generally bankrolled by the brewers, who were busy buying up pubs and beerhouses and redeveloping them. Those not acquired by the brewers – or acquired by the brewers but left undeveloped – tended to fall by the wayside. Change came much more slowly in the countryside, where lack of competition and little potential for increased trade meant that the brewers had little incentive to spend money on revamping their pubs. For town pubs, however, makeovers were the order of the day. Many, naturally, bewailed the changes. The *Building News* of 15 May, 1857, for example, included a piece of pure nostalgia lamenting the loss of the traditional boozer:

> Settles or backed benches, with a plank to each, sufficed in primitive times for the enjoyment of a cup of brown nappy, with a pipe and a joke; the light of a coal fire, or the glimmer of tallow fat, illumined satisfactorily the boozy meeting of ancestral artisans and swashbucklers. Tonight it is otherwise – the corner pub is radiant of gas, redolent of mahogany, and glittering in mirrors, there are no settles, no stools nor an easy smoking with hard drinking ... At the bar the dropper-in to drink must stand their drink and move on when tired.

A "cup of brown nappy" sounds just the sort of thing worth taking a long detour to avoid. Apparently, however, it was a term used to describe a pint of beer with a particularly vibrant head on it. But, with Eleanor Rumming's organic brewing methods rattling around at the back of your mind, would you want to check it out?

One thing that did remain constant throughout the nineteenth century was the rigid demarcation between the accommodation provided for middle-class and working-class customers. In the seventeenth and eighteenth centuries, rooms for respectable punters were often on the first floor, with the ground floor left to the rabble. In the nineteenth, it was more usual for all the principal public rooms to be on the ground floor, with the first floor given over to club or semi-private rooms. This description of a London pub in 1840 gives us a good idea what many of Bath's pubs would have been like in the mid-nineteenth century:

> In the parlour of a public house, properly kept, frequently assemble some of the most pleasant company. The same set generally meet every evening at the same hour. Although it is the landlord's interest that each man should drink much, most of the frequenters drink moderately, and it is a rare thing to see a drunken man in the parlour. The conversation is very instructive, and well expressed. The talk is mostly about politics, the news of the day, parish intelligence, and the like. A great deal of useful information may be gleaned there; and many a man in the present march-of-intelligence age, too idle to read at home, depends for his mental resources on what he can pick up in the parlour of a public house.
>
> The tap room is not so well conducted. Here collect the working men, male servants in and out of place, hackney-coachmen, omnibus cads, etc. These frequenters drink far more in proportion than those of the parlour. Many leave the place in a reeling attitude. These often linger at the bar, before they go out, and frequently insult most grossly the young women who are standing there to be served.

The bar is frequented by a motley variety of visitors. It is often in a most disgusting state. Here the servant girls from the neighbouring houses, and the wives of mechanics, poor tradesmen, and the broken-down gentlewoman who keeps a school, come to fetch their supplies of beer for dinner or supper. Here the washerwoman, the market-woman, the basket-woman, the gaudily-attired courtesan, the sad street-walker, with famine in her cheeks and sickness in her eyes, congregate at one and the same time, using language only fit for such a place. For a man, this is a hazardous scene of corruption; for a woman it is highly dangerous.

In the early nineteenth century, as we have seen, gin drinking became a major problem once again. This was due to a reduction of the duty on spirits from eleven shillings and eight pence to seven shillings a gallon in 1825. The reduction was partly a response to calls for Free Trade and partly an attempt to cut down smuggling. Its effects, however, were disastrous. In 1829, the Middlesex magistrates published a broadside, calling attention to "the demoralising consequences likely to ensue in the middling and lower classes from the alarming increase of gin shops in every direction, in and around the metropolis, by the conversion of what used to be quiet respectable public houses, where the labouring population could find the accommodation of a tap room or parlour in which to take the meals or refreshment they might require, into flaming dram shops, having no accommodation for persons to sit down, and where the only allurement held out was the promise of 'Cheap Gin.'"

It was, once again, cheaper to get drunk on gin than beer. The determined imbiber would often order a tot of gin to accompany a mug of beer, while the really determined one would add the gin to the beer and down the whole lot in one go. This concoction was known as a dog's nose, for reasons which are unclear, but are probably not worth inquiring too deeply into. Lacing beer with gin was, as far as most people were concerned, a definite case of overkill. It is a well-known fact (sometimes known as the "it went straight to my head, officer" syndrome) that it is far easier to get drunk on an empty stomach than a full one. Go back anytime before the First World War and you would find that most people were chronically malnourished and almost permanently hungry. It is not surprising that they could not hold their liquor. It was bad enough when they were just drinking beer. The sudden availability of cheap gin made matters much, much worse.

The solution, as far as the Duke of Wellington was concerned, was to get them to drink more beer. As we have seen, when Britain's rulers have encouraged people to drink more, they have been wildly successful – so successful, in fact, that attempts to encourage them to drink less have invariably followed. These, however, have been much less successful.

The 1830 Beer Act was no exception to this rule. To foster the drinking of beer, any householder was allowed, on payment of two guineas, to take out a licence for selling beer or cider on their premises. Local magistrates, the arbiters of licensing law from time immemorial, had no say in who was granted a licence. The money was paid directly to the Exchequer, and there was nothing the magistrates could do about it. As a further incentive, all duty on beer was abolished. Among those who greeted the

AWASH WITH ALE

proposals with a marked absence of enthusiasm was the editor of the *Bath Chronicle*:

> It is much to be feared that the great increase which is likely, in a short time, to take place in the number of cider shops in Somersetshire and the other western counties, is calculated to have a very injurious effect on the morals and general habits of the labouring classes. We have conversed with several country gentlemen who have opportunities of remarking the effect of those cider shops already opened, and we are informed that in numerous instances they have been productive of much misery among families in the humbler walks of life, instead of conferring the additional comforts which it was thought would result from the measure. We are among the last who would willingly curtail the enjoyment of the labouring poor; but we have long thought, and we still think, that the great increase which may be expected to take place in the cider shops will be found to create much serious mischief, where we well know only good was intended. . . . There can be little doubt that if the cider shops increase as we fear they will, our rural population will be demoralised in a degree which we have no wish to dwell upon. We sincerely trust that our anticipations may be groundless, and that good instead of evil may result from the measure referred to; but we cannot but feel persuaded that the consequences will be shortly found to warrant the expediency of returning to the old system, or at least of making some considerable modifications to the provisions of the new Act.

In September 1830 the *Bath Herald* announced that "it is intended to open no less than six new houses in the Twerton road alone for the sale of beer under the new Act, which comes into operation on the 15th of next month; and in some of the other outskirts of the city, they are likely to be still more numerous." A month later Sydney Smith wrote:

> The new Beer Bill has begun its operations. Everybody is drunk. Those who are not singing are sprawling. The sovereign people are in a beastly state.

Lord Palmerston added the observation that "the words 'Licensed to be Drunk on the Premises' are by the people interpreted as applicable to the customers as well as the liquor."

It seems inexplicable that, to solve a national drink problem, the Government should have sanctioned an explosion in the number of licensed premises, at the same time as taking many of them out of the jurisdiction of local magistrates. However, there was a method in their madness, even if it was the sort of method that only a politician could come up with. A couple of letters in Bath Record Office cast an intriguing sidelight on the thinking behind the 1830 Beer Act. The first was sent from SM Phillips, Esq., on behalf of the Home Secretary, to Mr Tugwell, the Mayor of Bath, on 18 February 1826:

> Sir,
>
> I am directed by Mr Secretary of State Peel to acquaint you that it has been intimated to him by a person, on whose accuracy he places considerable reliance, that there are at present in the City of Bath several Public Houses of notoriously bad character, and which were known to be so previously to the last renewal of their Licences. The Houses more particularly alluded to are the *Smith's Arms* and *Lord Nelson* in Avon Street, the *Pig & Whistle* and the *Cross Keys* at the bottom of the Market Place.

As Public Houses of bad character are generally the resort of the profligate, and thus tend materially to increase crime and impede the due execution of the laws, I am directed by Mr Peel to draw your attention to this subject, and to request that you will state to me, for his information, your opinion as to the mode in which these Houses are conducted, and also whether you are aware that any Public Houses in the City of Bath have had their Licences renewed by the Magistrates notwithstanding that they have been at the time known to be frequented by persons of bad character.

I am, Sir,

Your most obedient

humble servant,

SM Phillips

Mr Tugwell's reply was dated three days later:

Sir,

I have to acknowledge the receipt of your letter of the 18th inst. relative to the licensing of certain public houses in this city, particularly the *Smith's Arms*, the *Lord Nelson* (sometimes called the *Pig & Whistle*), and the *Cross Keys*, which have been represented as being, at the time, of notoriously bad character. The houses in question were licensed at the last general licensing day, but certainly not under the circumstances alluded to, the magistrates not being in the possession of any facts which would justify in their estimation the discontinuance of a licence. The neighbourhood of Avon Street is bad and the entire exclusion of persons of suspected character from these houses is almost impossible.

With regard to the general conduct of the public houses in this city, I can assure you that under the directions of the magistrates they are frequently visited by the police officers and that their attention is most promptly given to the investigation of any complaints which are made to them ... The increase of crime, particularly amongst the younger classes, is much to be deplored. Every exertion is made and no expense is spared by the authorities here to establish an effective police, as well for the prevention as for the punishment of crimes. It is a difficult undertaking, but the various calendars will show that by the activity of the police officers great numbers are brought to justice, who would otherwise escape.

What Mr Tugwell does not say – although it lurks in the subtext of both his and Mr Phillips' letter – is that these pubs were owned by powerful brewing interests in the city. The *Cross Keys* was owned by the Sainsbury family, while the *Lord Nelson* and the *Smith's Arms* belonged to John Grant Smith of the Anchor Brewery in Southgate Street.

What the government was worried about was the cosy relationship between powerful brewers and local politicians, largely because it meant that many disorderly houses went unchecked. It was a problem throughout the country. As long as the money flowed in, the brewers, safe in their villas well away from the city centre, were happy. And the same went for their friends, the local magistrates, who lived in the same leafy suburbs.

Meanwhile, the bad parts of town got worse, with little interference from on high. Mr Peel's interest in Bath's dens of iniquity can be seen, in retrospect, as the cautious placing of a toe in the water, to see what Mr Tugwell's reaction would be. Mr Tugwell's weaselling his way out of the issue must have confirmed what was already suspected in Whitehall, and was probably echoed by replies from local dignitaries elsewhere in the country. What Mr Tugwell may not have known, but which – with hindsight – seems clear, is that the government were toying with the idea of taking responsibility for licensing away from local magistrates and setting up a national licensing body. Four years later, they went part of the way towards this by bringing in the Beer Act, which introduced a new, nationally-licensed tier of pubs selling only beer and cider – not the demon gin. However, like many well-laid plans, this attempt to break the power of the brewers not only misfired, it led to a sharp increase in exactly the sort of pubs the government were trying to shut down.

In the first twelve months after the passing of the Beer Act, 30,000 beerhouse licences were taken out. By 1836, there were 46,000 beershops, against 56,000 fully licensed pubs. Somerset took to beerhouses even more eagerly than most other counties, and, within three years of the act coming into force, it had more beerhouses than fully licensed houses – 1,339 against 925. This was probably because Somerset had a larger proportion of unlicensed premises than most other counties before the Beer Act came into force. Many of these would have been cider houses, which traditionally regarded themselves as beyond the law. However, the passing of the Beer Act was accompanied by a crackdown on unlicensed premises, with reports like this, from the *Bath Chronicle*, appearing in local newspapers:

> A woman named Betty Perry has been committed for six months imprisonment in
> Wilton gaol … for default of payment of the mitigated penalty of £25 for selling
> cider by retail in her house at Cossington without having taken out a licence.

The problem was, of course, that in country districts, many households made cider, just as, in towns, many households made beer. Much of it was for personal consumption, or for servants and farm labourers, but the line between supplying friends, neighbours and passers-by with alcoholic refreshment and running a cider house was a difficult one to draw. Many people did not give much thought to it, and, as long as the house was not unruly and there was a welcoming mug whenever a guardian of the peace happened to pass by, nobody was too concerned. The government was keen to change all that, especially as one report from 1830 suggested that "Devon and Somerset are overrun with common sheds by the roadside in which cider is sold in great quantities to people of both sexes." With a choice between coughing up two guineas a year and being fined £25, most people opted for the former. Hence the explosion of beerhouses in Somerset.

Even if we discount the cider houses which legitimised themselves, the increase in the number of licensed premises in the wake of the Beer Act was phenomenal. Beershops – known as "Tom and Jerry Shops" after the rough characters in Pierce Egan's *Life in London, or Days and Nights of Jerry Hawthorn and his friend Corinthian Tom* – sprang up everywhere, although the overwhelming majority were in poorer areas. As for the government's main aim, to curb the power of the breweries and undermine their cosy relationship with local magistrates, it backfired – just as the Thatcher Government's attempt to break brewery monopolies backfired 160 years later.

It was not just the Government who resented the power of the brewers. Nineteenth-century breweries were like fortresses. Going into one was like entering a prison or naval dockyard. They were the most conspicuous symbols of capitalist oppression, their vast profits coming from the pockets of the workers who poured their brews down their necks, bitterly cursing each price rise. To many drinkers, driven to the pub because of the appalling conditions they lived in, the fortress-breweries were as much as a symbol of oppression as the string of castles Edward I built around the Welsh coast to subdue the natives. For their part, the brewers, at the end of a hard day's graft, climbed into their carriages and were carried home to palatial mansions high above the smoke and dust of the city. It is hardly surprising that so many nineteenth-century breweries were burnt down, not by angry mobs, but by lone and generally unapprehended arsonists.

Brewers initially opposed the Beer Act, fearing the competition it would foster. Once it was passed, however, it gave them an unprecedented opportunity for growth as new markets opened up. The 1830s and 1840s also saw the development of the rail network, facilitating the distribution of beer over greater distances. Between 1832 and 1841, the number of common brewers grew by a third, while many existing breweries expanded rapidly. In Burton on Trent, for example, the production of Bass rose by 600% in the 1830s. Brewers' agents went from door to door canvassing trade and offering to pay for licences if householders would open beerhouses for the sale of their beer. Advertisements like this one from 1835 were commonplace:

PUBLIC HOUSES WANTED

Wanted to purchase four or five good and well-accustom'd Public Houses in Bath and Bristol.

Particulars forwarded to the counting-house of the Bath Brewery, Kingsmead Street, addressed to Mr Pinch will receive immediate attention.

If the breweries were powerful before the 1830 Beer Act, after a couple of decades of consolidation, expansion and amalgamation, they were in a position to influence not just local but national politics. By the 1860s, the Tory party was firmly allied with the drink interest, while the Liberals were lined up with the temperance movement. But before we get on to the implications of that, we need to look at how the government sorted out the mess caused by the 1830 Beer Act.

The issue of the *Bath Chronicle* in which the Bath Brewery's advertisement for more pubs appeared also carried the following report:

> We are happy to learn that a Sunday School … has just been opened on Beacon Hill. A neighbourhood more infested by those pests to the community, beer shops, and other demoralizing influences, and in which the necessity of raising some counteracting barrier for the protection of the rising generation is more palpably apparent, it would, perhaps, be impossible to point out.

By this time the Government had acknowledged what people had been telling them all along – the Beer Act had caused more problems than it solved. Six years after the original Act another one reached the statute books. The *Bath Chronicle* announced that "there is a clause in the new Beer Act to the effect that no licence for a beer shop will be granted after 5 April 1836 for any house but what is rated at £10 per annum. This will be the means of closing many of the roadside concerns."

This amendment to the Beer Act was the result of persistent lobbying. Evidence to show that the introduction of beershops had been an unmitigated disaster also came from bodies like the Factory Commissioners. Among the factories they visited in 1833 was that of Charles Wilkins at Twerton. Mr Wilkins employed around 800 workers in his factory, plus around 300 outworkers. He told the Commissioners that:

> we cannot now avoid remarking the introduction of beerhouses in this parish has been attended with the most deplorable results; children of both sexes are now habitually frequenting them, whereas before their introduction such habits were quite unknown; nor can this excite surprise, when we state there were formerly only two public houses and two retail breweries, and directly on the passing of the Beer Bill, no less than 20 beer shops were opened in addition to the two regular public houses … and we find it impossible entirely to prevent the children and young persons in our employment from frequenting them, notwithstanding our most strenuous efforts to do so.

These efforts included a list of rules drawn up in 1832 with fines for those who broke them. They included the following:

> Any young woman found drinking in a public house at any time, whether during the hours of work or not, will be liable to a fine of one shilling, and such who make a practice of frequenting public houses will on no account be employed in any capacity whatsoever.

Today the memory of that rule lives on in the name of a group of female Morris Dancers who, not unnaturally, are in the habit of frequenting licensed premises – Mr Wilkins' Shilling. But Mr Wilkins was not some Gradgrind who wanted to stop people having fun. Paternalistic he may have been, but his paternalism embodied a concern for the welfare of his workers, and a keen awareness of how a few visits to the beerhouse could start young girls on the slippery slope to prostitution and destitution. The early nineteenth century was a much more unforgiving time than ours. Working class people – especially working class girls – did not get second chances, and the welfare state was the pipe dream of a few eccentrics. Mr Wilkins was not alone in his crusade. Groups of senior workers in his factory also helped keep teenagers on the straight and narrow by encouraging them to go to Church and Sunday School. Not a lot of fun, perhaps, but the alternatives were much, much worse.

Beerhouses came under attack from all sides. Colonel Blathwayt, whose family has given its name to an inn on Lansdown, equated their introduction with a breakdown in public order. "In the common alehouses," he declared,

> the master and man met together – the master behaved himself in order to keep up his dignity, while the man was ashamed to misbehave himself before his master. But, in these wretched places – beerhouses – there are no such influences, and poaching, felony, and crimes of every description are hatched.

Blaming beerhouses for an increase in crime was a common cry. At the Somerset

Spring Sessions in Wells in 1840, for example, the Chairman, Henry Hobhouse, said that he:

> never knew so many thefts committed as have recently been brought to light ... My experience teaches me to think that the beerhouses are the crying cause of this evil ... We have, session after session, bills introduced into parliament for the redress of this grievance, but I am sorry to say that no measure has yet been passed ... For centuries, the granting of licences remained with the magistrates. This course prevailed to within the last dozen years, but now the matter is put on a different footing, and it is entrusted to the Commissioners of Excise, whose duty it is to promote the increase of the revenue, and [have] no regard for the peace of the country or as to where pot-houses should be set up. I remember that in 1787 ... means were taken to reduce the number of alehouses, and exertions were made ... to suppress several altogether. Such houses were abolished as were situated in lone places, bye-lanes and on commons; but since the beerhouse system has been acted on, some of these houses have been again opened for the sale of beer. These are the receptacle for thieves and the places where felonies are planned [and] every facility is afforded for the secretion of stolen property.

By the mid-nineteenth century, the unfettered proliferation of beerhouses which the Beer Act had ushered in was being brought under control. The magistrates were also paying closer attention to fully licensed premises which failed to meet ever more rigorous standards. Reports like the following, from 1852, became commonplace:

> This day being the adjourned special sessions for granting wine and spirit licenses, a number of applicants whose names were ordered to stand over at the first meeting were now attended to. No application from parties already holding licenses was absolutely refused, but several houses against which complaints had been recorded in the police books were instanced by Mr Oakley as affording strong objections for a renewal of their licenses. These were the *Freemasons' Tavern*, Abbey Green; the *Grapes Tavern*, Westgate Street; the *Horse and Jockey*, Beau Street; the *Horse and Jockey*, Barton Street; the *Victoria Tavern*, Bridewell Lane; the *Shakespeare Tavern*, Orchard Street; and the *Hole in the Wall* [*Long Acre Tavern*], Walcot. Mr Oakley, in referring to them, said that the keepers of these houses, after repeated cautions, had some of them kept open their houses on Sunday mornings, and others allowed prostitutes and other bad characters to resort to them. On their licenses being renewed by the bench, they each received an admonition to be cautious for the future, and an intimation that, if they did not conduct their houses in a more orderly manner, they would be marked for next year, as likely to have their applications refused.

In the face of increasing official hostility, Bath's publicans decided they had to take the offensive, and in May 1852 they formed the Bath Licensed Victuallers' Association. Its objectives were "to protect members against frivolous and vexatious information; to watch over the interests of the trade in the legislature; to offer rewards for the detection of persons robbing its members, to persons coming to the aid and assistance of its members in cases of brutal assault or outrage, and also for such information as shall lead to the conviction of persons illegally selling excisable liquors;

to pay a certain sum upon the decease of any member; and to establish a fund for the relief of aged and decayed members, their widows and children" It started off with 30 members, but in less than twelve months the figure had risen to 70.

In the mid-nineteenth century, pubs were changing fast. Many of these changes can be dated to the Excise Act of 1846, which lifted the tax on glass. Bottled beer became much cheaper to produce and, as a result, more widely available. Beer glasses started to replace pewter and china mugs. This had two important consequences. The first was the gradual disappearance of the quart measure. Quart-size mugs were easy to produce and were standard in most alehouses. Quart-size glasses, robust enough to take the rough handling they invariably received, were not only heavy and cumbersome, but also costly to produce. As a result, pint or half-pint measures quickly became the norm. Glasses also meant that drinkers could see the quality – and clarity – of the beer they were drinking much better than they could before. Before long, they began to develop a taste – or an eye – for lighter-coloured bitter or pale ale, which they could hold up to the light and scrutinise for any hint of cloudiness or foreign matter. Thick, dark, opaque porter, the most popular style of beer for well over a century, suddenly began to lose its appeal. By the end of the nineteenth century, bitter – with mild trailing in its wake – had knocked porter into third place. In the twentieth century, bitter gradually consolidated its position as the nation's favourite tipple, until, in the closing decades of the century, it yielded the title to a beer which was lighter still – lager.

Apart from lager, the overwhelming bulk of beer drunk today is either bitter – ranging from the intensely malty to the intensely hoppy – while porter, of a sort, lives on in the form of Irish Stout, which is almost invariably referred to by its trade name – Guinness, Beamish, Caffreys or whatever. Mild, which still maintains a loyal following in some parts of the country, is almost unknown in the Bath area, while the number of pubs in the city which serve true English porter can be counted on the fingers of one hand.

An even more spectacular consequence of the lifting of the glass tax was the new freedom given to pub designers. Glass – frosted, stained, engraved, silver-backed or whatever – suddenly became much cheaper. The Excise Act of 1846 made the glittering beer halls of late Victorian England – such as the *County Wine Vaults* (now *Flan O'Brien's*) in Westgate Street and the *Hat & Feather* in London Street – possible. The new bars were infinitely more light and spacious than the wood-panelled rooms they replaced. For the working class drinkers who made up a large proportion of their customers, they were a revelation of a glittering world which until then they could only have dreamed of. Getting tanked up in one of these for the first time, surrounded by unaccustomed noise, light and activity must have been a heady experience, even if it was followed by a slow walk back to some damp hovel at the end of the evening.

It was at about this time that alcohol consumption started to rise dramatically. The "hungry forties" gave way to a period of steady economic growth. As drinking increased, so did calls for reform. Beer was no longer seen as a panacea for society's ills, but joined gin as a bogeyman of the temperance movement. The high point for beer consumption in this country – at least since reliable records began – was reached in 1876 with an average of 275 pints downed annually by every man, woman and child. Consumption of spirits peaked a year earlier – in 1875 – with 10.4 pints a year put away per head of population. Today, we manage a mere 180 pints of beer a year each, plus a miserable 2.3 pints of spirits. So, the next time somebody tells you that alcohol consumption has reached crisis levels, you could be forgiven for quoting the words of Sunny Jim – "crisis, what crisis?" – and informing them that, just over a hundred years ago, our great-great-great grandparents were not only putting away three pints of beer for every two we manage to get through today, but were downing over four times the amount of spirits as well. On top of that, beer was much stronger, averaging around 5.7% alcohol by volume, the same as Theakston's Old Peculier.

Alcohol consumption started falling after 1876 for four reasons. First, there was a gradual improvement in working-class living standards as slum clearance got under way. The result was that an increasing number of people had a reasonable place to live, and therefore less incentive to seek the sanctuary of the pub. Second, there was an increasing number of alternatives to the pub as a place for working men to meet and be entertained. Third, there was an industrial slump in the late 1870s and an agricultural slump in the 1880s, both of which left people with less money to spend. But the most important reason was the increasing power of the temperance movement, many of whose members were also instrumental in improving working-class living standards.

In 1869, thirty-nine years after it was introduced, the Beer Act experiment was abandoned. Beerhouses remained, but responsibility for them was transferred to local magistrates. This was the second great watershed in the history of nineteenth-century drinking. In the wake of the 1830 Beer Act, the number of licensed premises had almost doubled. Refinements to the Act had mitigated its worst effects, but, while responsibility for around half of all pubs lay beyond the remit of local magistrates, there was little incentive for them to instigate reform. The keeper of a fully-licensed pub who had his licence revoked on the grounds that his house was disorderly could simply get a beerhouse licence and put two fingers up to the magistrates. Now the magistrates had control over all the licensed houses in their area, a clean-up campaign could begin in earnest.

The 1869 Act marked the beginning of a pub closure programme which extended well into the twentieth century. It did not go far enough for many temperance campaigners, however. In 1871, the Liberals, who by this time were firmly identified with the temperance movement, tried to push through a bill to cut pub opening hours and introduce government inspectors to weed out unruly houses. Their most far-reaching proposal, however, was that local ratepayers should vote to determine how many licensed houses there should be in each area, with closures following hard on the heels of the ballot. Such was the outcry from brewers, publicans and the drinking classes that the bill was dropped and replaced by a watered-down version, which reached the statute book in 1872.

The 1872 Licensing Act was, nevertheless, a major piece of legislation. It outlawed the adulteration of beer (adding salt to make drinkers thirsty seems to have been a common ploy at the time). It banned the sale of spirits to children under the age of 16. It codified the law relating to drunkenness, differentiating between "simple drunkenness" (the sort where you just sit in the corner dribbling into your beer and minding your own business) and the disruptive or dangerous sort. Now you could be done for being drunk in a public place, drunk in charge of a carriage or steam engine, drunk in charge of a loaded firearm, or drunk in charge of cattle. The law also gave magistrates more power to close pubs in areas where they were too thick on the ground and cut the number of hours pubs could open.

Local magistrates now had complete control over the licensed houses in their area, but it was generally accepted that they could not refuse to renew a licence if the landlord had kept his house in order during the previous twelve months. There was one way round this difficulty, however. The last quarter of the nineteenth century was an era of massive urban growth. New estates of terraced houses sprang up on the edges of towns and cities. Brewers were keen to open new pubs in these areas; local authorities were much less enthusiastic. Before new licences were granted, therefore, they insisted that the licences of other pubs be surrendered. The Bath Brewery Company, for example, had to surrender the licences of the *Bird in Hand* in Dolemeads, the *Engineer's Arms* on the Lower Bristol Road, and the *Malakoff Tavern* in Claverton Street, in order to get a licence for the *Moorfields Park Tavern* in Oldfield Park.

In 1891, however, the hand of the magistrates was strengthened by a ruling in the House of Lords in the case of Sharp v Wakefield. This established that justices could refuse to renew a licence at their own discretion, regardless of the conduct of the licensee or his customers. Naturally, the magistrates still tried to weed out disorderly houses, but "redundancy," or lack of business, was increasingly cited as grounds for refusal. Running a respectable house was no longer enough to ensure that its licence would automatically be renewed. Beerhouses and fully-licensed houses were assessed not just on their individual merits, but on the number of other pubs in the area. If there were too many, then some of them had to go, and inevitably those with antiquated facilities, a dubious reputation, or little trade were the first to disappear.

The breweries, who owned most of the pubs by this time, opposed pub closures not just because of loss of trade, but also because of loss of property value. In the early twentieth century, pubs which lost their licences were worth far less when they became private houses or ordinary commercial premises – in direct contrast to the situation today. However, a compensation scheme, set up by Act of Parliament in 1904, guaranteed to make up the shortfall when pubs closed, thus countering the objections of the brewers.

In 1891, the Liberal government tried once again to introduce a new system of licensing, by which control would be devolved from magistrates to local councillors. Local referendums would be held, in which a two-thirds majority of local ratepayers could vote to reduce or even close all the pubs in a particular area. The prospect of large swathes of the country going dry was only averted by a series of political crises which deferred the passage of the bill through parliament and led ultimately to the collapse of the Liberal Government and the re-election of the Tories.

In the 1880s, the warrens of small rooms which many pubs had acquired started to drop out of favour, to be replaced by partitions. New or redesigned pubs went back to a basic two-bar design, with a saloon and a public bar. Most pubs had a jug and bottle department as well, although this often amounted to no more than a hatch in the corridor. Off sales, generally in the form of jugs of beer, were a staple of many pubs' trade until well into the twentieth century. Women, in particular, would call in or send out for a jug of beer, as many pubs discouraged female customers. The lack of ladies' toilets in the vast majority of pubs was a clear sign that their presence beyond the jug and bottle was not welcome. Nevertheless, there is ample evidence that ladies were frequently to be found in pubs, especially those at the less respectable end of the market. There is also evidence that many of them, including those who followed the oldest profession of all, drank copiously. The record books, however, are silent on how they coped with the lack of lavatorial facilities.

Inside the late Victorian pub, clutter reigned supreme. Shelves of books, clocks, jugs, bottles, stuffed birds and animals, pot plants, épèrgnes, prints, water colours, advertising mirrors, and china ornaments jostled for position. Ironically, after all the clutter had been cleared away and the pubs were gutted in the late twentieth century, this sort of stuff suddenly became popular again and fortunes were made by antique dealers who specialised in filling pub interiors with old bric-a-brac that had no connection with the pub or the town it stood in.

Another important change to pub design in the second half of the nineteenth century was the provision of different entrances for the various bars. It was not just that late-nineteenth century England was growing more class conscious. It was also because brewers were trying to make their pubs appeal to as wide a cross-section of the public as possible. They did this by ensuring that working- and middle-class punters did not mix, even on their way into and out of the pub. For those who wanted even greater privacy, snob screens – swivelling panes of etched or frosted glass – were provided along the bar to shield them from the gaze of fellow drinkers. Curiously, though, nobody seems to have been particularly bothered about providing separate toilet facilities. Then as now, a trip to the gents was a great leveller.

Outside, the typical late-Victorian pub had large, garish advertisements painted on its walls, bearing the name of the brewery that owned it. Large gas lamps or ornamental gas holders, bristling with naked flames arranged in the shape of a star or a crown, were like beacons in the dimly-lit streets. In the late 1890s, following the defeat of the Liberals and the re-election of the beer-friendly Tory Party, there was a boom in the brewing industry which led to a rash of pub rebuilding – often accompanied by road widening – on a scale never seen before. The *Hat & Feather* and the *Three Crowns* in London Street, the *Old Farmhouse* on Lansdown Road, the *Crown* in Bathwick, the *New Inn* in Southgate Street, the *Castle* in Forester Avenue, and the *Royal Oak* (now the *Brains Surgery*) in Larkhall were all pulled down and rebuilt in the late 1890s or early 1900s. On top of that, massive pubs like the *Weston Hotel* and the *Victoria Hotel* in Oldfield Park were built to serve the expanding suburbs, while many other pubs were remodelled internally or had elaborate extensions added.

The nineteenth century also saw the first moves to cut licensing hours. At the beginning of the nineteenth century, just about the only time pubs had to shut was during Divine Service on Sundays. This rule was centuries old, as was a tradition of ignoring it. As long ago as 1615, for example, John Humphrey of Batheaston, Edward

Then as now, a trip to the gents was a great leveller

Brewer of Freshford and John Tucker of Bath were all summoned for opening their alehouses for "tiplinge and drinkinge ... at the time of divine service on Sunday."

A reduction in opening hours was first tried in London in 1854. Pubs had to shut between 2.30pm and 6pm and call last orders at 10pm. When the new regime was introduced, many people refused to leave the pubs until forcibly ejected by the police. The new measures were soon abandoned after concerted lobbying by the brewers. Twenty years later, in 1874, the Liberal government imposed national closing times of midnight in towns and cities and eleven o'clock in the countryside. The earliest time a pub could open was six o'clock in the morning. Sunday opening times were from 12.30pm to 2.30pm, and from 6pm to 10pm.

Further legislation followed. The Habitual Drunkards Act of 1879 and the Inebriates Act of 1898 tried to set up a system whereby habitual drunkards would be sent to reformatories to dry out. The Licensing Act of 1902 made it an offence to be drunk in charge of a child. There was, however, no further reduction in opening hours until the First World War, when Lloyd George, claiming that munitions workers were spending their afternoons drinking, brought in an emergency measure to make pubs close after lunch. It was an emergency measure that lasted, as we will see, for most of the twentieth century.

Men who are good singers are very apt to become drunkards

AWASH WITH ALE

CHAPTER FIFTEEN

THE TEMPTATIONS OF TEMPERANCE

Abstainer: a weak person who yields to the temptation of denying
himself a pleasure.
Ambrose Bierce, The Devil's Dictionary

In April 1789, there was a day of rejoicing for the restoration of the health of His Majesty, the formerly mad King George. At Marshfield, over the border in Gloucestershire, the charity boys sat down to a splendid repast – roast beef, plum pudding, and a pint of strong beer each. Free beer was also available for all and sundry. Three years later, in 1792, at the opening of a new mill in Twerton, the entire workforce of around 280 were regaled with "wine, punch and strong beer." It is a measure of how attitudes to alcohol changed in the early nineteenth century that, less than 30 years later, such scenes would have been unthinkable.

Although there was a great deal of official concern about the consumption of alcohol in the late eighteenth century, it focused on the problem of working-class drinkers getting together in disorderly houses and plotting mischief. The health of the workers or the economic well being of their families was of scant concern to the authorities. The temperance movement, which got under way in the early years of the nineteenth century, was, for all its faults, its paternalistic piety and its doom-laden morality, an attempt to improve the condition of the working classes.

Concern for the welfare of the working classes, however, sometimes took a back seat to a concern for their productive capacity in an increasingly industrialised, capital-intensive market place. In 1816, Walter Sidgwick wrote that he had known weavers, "when the wages have been great, play on Monday and Tuesday, and then work on Wednesday, Thursday and Friday during half the night, take their work home on Saturday, receive their money, and then go to drink again." This sort of thing was fine when weaving was a cottage-based industry, but, when it moved into factories, no industrialist could afford to have his looms standing idle half the week and working flat out the other half. For all their pious pronouncements, Victorian factory owners were less concerned with the spiritual welfare of their workers than they were with getting the maximum return on their capital investments. It was a matter of hard economics. If they let their workers retain pre-industrial patterns of working, including lengthy binges, they would lose out to their competitors and go bust.

There was also the question of safety. Factories were vastly more dangerous than cottage workplaces, and the bigger they got, the more dangerous they got. Accidents were commonplace, and drunken machine hands were a danger not only to themselves, but to everyone around them. Even though health and safety was almost non-existent, compensation payments unheard of, and coroner's inquests almost certain to produce a verdict of death by misadventure, it was not a good idea to have people falling into the machinery willy-nilly. Even if they did not damage it, work would have to come to a halt while they were pulled out, and the chances are that other workers would be so upset by such accidents that productivity would suffer as a result. So captains of industry had good reason to support the temperance movement.

The first temperance societies were anti-gin, not anti-beer. Although they called for total abstinence from spirits, they were quite happy for people to drink beer in moderation. It was Ireland that led the way. Temperance societies were founded in Belfast and New Ross in 1829. Bradford and Leeds followed a year later, with the Bath Temperance Society starting up in 1832. This was, however, only one of several organisations in the city which had ill-regulated houses – and ill-regulated drinkers – in their sights. One of the most vehement was the Bath Anti-Immorality Association, which had as its objectives:

> the suppression of houses of notorious evil resort; the detection and punishment
> of panderers to vice; the protection of young persons, strangers to the city, and
> who may be in poverty, and out of place; the prevention of street importunity;
> and the reclamation of degraded females.

One of the temperance movement's trump cards was the availability of alternatives to alcohol. Until the end of the eighteenth century, working people had little choice but to drink beer or cider if they wanted to quench their thirst. Water was too dangerous, tea or coffee too expensive. Tea – which Dr Johnson described in 1755 as "a Chinese plant, of which the infusion has lately been much drunk in Europe" –was the preserve of the well-to-do, partly because it cost a lot to bring it from China, and partly because it was heavily taxed. Towards the end of the eighteenth century, tea cultivation started in India. This, combined with a reduction in duty, brought it within reach of all but the poorest in the land. Coffee prices fell at around the same time, for similar reasons. Temperance campaigners took full advantage of these falling prices. By 1837 there were *Temperance Tea & Coffee Rooms* at 12 Lower Borough Walls, a *Temperance Coffee Hotel* at 25 Union Passage, and a *City Temperance Hotel & Reading Rooms* at 10 Sawclose.

The first meeting of the Bath Temperance Society took place in the Bazaar in Quiet Street (now the Eastern Eye restaurant) in January 1832. Lieut Gen Sir W Cockburn, Bart, urged those present "to unite in an act of charity and benevolence to the lower classes, in rescuing them from the hurtful effect of drinking ardent spirits." A second meeting was held later the same evening, at which around 4,000 people, "chiefly of the working classes, were present, where the principles, upon which the institution was founded, were zealously advocated, and which appeared to be pervaded by an unusual degree of attention and interest."

Some conversions to the cause of temperance were dramatic, as this report from 1836 indicates:

> On the 1st of November…a whole company of tipplers, who had been carousing for a fortnight at the old *Lamb & Cottage* in Stall Street, where they had spent all their money, were reduced to the greatest straits – their wives in most cases being obliged to go out to work to procure food to keep themselves and their children from starvation. In this dilemma they were driven to their wits' end to know what to do. It so happened that some of them, having noticed placards announcing that a Temperance meeting would be held that evening, they mutually agreed among themselves to abandon their dissipated habits, and they accordingly left the tap room in a body, and signed the pledge. Several of them became zealous and faithful advocates of the cause which they espoused.

Not all temperance meetings were so successful. In the same month,

> a very noisy and turbulent meeting took place at the Friends' Meeting House, when the opponents of the movement mustered in strong force, and not only shouted and sang to drown the voices of the speakers, but broke up some of the forms. Additional attention was called to this meeting by a letter in the press, written in a vein of satirical humour, attacking the speakers, the cause, and the whole proceedings with unsparing ridicule, signed "Sam Sly."

The temperance movement had plenty of hard evidence of the evils of drink. Nevertheless, they propagated some bizarre untruths, such as the following from a temperance tract of 1829:

> Men who are good singers are very apt to become drunkards, and, in truth, most of them are so, more or less, especially if they have naturally much joviality or worth of temperament.

The temperance movement managed to shoot itself in the foot in other ways as well. Take, for instance, the issue of Sunday opening – or to be more precise, Sunday closing. Temperance campaigners insisted that the rules governing the closure of licensed premises during the hours of divine service should be strictly enforced. Their idea was that the miserable drunken sinners who were slung out of pubs would spend the time contemplating their evil ways – preferably in a church or chapel – and turning their feet unto the ways of righteousness, even for the Lord's sake. What actually happened was that they got as much down their necks as possible before being turfed out onto the street just when they could cause the maximum nuisance, instead of being left to slide under the table of their favourite hostelry well out of harm's way. It was a home goal of stupendous ineptitude and there were plenty of reports like the following from the *Bath Chronicle* of 20 October 1842:

> Edward Thomas, found in a state of drunkenness on Sunday morning about eleven o'clock by Inspector Cox near Walcot Church, was fined five shillings and costs. On the 17th ult. the same man was brought before the magistrates, charged

with a similar offence, on which occasion he was discharged … The prisoner was turned out of the *White Horse Cellar* in a state of beastly intoxication shortly before the commencement of Divine Service at the church, and behaved in so violent and disgraceful a manner as to render it necessary to give him into custody. Mr Wilkinson thought it would it would be advisable to take some notice of the landlord's conduct when he should apply for the renewal of his licence.

One of the biggest challenges faced by the temperance movement in Bath in its early years was the coming of the railway. With the railway came an army of navvies – overpaid, over-intoxicated and with muscles like iron. Admittedly, Bath did not suffer as badly as the rural communities through which the railway passed, where locals were outnumbered by navvies many times over, especially when large earthworks were needed. In November 1839, for example, the *Bath Chronicle* reported "serious disturbances . . . in that part of the GWR which passes through Christian Malford, between the navigators and the village labourers, and that several of the labourers have been severely beaten, and robbed of their watches, etc." Assaults in Bath tended to be of an isolated nature, as when "three supposed navigators robbed violently a man on the canal bank near Widcombe" in May 1840.

The arrival of the navvies had another unfortunate consequence as far as the guardians of public morality were concerned. Prostitution soared. The following report from 1841 gives some idea of the extent of the problem:

With the railway came an army of navvies – overpaid,
over-intoxicated and with muscles like iron

AWASH WITH ALE

James Bissell, landlord of the *Crown & Thistle*, Avon Street, was charged with keeping his house open during the hours of divine service ... Inspector Norcross stated that he was on duty in Avon Street between the hours of three and four o'clock, when, on perceiving the door of the *Crown & Thistle* open, he went in, and in one of the rooms he saw between 30 and 40 persons, railway men and prostitutes, assembled, and some of them had beer before them.

An item from the *Bath Chronicle* for 19 December 1841 gives a vivid description of the all-day drinking which went on at several of the pubs in Southgate Street – and of its consequences:

Sarah King and Mariah Hopkins were charged with stealing from the person of a railway labourer, named Matthew Leonard, a purse containing eight sovereigns, two half sovereigns and two half crowns. Leonard and another man named Whitelock had been sitting with the prisoners nearly all the day on Wednesday at the *Plough Inn* in Southgate Street, having first met them at the *Bell* in Stall Street. In the evening Whitelock missed a cheque for £40 from his pocket; but he could not discover by what means he had lost it. About seven o'clock, Leonard also missed his purse and money. An elderly woman saw Hopkins take the purse from his inside waistcoat pocket and hand it over to King at the door. She went out for a short time, and on her return accused them of the transaction, when King fell on her; a row ensued, which brought the police, when the prisoners were given in charge; but neither purse nor money was found on them. The prisoners were remanded.

The most remarkable thing about this account is the amount of money the two men were carrying around with them. Navvies earned, at most, eight shillings a day. Leonard and Whitelock must have received their final wages after the completion of the railway and gone on a binge to celebrate. A pity they were not more cautious about the company they chose to celebrate with.

The navvy problem may have been one of the reasons for building a Temperance Hall on Claverton Street, just along from the railway, in 1839. Even more elaborate provision was made at Batheaston. In January 1840 a sermon was preached at St Saviour's, Larkhall, "in aid of a fund to ameliorate the destitute spiritual condition of the men working on the railroad." By June 1840, a "Railway Episcopal Chapel" had been opened at Batheaston and the Rev WC Osborn placed a notice in the *Bath Chronicle* stating that, "considerable expence having been incurred in setting up an Episcopal Chapel, and further expence being contemplated to provide a home for railway boys, and a retreat for the men on wet days and Sundays, contributions are earnestly solicited." The report of the opening ceremony, which appeared at the same time, indicates that, although the temperance movement was a guiding light behind the chapel, they did not have the knee-jerk reaction to alcohol of later campaigners:

On Monday last, about 100 men and boys employed on the GWR had a supper of beer, bread and cheese provided for them in the room underneath the Railway Episcopal Chapel at Batheaston. The building, originally the poor house, is divided into three floors. The middle floor is licensed by the Bishop for the purposes of a chapel, where service is performed on Sundays and Friday evenings, and the men are instructed in reading. The lower floor is intended as a retreat for the men on wet days, where they will be furnished with books and tracts. The upper floor the Chaplain wishes to convert into a dormitory for the boys engaged on the line, many of whom now sleep in and around the stables, or in, or under the waggons, or by the side of the fires in the road.

By the mid-nineteenth century, temperance campaigners had disorderly houses well and truly in their sights. At the meeting for the renewal of public-house licences in 1852, they handed the following petition to the Mayor:

From a register kept during 41 weeks since the last annual licensing day . . . it appears there were 660 persons brought before your worshipful bench. Of these 83 were charged with being drunk; 39 were licensed victuallers or beer-house keepers, who were summoned for infractions of the law; 61 were charged with offences of different descriptions, including theft, felonies and assault, and which were shown by the evidence to have been committed under the evidence of strong drink, or which were indirectly connected with it.

Your memorialists are feelingly alive to the amount of rates they are called upon to contribute for the prevention and punishment of crime, nearly £10,000 being annually required to meet the expenses of our police and prisons. Viewing this fact in connection with the returns now brought forward (which show that considerably more than one-fourth of those cases brought up are known to arise from intoxicating drink), and remembering also that it has been given in evidence in the House of Commons, and the same opinion has been expressed by several of our Judges, that three-fourths of the crime, poverty and disease in the nation arise from the sale of intoxicating liquor -

Your Memorialists deem it their duty to protest against any step being taken to increase the heavy payments they have to make on this account, and to afford greater facilities for the increase of crime, which would undoubtedly be the case with an increased number of licensed houses.

Your Memorialists would further urge upon you the fact that there are now existing one-third more places for the sale of strong drink than the number of bakers and butchers combined; and that the houses already licensed are in proportion of one for every two hundred of the population.

In response, the Magistrates made it more difficult for licences to be transferred, requiring no less than six certificates of good character from upstanding citizens before a new landlord could take over. Yet, despite an increasing willingness on the part of the authorities to close down ill-conducted houses, their numbers fell much more slowly than the campaigners would have liked. In 1867, they went back to the bakers and butchers argument, pointing out that, while there were only 74 bakers and 51 butchers in Bath, there were "300 places for the sale of intoxicating drink ... Poverty, immorality and crime are in proportion to the facilities afforded for the sale of spiritous liquors."

Other things went wrong for the temperance movement as well. In July 1869, they fell victim, ironically, to water, when a Temperance Fete at Cranwells, Jerom Murch's house on Weston Lane, was marred by a sudden downpour of rain. Many people took shelter under a temporary platform, which, unfortunately, proved more temporary than was intended, and collapsed, causing several injuries. Perhaps Mr W Mancip, the Secretary of the Bath Temperance Association, was still smarting from his injuries six weeks later when he wrote this rather intemperate letter to the *Bath Chronicle*:

HOUSES OF BAD CHARACTER:

Anyone who has been unfortunate enough to live near one of these pestilential sinks of vice, can form some faint estimate of the appalling consequences, when informed that in this beautiful city so favoured with religious appliances, there were, during the past year, no less than 42 places licensed as public houses and beerhouses, the resort of "thieves and prostitutes." One such moral pest which stood within a stone-throw of our venerable abbey, is fresh in my own recollection. To describe the nuisance only as it appeared from the outside would be unfit for publication. Clergymen and neighbours sought again and again through the landlord to replace this den of infamy, but for more than 12 years it withstood every such effort, until by doubling the rent, to the great joy of the neighbourhood, it suddenly collapsed.

The house referred to by Mr Mancip was almost certainly the *Cross Keys*, one of the "houses of notoriously bad character" which the Home Secretary had contacted the Mayor of Bath about in 1826. The site of the *Cross Keys* is today marked by the Rebecca Drinking Fountain, a lasting symbol of the temperance campaigners' triumph. This fountain was handed over by JH Cotterell, the President of the Bath Temperance Society, to the Mayor at a ceremony on Saturday, 8 June, 1861. In his acceptance speech, the Mayor expressed the hope that the drivers of the cabs queuing for custom in the Orange Grove would take advantage of the refreshing waters of the fountain, rather than nipping into one of the nearby pubs. However, this being Bath, it was only a matter of time before someone wrote to the paper complaining about the fountain. Just over two months later, a letter from an irate lady appeared in the *Chronicle*. She had taken some visitors to admire the fountain, only to find that the cup – which was too small anyway – took several minutes to fill, so meagre was the dribble of water which issued forth.

Slowly the temperance campaigners grew more powerful and extended the scope of their condemnations. In 1878, the Bishop of Bath & Wells, in a report to the Church of England Temperance Society drew attention to "the condition of many holidaymakers in excursion trains … to the great annoyance of their sober companions and fellow travellers."

Many pubs that closed in the late nineteenth or early twentieth century became temperance dining rooms. These included the *Freemason's Arms* in Abbey Green, the *Clarence* in Kingsmead Square, the *Cornmarket Tavern* in Walcot Street, the *Manege Horse* in Julian Road, and the *White Hart* in Twerton High Street. The *White Hart* was abandoned by the Bath Brewery Company in exchange for the granting of a licence to the *Victoria Hotel* in East Twerton. It was bought by the Twerton Lodge of Good Templars for £355 and turned into a Temperance Institute and Restaurant. At the opening ceremony in May 1899 there was an unnecessary and rather chilling display of triumphalism when the Templars "burst the old vats and other things connected with alcohol."

By now, the moderate aims of the original temperance campaigners had given way to an intemperate fanaticism which sought nothing less than total prohibition. Calls for a total ban on the sale of alcohol had started in earnest in 1853, when the United Kingdom Alliance for the Suppression of Traffic in Intoxicating Liquors was founded in Manchester. By and large, teetotallers were an pretty unpleasant bunch. Samuel Butler, the novelist, said that "there should be asylums for such people. But they would probably relapse into teetotalism as soon as they came out." Teetotallers claimed to take their lead from the Bible, conveniently ignoring the fact that Jesus had performed the party trick to end all party tricks by turning water into wine. When this was pointed out to Abraham Coles, an American teetotal preacher, he came up with an example of convoluted logic that would put the most inventive spin-doctor to shame:

> Taking our stand on the immovable rock of Christ's character, we risk nothing in saying that the wine of miracle answered to the wine of nature, and was not intoxicating. No counter proof can equal the force of that drawn from his attributes. It is an indecency and a calumny to impute to Christ conduct which requires apology.

There are, of course, plenty of other quotes in the Bible to give the lie to the teetotal movement. For instance:

> Wine is good as life to a man, if it be drunk moderately. What is life then to a man who is without wine? For it was made to make men glad.
> (Ecclesiasticus, 31:27),

or:

> Give beer to those who are perishing, wine to those who are in anguish; let them drink and forget their poverty and remember their misery no more.
> (Proverbs, 31: 6-7)

or:

> Drink no longer water, but use a little wine for thy stomach's sake.
> (1 Timothy, 5:23)

Then there are Benjamin Franklin's simple words of wisdom:

> Beer is proof that God loves us and wants us to be happy.

and this wonderful last request from the seventh century St Columbanus:

> It is my design to die in the brewhouse; let ale be placed to my mouth when I am expiring, that when the choirs of angels come, they may say, "Be God propitious to this drinker."

It is unlikely, however, that any of this would have cut much ice with a temperance campaigner called Tennyson Smith, who turned up in Bath in March

1899 for a week-long crusade. He was a rabble-rouser of the worst type. In his opening rally, held in the Guildhall, he declared that "there was not a hotel in Bath which was not the centre of evil influence." He urged his audience, "when the time for election came, to turn out of the Bath council the two members who were engaged in the liquor trade." Give Smith his due, he was not afraid of upsetting people. The "two members" he referred to were among the most influential men in the city. Alfred Taylor and John Rubie were both aldermen, and both owned upmarket wine merchant's in New Bond Street. John Rubie also held the lease of the *Castle Hotel* in Northgate Street, the *Bladud's Head* in Walcot Street, and the *Saracen's Head* in Broad Street. Mr Smith was summoned before the Mayor and invited to retract his remarks or forfeit the use of the Guildhall for the rest of his meetings. Not surprisingly, he took the latter option, leaving the powers that be to ponder on how, by fostering the temperance movement, they now had a tiger by its tail.

Today, when we think of the temperance movement, it is of people like Tennyson Smith that come to mind, rather than the early campaigners, who saw nothing wrong in a pint or two of beer and whose watchword was moderation. It is well for us to look back beyond zealots like Tennyson Smith and raise a glass to the pioneers of temperance whose concern was for the welfare of the working classes – physical as well as spiritual – rather than blinkered allegiance to the life-denying doctrine that drinking alcohol was a sin.

The evils those early temperance campaigners fought against were very real. A few nineteenth-century stories from the *Bath Chronicle* will serve to highlight how great the misery caused by drinking was. The first comes from May 1814:

> A fatal instance of the sad facts of inebriety and unrestrained passion has occurred. Mr Henry Adlam and his wife, who kept a straw hat manufactory in Bath Street, had long indulged in habits of mutual recrimination, and blows occasionally passed between them. On the morning of Wednesday, they renewed their dispute, and immediately after breakfast Mr Adlam left the house. He returned late in the afternoon in a state of intoxication, when the quarrel was revived, and very opprobrious words being applied by Mr Adlam to his wife, the exasperated woman plunged a cake knife into her husband's arm, by which the main artery was severed, and a mortification ensuing, he expired on Thursday night, in the thirtieth year of his age. The Coroner's Jury, after an investigation of six hours duration, returned a verdict of wilful murder against the wretched wife, who was accordingly committed for trial.

At her trial, three months later, she was found guilty of manslaughter and sentenced to six months imprisonment.

There were, of course, many tales of men spending all their money on beer and leaving their wives and children to starve. Here is a typical one from 1852 which only made the papers because the woman concerned took matters into her own hands:

> Mary Backhouse, the wife of a mason, living in Gibb's Court [off Walcot Street], was charged with being drunk and wilfully breaking three panes of glass at the *Lambridge Tavern*, a beerhouse. The prisoner, in answer to the charge, said that

she went to look for her husband, who, she complained, spent all that he earned in drink, leaving her to live upon what small sums she could get by going out to work. When she found him in the house she quarrelled and he beat and kicked her. In her exasperation she committed the act complained of, for which she said she was sorry and, if a few days were given her, she would pay the damage (two shillings). The Magistrates, in compassion to her, consented to adjourn the case till Thursday, to give the prisoner an opportunity of paying; but, before she left the room, a gentleman, from kindness, gave her the money, which she immediately gave to the landlady, the clerk's fees not being demanded.

We should not run away, however, with the idea that it was only men who liked to put it away in the mid-nineteenth century. Intemperate women were a major problem, especially as they often had children to look after. In 1851, a woman called Mariah Clark "of intemperate habits" was found drunk by her husband when he returned home unexpectedly at eight o'clock one Tuesday night. He was working in Bristol and generally lodged there all week, only returning home at weekends. He flew into a rage and killed her with a stick, despite the presence of their three children. The oldest one, a boy who had celebrated his ninth birthday the day before, gave evidence at the inquest. It emerged that she was almost always drunk and that, although she normally sent out for beer and drank it alone, sometimes she would be missing for "two nights and days," leaving the children to fend for themselves. According to the shopkeeper downstairs, "she was enticed to intemperance by the women." It emerged at the inquest that she came from a respectable Roman Catholic banking family in Cheltenham, but had started drinking at an early age and married beneath her. An autopsy revealed that, even if she had not been killed, she would not have lasted much longer as her liver was badly affected by alcohol. She was 40 years old. Her husband was charged with wilful murder.

For a real flavour of what life was like for women who "went wrong" in early Victorian England, this report, from 1842, is worth quoting in full:

An inquest was held on Saturday evening ... at the Bath Union Workhouse, on the body of Eliza Tarlton, aged 52, a woman of very dissipated habits, who was being removed from her residence, 16 Avon Street, to the Workhouse on Thursday, when she was suddenly seized with illness and died on the road. It appeared from the evidence of Mr Seale, sergeant to the Walcot District of the Union, that he had been in the habit of attending the deceased since the 5th inst., where she was visited by order of the relieving officer, Mr Douglas. She was then labouring under the influence of drink, and was surrounded by several respectably-dressed females, who were surprised at Mr Seale's entrance. She denied having been drinking to any great extent. Mr Seale asked her the necessary questions, and left her, desiring her to send for medicine. On coming downstairs, Mr Seale learnt that the deceased was addicted to drink; and on Wednesday the 7th his assistant visited her and reported her to be drunk. On the 9th, Mr Seale visited her himself and again found her drunk. On remonstrating with her, Mr Seale found she took an immense quantity of medicine, which she drank when she could not get liquor. Between the 9th and the 14th, the assistant again saw her, and reported that she was then seated at a table, surrounded by females, and with cards before her. On the 14th Mr Seale again saw her, and she was then as drunk as ever; on which she was told by Mr Seale that she would be reported to the Board, and to the Magistrates, as an improper character. On the 19th the assistant again called; on the 20th Mr Seale saw Mr Douglas, the relieving officer, to whom he reported her conduct, requesting he would name it to the Board, and at the same time recommending her removal to the House as the fittest place for her. Mr Douglas said the money he had paid the deceased was not allowed by the Board, but was remitted by her husband. Mr Douglas said, however, he would not lose sight of the case. On the 22nd an application was made by the deceased to Mr Seale to call on her. Mr Seale told the messenger it was folly for him to prescribe medicine for her, and that he had made up his mind to report her. In the afternoon Mr Seale called on her, and heard she had been removed, and had died on her way to the Workhouse. Her malady was undoubtedly *delirium tremens*; and the quantity of physic she took was counteracted by the amount of beer she drank. The cause of death was attributable to the want of energy in the action of her heart, arising from its usual stimulus being withdrawn; she had not been known to be sober for the last eight or ten weeks. The day before her death she was deprived of nearly all her drink; on Tuesday (the 30th inst.) and the day preceding, she had drunk from 18 to 20 half pints of beer. Death resulted from the total withdrawal of all drink.

Mary Lacy of 37 Avon Street, the renter of the house in which the deceased lodged, proved that she had three shillings a week allowed her from her husband, of which two shillings and sixpence was paid for lodging. She gained her subsistence by fortune telling and writing letters. She was removed to the Union on Thursday, at the request of Mr Fowler of the City Mission. Witness had frequently seen her drunk and had heard that she had been drunk for the last 10 weeks. On Tuesday she was forced to drink some broth and on Wednesday she ate an egg. On Thursday, as she was being removed, she put her hand out of the fly, and asked witness to get her a pennyworth of beer.

Ann Kirk, a lodger in the same house with the deceased, who had been in the habit of waiting on her, said she had lived a very drunken life, and that she had been drunk for the last 10 weeks. She had not taken any food for some weeks. She was drunk on Wednesday last, and on the Thursday she was moved witness fetched her beer several times. She was in the habit of having a quart of beer placed at her bedside at night. The Coroner very properly reprimanded this witness for her improper behaviour, in which the Jury unanimously concurred.

Ann Barnett, of 18 Avon Street, accompanied the deceased in the fly which removed her to the workhouse, at which time witness believed she was sober. She died just as the fly got beyond the *Bear* public house, and had appeared very ill all the time she was in the fly. Rachel Clark, another witness, was also in the fly at the time of the deceased's death.

Mr Douglas, relieving officer, stated the husband of the deceased was a respectable man in Cheltenham, who allowed her three shillings a week, which was regularly paid. The Jury briefly consulted and returned a verdict of "Died from *delirium tremens* resulting from habitual drunkenness."

The Victorians certainly had an uphill struggle on their hands getting people off the bottle. Even christening girls Temperance – a favourite name for pious working-class parents – was no guarantee that they would live sober lives. In 1842, for example, the *Bath Chronicle* reported the death of a 46-year-old domestic servant "of intemperate habits" with the unfortunate name of Temperance Taylor. Nine years later, Temperance Doddimead, a servant at 1 Lansdown Place East was charged with stealing three bottles of wine from her mistress.

But enough of fair-handedness and cautionary tales. This is, after all, a book about drinking, not about reasons for stopping drinking. The last word on temperance, therefore, should go to the great Irish poet, Louis MacNeice:

Coming of a temperance family, drunkenness had always been for me a symbol of freedom. It was a kicking overboard of the lumber of Puritan ethics; it was a quick road to fantasy; it achieved a communion among those whom sobriety divided. I had heard a temperance lecturer explain that alcohol impairs the mind through weakening the synapses of the brain, and I was willing to believe this; we have more mind than is comfortable anyway, the same again and to hell with the synapses ... My father had never mentioned synapses but I knew that *his* chief objection to drink was that the drunkard loses his self-respect. But that again from my point of view was all to the drunkard's credit, self-respect being one of the roots of evil ... Self-respect was the Evil Genius of half the world's troublemakers – of the sectarians and the militants, the nationalists and the imperialists, the captains of industry and the moral reformers. To get tight therefore, to stagger round the quadrangles being sick or making water, even if it was not always enjoyable, was all in a good cause; one was laming and debilitating one's private Satan, one's Tempter, one's self-respect.

CHAPTER SIXTEEN

A DIGRESSION ON WATER

I never drink water because of the disgusting things that fish do in it.
*WC Fields**

"Water is Best" is a rough translation of the Greek motto on Bath's Pump Room. It also appears on the Rebecca drinking fountain. It was not a sentiment shared by the twelfth-century Abbess Hildegarde of Bingen:

> Whether one is healthy or infirm, if one is thirsty after sleeping, one should drink wine or beer, but not water. For water might damage rather than help one's blood and humours.

The image of a yawning nun groping around for a glass of beer as the angelus rouses her from sleep is probably not one the Catholic church of today would wish to foster. The idea that water is bad for you was still current 500 years later, however, when a seventeenth-century doctor called Tobias Venner published a treatise on how to live longer. He advised his readers to steer clear of water, which "doth very greatly deject the appetite, destroy the natural heat, and overthrow the strength of the stomach."

The main problem with water was not – despite WC Fields' dictum – the disgusting things that fish did in it, but the disgusting things that other people did in it. This was certainly the case in eighteenth century Bath, as Smollett's Matthew Bramble discovered:

> After a long conversation with the doctor, about the construction of the pump and the cistern, it is very far from being clear with me, that the patients in the Pump Room don't swallow the scourings of the bathers. I can't help suspecting that there is, or may be, some regurgitation from the bath into the cistern of the pump. In that case, what a delicate beverage is each day quaffed by the drinkers! medicated with the sweat, and dirt, and dandruff, and the abominable discharges of various kinds from twenty different diseased bodies, parboiling in the kettle below. In order to avoid this filthy composition, I had recourse to the spring that supplies the private baths on the Abbey Green; but I at once perceived something extraordinary in the taste and smell: and, upon inquiry, I find that the Roman

---

* This, of course, is the clean version of this quotation.

baths in this quarter were found covered by an old burying-ground belonging to the abbey; through which, in all probability, the water drains in its passage: so that as we drink the decoction of living bodies at the Pump Room, we swallow the strainings of rotten bones and carcasses at the private bath. I swear to God, the very idea turns my stomach!

Determined, as I am, against any further use of the Bath waters, this consideration would give me little disturbance if I could find anything more pure, or less pernicious, to quench my thirst; but, although the natural springs of excellent water are seen gushing spontaneous on every side, from the hills that surround us, the inhabitants, in general, make use of well-water, so impregnated with nitre, or alum, or some other villainous mineral, that it is equally ungrateful to the taste, and mischievous to the constitution. It must be owned, indeed, that here in Milsom Street, we have a precarious and scanty supply from the hill; which is collected in an open basin in the Circus, liable to be defiled with dead dogs, cats, rats, and every species of nastiness, which the rascally populace may throw into it, from mere wantonness and brutality.

Despite Matthew Bramble's criticisms, the problem with well water was not its mineral composition but the sewage that filtered into it. It was fine if you lived at the top of the hill, less so if you sank a well downhill from somebody else's cesspit. The wells at the bottom of Morford Street or Holloway must have been particularly flavoursome. Worst of all was the drinking water in the Avon Street area. Here, even when the river was low, the cellars were damp and sewage had no difficulty percolating upwards. When the river flooded, as it often did, sewage swirled around in the street, augmented by refuse from the slaughterhouses and piggeries in the area. People in Avon Street did not just drink beer because they wanted to get drunk. They drank it because they did not want to catch cholera, typhoid or whatever disease was doing the rounds at the time.

As Matthew Bramble pointed out, however, Bath was also supplied with fresh water from the springs which flowed off the surrounding hills, and which from the earliest times were diverted to feed conduits around the city. Some of these were very elaborate. The one that stood just within the North Gate, for example, was described by John Wood as "a handsome quadrangular reservoir of water, built in the Dorick style, with a cymatium roof terminating in a point, and decorated with pinnacles at the angles." But even spring water could not always be relied upon. As late as 1928 there was a typhoid outbreak on Bathwick Hill, leading to five deaths, after the springs which fed its water supply were contaminated.

And then there was the river. Imagine looking down on Bath one May morning in the late middle ages, with the dew on the grass, buttercups dotting the shining meadows with gold, and the abbey tower rising high above the city walls. Around the great church, wreathed in steam from the hot springs, stand pear and apple orchards, the branches of the trees heavy with blossom. Bells echo and re-echo across the valley. The silver river flows silently on, curving gently round the city, while, from high, sheep-cropped hills, sparkling rills run down to meet it, glinting in the rays of the rising sun.

That would not have been how most people saw it. For generations of Bathonians, the river was a savage, unpredictable, unappeasable god, to be used if necessary, but never to be loved. Until well into the nineteenth century, there were few years when the number of people who met their end in its muddy, swirling waters did not run into three figures. Many of those who drowned accidentally were children – generally boys – who lost their footing while messing about on the bank or taking horses down to drink at the water's edge. Many of the adults who drowned were drunk and strayed too close to the bank on their way home from the alehouse in the dark. Reports like the following, from the *Bath Journal* of 1749, were commonplace:

> Last Monday the body of Michael Portice, a cooper of this city, was found in the river near Monk's Mill. He had been missing ever since Thursday night, the 26th of January; at which time he was much disguised in liquor, so 'tis thought that he accidentally fell into the river.

In June 1851 a butcher from Downside, having visited Bath for the day, stopped off at the *Full Moon* at the bottom of Southgate Street. He imbibed rather too freely and, although entreated to stay the night when last orders were called, insisted on walking home. He got no further than the bridge across to Widcombe, where he lost his footing. His body was fished out of the river the next morning.

Drink featured not only in many accidental deaths, but also in many suicides. In June 1851, for example, a "woman named Tilley" jumped into Avon "while maddened with drink." In July 1841 the following bizarre report appeared in the *Bath Chronicle*:

> About half past seven a man named George Atkins, servant to Mr Sainsbury, soda water manufacturer of Burton Street, leaped from the parapet of Bathwick Bridge. We are informed that he had leave of absence for a few hours, and that whilst at a public house he had his pocket picked of eight half crowns, on discovering which he became frantic, and immediately proceeded from the house to the bridge, where he divested himself of his hat and neckerchief and then mounted the parapet and leaped off into the water, exclaiming, "Good bye, my name is George Atkins." Mr Jennings of Walcot House, hearing an alarm raised by those who witnessed the act, ran to the river and got into Mr Sheal's (the blind fisherman's) boat, and being supplied by Mr Sheal with a crook, he hitched it in the man's frock as he was sinking for the last time and brought him ashore.

In 1816, the river featured – as was all too often the case – in a coroner's inquest:

> David Price, labourer, gave evidence that he had known the deceased, eighteen-year-old Fanny Dayer, for two months: On Saturday evening last he was sitting in the kitchen at the *Ship & Nelson* in Horse Street and she came in and drank with him. While there they agreed to go and sleep together. As they were going from thence to Avon Street along the way she complained her friends had behaved very ill to her in consequence of her going to Bristol with a man. They went to Mr Yearsley's in Avon Street and went up the stairs into a room where she took

Several publicans residing within the neighbourhood of the river have suffered

off her clothes and sat on the bed crying very much. He asked her what she was crying about but she would not tell him and said he knew nothing about her trouble. She continued crying and he told her if she did not leave off he would go away. He was attempting to go when she said if he did not stay and sleep with her she would make away with herself. He went downstairs and she followed him as soon as she had put her clothes on. She was very much in liquor. They went down the street together and at the bottom of Avon Street as he was going home to the *Ship & Nelson*, he wished her goodnight and they parted. It was about ten o'clock. She often talked of destroying herself. She appeared very uncomfortable about having left her friends and if it had not been for them she would not have been on the town. She drank two glasses of rum and water and a part of a quart of beer.

Fanny Dayer, who been thrown out by her parents for bad behaviour only a few months earlier, was later found drowned in the river.

The river also harboured disease. In the summer of 1849, with cholera raging in Bristol and parts of Gloucestershire, the Avon was drained near the Old Bridge and accumulated mud removed. Some of the exposed sewers were found to be in a very bad state, "with no current to carry off the accumulated soil." As late as 1870, the Surveying Committee reported that the river was heavily polluted by "woollen cloth manufacturers above and below Bath" as well as by slaughterhouses in the Avon Street area.

Bathonians had another reason to hate the river. Within the old city walls there was little risk of flooding, but in Southgate Street and other low-lying areas adjoining

AWASH WITH ALE

the river it was a different story. In 1774, a "great flood" hit Bath, undermining Newton Bridge and leaving the Lower Bristol Road and Avon and Southgate Streets under several feet of water. A flood of 1809, caused by melting snow, was worse still. "The inhabitants of the Quay, Southgate Street, Milk and Avon Streets, and the old lower parts of the city, were obliged to retreat to their upper apartments; and many were deprived of food and fuel during that day and the following night." Dolemeads was badly affected, as were Walcot and Bedford Streets, "where some of the houses near the river collapsed burying the inhabitants." On 25 April, 1809, Mrs Jordan, the celebrated actress, wrote to the Duke of Clarence (later King William IV):

> Bath looks as if it was encompassed by a muddy sea. It is indeed a melancholy sight to see nothing in the lower part of the town but the miserable tops of the cottage chimneys appearing above the water, which is so rapid in its course as to carry everything it meets with it. The noise is *tremendous*.

In October 1823, "there was such an overflow of the banks of the Avon, that much damage was done to property and many lives were placed in danger." The pubs suffered as well, as this extract from the *Bath & Cheltenham Gazette*, reprinted with glee in a nineteenth-century temperance tract, explained:

> Several publicans residing within the neighbourhood of the river have suffered by their casks floating and either from "staving," or from losing the cocks the contents were wasted. In one or two instances, on working the beer engines, foul water followed the pump instead of beer, and it was found that the casks had literally changed their contents.

To see the river on a sunny summer's day, with barges and pleasure boats puttering up and down it and the water slipping over the weir, it is hard to imagine how much death and misery it has caused. But still each year it claims its quota of victims, reminding us that, despite everything, it is still the sullen, untamed, intractable presence that it ever was.

Finally, to end this digression upon water on a lighter note, here is a cure for drunkenness from a tract on *The Curiosities of Common Water*, published by John Smith in 1725:

> If a drunken man be plunged over head and ears in cold water, he will come out of it perfectly sober: and some I have known, that in such cases have been recovered by barely washing their heads in cold water.

And, in case you are wondering, it doesn't work.

He did clutch up a handful of apples and eat and
presently he grew happy again

CHAPTER SEVENTEEN

FORBIDDEN FRUIT:
A DIGRESSION UPON CIDER

… then did the young Prince Bladud, being cured of his leprosy, set off for his father's house, driving the Herd of Pigs before him. And at length, being weary, he lay down in an apple orchard to rest awhile. And for a while he did sleep sound, but ere long he was roused from his slumber by a fearsome noise that caused him to start up and look around, for fear that some wild beast had got into that orchard to slaughter his pigs. And as he gazed around, there he did behold a sight most uncouth to his eyes, for there the whole Drove of Pigs were seized as if by a Phrenzy, lying on the ground, kicking their Forelegs in the air, and making a most fearful sound. Those not yet inclined to the horizontal plane, staggered upon their feet as if wounded. Yet no assailant did Prince Bladud see, which confused him mightily, as why should there be such sounds of wailing and crying if no trouble was there. And as he looked he did see that each pig had around its mouth scraps and froth from the soft apples that lay upon the sward. And then did he realise that the sounds he heard were not those of pain but of a surfeit of glee as they wallowed joyously in the trodden fruit.

The Prince, minded to think that their ecstasie perforce came from partaking of these same apples that lay about, was struck with astonishment, and, considering with himself why he should not partake of the same Elixir, instantly resolved to do so. Thereupon he took up some of the apples that lay around and ate, and grew forthwith exceeding happy. And after a little space, his legs growing weak and staggering under him, he sat upon the ground and there did sing a song and fall asleep. And when he at length awoke he was sore troubled in his head and said, Where am I? And then he did espy the apples lying round about him and the pigs blowing noisily off, and recalling his former state, he did clutch up a handful of apples and eat and presently he grew happy again.

At length, he considered that he should bring these wonderful apples to his father's house and so did gather up of them well nigh four score and place them in a satchel. And driving his pigs before him, he set off for his father's house, but by the constant shuffling and jostling as he walked thither, these same apples did at length turn to a rich liquor, or *Pommice*, frothing at the seams of the bag. And when he arrived at his father's house he did there unbuckle the satchel, and those that stood by saw the sloppy mixture and did turn away saying: This is but some tiresome jape. Begone!

But Prince Bladud did there take up a cup and dipped it in the liquid and drank deep and did thereupon smile so sweetly and laugh and fall to singing, that very soon those that stood nearby and saw these wonders come to pass did drink also. And then did they repent their former words and agree it to be a liquor of most surpassing goodness and a sovereign Elixir to cast away the troubles of this world, and to dispel all sighs. By which they did call it by the name of *Sigh Dispeller*, from which we see it is called *Cyder* to this day.

The account of Bladud's discovery of cider may be taken with a pinch of salt – or a sliver of orange peel – but there is no doubt that Somerset was one of the counties where cider drinking first took hold and where it still maintains a firm, if somewhat tremulous, hold. Not that you would know it from most of the pubs in Bath. You do not have to go far out of town to find a cider pub – the public bar of the *Fox & Badger* at Wellow, for example, one of the best country pubs near Bath, is a stronghold of the opaque orange liquid – but in Bath, although some pubs still stock Somerset cider, drinking it is a minority activity. It was not always so – cider houses survived in Bath until well into the twentieth century. There was the *Devonshire Arms* on St James's Parade (now the *Bath Tap*), the *White Horse* in Northampton Street (now the *Dark Horse*), the *York Street Wine Vaults* on York Street (now the *Alehouse*), the *Charmbury Arms* in Brook Road, and the *Beehive* on Belvedere, Bath's last cider house, which closed in 2001. Until the late nineteenth century, several pubs, such as the *New Inn* in Southgate Street, even made their own cider.

It is sometimes said that, while a few glasses of wine make you forget your worries and a few pints of beer make you forget your inhibitions, a few pints of cider make you forget how to walk. Cider drinkers in the past had other things to worry about as well. A painting of 1742 by William Hoare in the Mineral Water Hospital shows two doctors examining patients. The one at the head of the queue is a labourer with paralysis caused by lead poisoning. This was a common complaint among farm workers in Somerset and was caused by drinking cider. The cider itself was not to blame – it was the lead-glazed pitchers they put it in. The cider was so acidic that it stripped the lead off the pitchers, and when the farm workers drank it they got a good dose of lead as well.

As long ago as 1230, cider presses were listed, in a Royal Charter, as one of the sources of income of Bishop Jocelin of Bath. By the seventeenth century, writers were praising cider's health-giving qualities. Francis Bacon, writing in 1626, declared that "cider and perry are notable beverages on long sea voyages." Cider, he went on, was "a wonderful and refreshing drink … an assured remedy for sicknesse taken at sea." If the cider ran out, then "those ill with scurvy [should] be given cider and oranges as an instant cure upon landing." In 1664, John Evelyn wrote that, "cider, generous, strong, sufficiently heady, excites and cleanses the stomach, strengthens the digestion and infallibly frees the kidney and bladder from breeding the gravel stone." In 1676, John Worlidge published his *Vinetum Brittanicum*, in which he stated his belief that "constant use of [cider] hath been found by long experience to avail much to health and long life; preserving the drinkers of it in their full strength and vigour even to very old age." So those farmers who paid some of their workers' wages in cider were not only saving themselves money; they could also sleep comfortably in the knowledge that they were doing their workers good as well.

Cider was not just for farmworkers, however. The gentry drank it too. In 1676, a Mr Beale of Yeovil told John Evelyn that, "some months ago, Mr Phellips of Montacute in Somersetshire shewed me a very fair large red-strake apple. . . . Mr Phellips, making cider of it, invited me to it, assuring that it already excells all high country wines." Bottle-fermented cider also started to appear at around this time. Glasshouse Farm at Odd Down marks the site of a glass manufactory, first recorded in 1696, which was almost certainly set up to make bottles for cider. In 1762, an advertisement appeared in the *Bath Journal* for "fine cyders either in cask or bottles, likewise fine old Taunton Squash Perry and Barlam Perry, in Bottles." According to John Evelyn,

> bottling is the next improver, and proper for cider; some put two or three raisins into every bottle, which is to seek aid from the vine. Here in Somersetshire I have seen as much as a walnut of sugar used for this country cider.

John Worlidge, who recommended that fine cider should be kept in racks in water-cooled cellars, declared in 1678 that "a barrel of Redstreak surpassed the best Spanish and French wines."

So popular was cider that, in the mid-eighteenth century, the government decided to raise some extra money by slapping a hefty tax on it. Cider had first been taxed in 1643, when the duty payable was one shilling and threepence a hogshead. In 1660 the tax was doubled. A century later it had crept up to four shillings a hogshead, but then, in 1763, the Tory Prime Minister, Lord Bute, decided to raise it to ten shillings. This was a step too far. Sir Charles Kemeys Tynte, MP for Somerset, was among those who spoke out vehemently on behalf of his cider-drinking constituents and voted against it. William Pitt the Elder, MP for Bath, and leader of the Whig opposition, was another. The Act was passed, however, largely because there were great swathes of the country where little cider was drunk. MPs from Essex or Northumberland could not give a fig whether cider was taxed or not, and if taxing it meant that something dear to the hearts of their constituents went untaxed, then naturally they were all for it.

The government had, however, reckoned without the cider drinkers. A few days after the Act was passed, the miners of the Forest of Dean resorted to direct action:

> Great numbers of Excisemen took up their qualifications at [Gloucester] Quarter

Sessions this week. Some of them may perhaps repent of their employ, as we are told the Subterranean Gentry of the Forest of Dean are determined to take all that come within their reach to the regions below. One of the Brethren of the Stick was last week catched by these Sons of Darkness in going his Rounds to the Cyder Mills, and was instantaneously hurried down two or three hundred feet under ground, where he now takes up his abode. The Colliers, it is said, use him very well, and he lives as they do; but they swear the Day of his Resurrection shall not come to pass till the Cyder Act is repealed; or, at least, till Cyder-making is over. Whether the Exciseman will, after the Mode of the Times, bring his action for false imprisonment, must be left to Futurity, which will, perhaps, bring this Question and him to light again.

In Somerset, opposition was more decorous, yet no less determined:

At a meeting of the High Sheriff, Grand Jury, Gentlemen, Clergy and Freeholders of the County of Somerset, at the Assizes in the City of Wells, on the 6th of August, a petition to Parliament was produced and signed, setting forth the inconveniences and grievances which they are subjected to by an additional duty now laid on cyder and perry, and praying a repeal of that act; which petition, we hear, will be transmitted to the public meetings in Bristol, Bridgewater Races, and the next General Quarter Sessions at Taunton, for the conveniency of obtaining a proper subscription thereto.

The Cider Act was not unpopular just because it made cider more expensive. It also created a new corps of excisemen with the power to enter people's homes without a warrant in search of untaxed cider. This was seen as an affront to traditional liberties and led Pitt the Elder to coin the phrase, "an Englishman's home is his castle." When Pitt became Prime Minister in 1766, he repealed the Act, abolished the excisemen's prerogative and slashed the tax. Naturally, he became the toast of Somerset. One landowner was so grateful that he left him his estate in his will. When Pitt inherited the estate he raised a massive column to the memory of his benefactor. Known as the Cider Monument, it can still be seen at Burton Pynsent near Langport.

There can be little doubt that farm workers, who received part of their wages in cider, were often blitzed out of their heads on a more or less permanent basis. They did not, of course, drink "fine cider." That was reserved for the gentry. Celia Fiennes, writing at the end of the seventeenth century, described how rough cider was made by throwing good and bad apples indiscriminately into enormous presses:

They pound their apples, then lay fresh straw on the press, and on that a good lay of pulp of the apples, then turn in the ends of the straw over it all round, and lay fresh straw, and more apples up to the top.

The unfiltered cider traditionally drunk by farm workers is today referred to as scrumpy, although originally this was a derogatory term for cider made from apples which had been "scrumped" or stolen.

The practice of paying part of the wages of farm labourers in cider survived until well into the nineteenth century. In 1843, a Poor Law Commissioner reported that:

AWASH WITH ALE

in the cider counties part of the wages of women is paid in cider; this is also the case with the wages of men, and also boys from the earliest ages at which they begin to work. A man has three or four pints of cider a day, a woman half that quantity. The man's cider is reckoned worth from one shilling and threepence to one shilling and sixpence a week ... The cider received by the women as part of their wages is not commonly drunk by them; it is more frequently kept for their husbands, though there are cases where it is partly, or even wholly consumed by the women themselves.

Some farm labourers put away far more than the average. In 1828 the *Bath Chronicle* reported "the fact (incredible as it may seem) that five men in the employ of Messrs Brown, Champion & Co. of Bridgwater, drank, on an average, in one week of the present summer, 122 quarts of cider each." That is equivalent to 34 pints a day. No wonder people like Sir Thomas Dyke Acland tried to stop the practice. "The liquor refreshes and stimulates [the farm labourer]," he wrote, "but wears him out, for common cider is not nourishing but exciting, like spirit and water. West Country labourers will never be what they might be as long as this system goes on." Part-payment of wages in cider died out for two reasons – pressure from the temperance movement and the mechanisation of farming. Going round half-drunk when all sources of power had either two or four legs was one thing; going round half-drunk when you had to operate machinery was quite another.

Cider – if you will pardon the pun – has had a bad press. It is hard to think of another drink that means so many different things to different people – from rough farmhouse scrumpy with bits floating in it, through sterilised, fizzy bottled versions aimed at the alcopop market, to farm-produced varieties which bear comparison, as they did three centuries ago, with fine wines. Sadly, many people still associate cider with puking teenagers, rambling scrumpy heads, or Adge Cutler fans. It is definitely a minority interest. In 1988, for example, we each drank, on average, just 14 pints of cider a year – compared to 175 pints of beer, 31 pints of wine and two pints of spirits. The words of Percy Bulmer, who wrote to Edward Elgar over a century ago of his struggle to re-establish cider as a drink for refined palates, have yet to be fulfilled:

Cider no doubt has a future before it and will take its place one day as a great national drink. We have overcome a great many difficulties and hope to work the subject out entirely before very long. Trusting you will have a pleasant winter in the south and will find time to write a cider symphony to encourage this struggling industry.

Elgar never did get round to writing a Cider Symphony, although part of his symphonic poem, *Falstaff*, was set in a Gloucestershire cider orchard. Perhaps one of today's composers will take up the challenge. Peter Maxwell Davis's *Variations on I am a Cider Drinker (Ooh-Ar, Ooh-Ar, Ooh-Aye) for Squeezebox, Washboard, Spoons and Chamber Orchestra* would surely go down a storm at the Last Night of the Proms. Perhaps then a few more people would track down some of Somerset's independent cider makers, such as that at Burrow Hill near Kingsbury Episcopi, and, like Bladud, find it to be "a liquor of most surpassing goodness."

There is no nation that drinks so hoggishly as the English

CHAPTER EIGHTEEN

THE MUDDY ECSTASIES OF BEER

There is no nation that drinks so hoggishly as the English. What passes for wine among us, is not the juice of the grape; it is an adulterous mixture, brewed up of nauseous ingredients, by dunces, who are bunglers in the art of poison-making; and yet we, and our forefathers, are and have been poisoned by this cursed drench, without taste or flavour. The only genuine and wholesome beverage in England, is London porter, and Dorchester table-beer.

Matthew Bramble in Tobias Smollett's Humphrey Clinker, 1771

Despite Matthew Bramble's stirring defence of our national beverage, it has, since the Norman Conquest, taken a back seat to wine. George Crabbe, in a rambling poem calling *Inebriety and the Candidate*, published in 1775, summed up genteel society's attitude to the beer drinker:

> Lo! The poor toper, whose untutor'd sense
>
> Sees bliss in ale, and can with wine dispense;
>
> Whose head proud fancy never taught to steer
>
> Beyond the muddy ecstasies of beer.

Crabbe's attitude still prevails in many so-called enlightened circles today. Lady Churchill was only reflecting genteel society's opinion of beer when she prepared the way for one of her husbands lesser-known ripostes:

> Lady Churchill: I hate the taste of beer.
>
> Sir Winston: So do many people – to begin with. It is, however, a prejudice that many have been able to overcome.

Since the Norman Conquest, beer has never seriously challenged wine as the gentry's chosen tipple. Small beer may have been all right at breakfast, but, for dinner, wine was the natural choice. Until very recently, wine has always been much more expensive than beer. In the mid-eighteenth century, for example, the cheapest bottle of wine cost around two shillings, compared to twopence for a pint of best porter (and a halfpenny for a tot of rotgut gin).

Quite why there should have been such an institutionalised prejudice against beer is hard to say, but it is still as strong as ever. Malcolm Gluck believes that the thought of serving beer instead of wine with a meal is "a disgusting idea," while

Derek Cooper will tell you that "a glass of beer, however excellent, can't compare with a premier cru claret." To such attitudes, all one can do is doff one's cap and mutter that, of course, they must be right – or, alternatively, tell them they are talking a load of elitist nonsense. It would make as much sense to say, "a pineapple, however excellent, can't compare with a runner bean," or, "a rump steak can't compare with a gooseberry." It is hardly surprising that brewers of high-quality beer in this country have such a difficult time. Just imagine what state the French wine industry would be in if the cognoscenti said things like, "a glass of grand cru, however, excellent, can't compare with a premier pint of Bellringer."

Crabbe's poem also highlights another peculiarity of our national beverage. Within the space of four lines, he manages to give it two names – ale and beer. This crisis of identity still survives today – the bible of the Campaign for Real Ale, for example, is the *Good Beer Guide*.

Ale and beer both predate the Norman Conquest. Ale is a particularly ancient word, and several others – most notably Yule – are derived from it. It was introduced into this country by the Danes and was mainly used in the eastern and northern parts of England where Danish influence was strongest. Danes and Norwegians still drink øl, while Swedes drink öl, and Latvians and Lithuanians drink alus. In England, ale eventually came to signify not only a drink but any special occasion at which it was drunk. There were, for example, "bride ales" – forerunners of today's wedding receptions – which have given us the word "bridal." "Scot Ales" were where people paid "scots" or taxes, drink being provided to soften the blow. If you were lucky enough to get away without paying anything, you were said to have got away "scot free."

The word beer was brought over to this country by the Anglo Saxons, and was mainly used in the south and west, where Saxon influence was strongest. It was probably derived from the Latin word biber (drink). The word beer – or something very similar to it – not only survives in Dutch, Flemish and German, but has also been introduced, over the centuries, into languages as diverse as Arabic, French, Kurdish, Japanese, Yiddish, and Vietnamese.

The existence of two words to describe the same thing is, therefore, a legacy of the struggle for control of the country in the centuries leading up to the Norman Conquest. Although there would have been local variations in brewing methods, ale and beer were essentially the same. The word you used to describe it when you turned up at the ale – or beer – house at the end of a hard day's graft depended on where you lived and who your lord and master happened to be at the time. When Swein the Dane, who had conquered most of England, turned up in Bath in 1013 to accept the surrender of the thanes of the western shires, he toasted his success with ale – although what he was drinking would have been called beer the day before.

After the Norman Conquest, beer – as a word to describe fermented liquor – rapidly fell out of favour. There was a very good reason for this. The Normans had brought their own language – Norman French – with them. It too contained the word beer; this, however, referred not to a drink, but to a frame for putting a coffin on. The potential for making a serious gaffe was obvious, and, as the Norman word eventually found its way into that curious hybrid of Anglo Saxon and Norman French we know as Middle English, it is hardly surprising that people stopped ordering beer. Chaucer's *Canterbury Tales*, written in the late fourteenth century, is awash with ale, but of beer – apart from the sort you put coffins on – there is not a mention.

A tankard of foaming nut-brown ale, forsooth, mine genial host

When hopped ale was introduced to England from Flanders, at around the same time that Chaucer's pilgrims were downing their ale on the road to Canterbury, it was called by its Flemish name – bier or beer – to differentiate it from unhopped English ale. Thus an Old English word which had not been used for centuries was reintroduced into the language to describe a foreign import. John Taylor, the "Water Poet," was among those who failed to recognise the history of the word, branding it "but an upstart or a foreigner or alien." Coincidentally, it was at around this time that the use of the word beer (now generally spelt bier), to describe a frame for putting a coffin on, started to fall out of use. It continued to be used by poets and undertakers, and still appears in dictionaries today, but before long there was very little chance of being misunderstood when you asked for a beer.

For the next three and a half centuries or so, beer and ale had distinct meanings – beer was hopped, ale was not. After hopped beer became universal in the late eighteenth century, however, the words became interchangeable, although ale was now the poor relation. By the end of the nineteenth century, there was another move to distinguish between the two, with darker, malt-flavoured beverages being called beers and lighter, hoppy kinds being called ales, but this failed to catch on.

Generally speaking, beer is now the generic term to describe the whole range of beverages brewed with malt and hops, except for lager. Ale fell out of general use a long time ago, except in the names of certain bottled beers, such as brown, pale and light ale. It has also, of course, given rise to the term "real ale." Walking into a pub, however – especially a real ale pub – and asking for a pint of ale would mark you as either: a) eccentric; b) foreign; c) taking the mick. Although we did once stumble across the chairman of a local CAMRA branch, resplendent in cravat and tweeds, his head wreathed in clouds of pipe smoke, who strode up to the bar uttering phrases like, "a tankard of foaming nut-brown ale, forsooth, mine genial host."

Even after the battle of the hop had been won, and unhopped ale disappeared, many other things continued to be added to beer to improve its flavour or hide the taste of substandard ingredients. Chamomile, liquorice, myrtle, chillies, caramel, caraway, coriander, juniper, cassia and ginger were all used, along with several other potions which, while they may have induced a more euphoric high, were lethal. Opium, digitalis, belladonna and *nux vomica* were all used by small brewers in the early nineteenth century. Cocculus Indicus, or India Berry, a relative of Deadly Nightshade, was particularly popular. It is not known what sort of hangover you'd have ended up with after a heavy session on beer adulterated with one of these little charmers. Nor is it known how you'd have reacted while under its influence – and, as for its addictive qualities, the less said the better. Curiously, though, these illicit brewing practices marked a return to the kind of hallucinogenic beverages quaffed by shamanistic priests several millennia earlier. Sulphuric acid was also commonly added to beer in the nineteenth century. As late as 1900, 70 people died, and many thousands became seriously ill, when there was an outbreak of arsenic poisoning in Salford. The arsenic was eventually traced back to a contaminated batch of sulphuric acid in a brewery.

By the mid-eighteenth century, porter – a dark beer made with slightly scorched malt, first produced in the 1720s, and so-called because London porters were the first to drink it – was the most popular tipple in the country. This was just one of the changes which overtook the brewing industry in the eighteenth century. Technological innovations – such as the introduction of isinglass finings in 1758 and the invention of the saccherometer in 1760 – made the whole process much less hit and miss. The main change, as we have seen, was that breweries became much bigger. Vats for storing beer got bigger as well. They were one of the wonders of the age – until they burst, as they occasionally did. One of the most spectacular disasters occurred in 1814, when a vat holding over a million pints burst at Meux's brewery in London. Eight people died in the deluge, either drowned in basements or overcome by the fumes. Several houses were also demolished by the flood.

Brewing could be a risky business even in smaller establishments. Bath had its share of accidents. In 1761, "as Isaac Wycombe, servant to Mr Cottrill at the *Packhorse* near St Michael's Church, was pumping some boiling wort out of a furnace, he fell into it and was so terribly scalded that he died Sunday." In 1842, George Morris was working at the Grosvenor Brewery when the flooring of the tun room gave way and "the whole mass with two long stillions and nine puncheons of beer fell into the store cellar below, trapping him." All the beer – between 800 and 900 gallons – ran away, but Mr Morris survived the ordeal. A man who climbed into a cask of beer at Marlborough a few years later was not so lucky:

> On Wednesday last a young man named Strood was found dead in a large beer cask at the *Kings Arms Inn*, Marlborough. It is supposed that while dipping out some beer with a bucket he was overcome with carbolic acid, and falling in head foremost was drowned. The beer was about eighteen inches deep and the whole of it, worth £19, was thrown away next day.

From the tone of the report it seems that the loss of the beer was a bigger source of regret than the loss of the young man.

Despite the growth of breweries in the eighteenth century, virtually every inn and alehouse, and most larger households, continued to brew their own beer. Although today's micro-breweries, with all the hi-tec gadgetry at their disposal, can brew beer as good as, or better than, large breweries, most of the beer brewed by small breweries in the eighteenth century would probably be considered undrinkable today. Few, if any, small breweries brewed porter. Their staple brew was a type of pale ale, heavily hopped to help it keep, and with who knows what secret ingredients added to make it palatable. While this was considered good enough for the tap room, the better-off turned increasingly to supplies of bottled or cask beer from the bigger breweries. Surprisingly, beer travelled vast distances, long before the coming of the railways. A writer in 1727 listed the variety then on offer in London:

> Beer of Dorchester, Burton Ale, Lincoln Ale, Derby Ale, Litchfield Ale, Yorkshire Ale, Yorkshire Stingo, Doncaster Ale, Basingstoke Beer, October Beer, Nottingham Ale, Boston Ale, Abingdon Beer, Newberry Beer, Chesterfield Ale, Welch Ale, Norwich Nogg, Amber Beer, Sir John Parson's Beer, Tamworth Ale, Dr Butler's Ale, Devonshire Beer, Plymouth White Ale, Oxford Ale, Sussex Beer, Johnson's Julep, or Lyon's Blood, Twankam, Coal Heaver's Cordial; and lastly plain humble Porter.

A similar range would have been available in Bath. In the *Bath Journal* of 3 May 1758 it was announced that Mr L Lee had opened *Old Wine & London Bottle Porter Vaults* in Trim Street. Bottled London Porter was available at "six shillings per dozen in full quarts," while Taunton Pale Beer sold at seven shillings and sixpence per dozen. Bottled beer was not only sold for home consumption. Any inn or alehouse that hoped to attract a better class of customer had to lay in stocks of bottled beer. In pre-railway days this was shipped up the Avon from Bristol, or later along the Kennet & Avon Canal, and offered for sale to the trade at riverside warehouses. Advertisements like this, from the *Bath Journal* of 19 April, 1773, appeared regularly:

> To the Publicans in General, there is now on sale at a cellar near the Key a large quantity of exceeding fine Ringwood and Taunton Beer, which may be seen and tasted by applying to Mr Thomas Walford in Broadley's Buildings.

Burton on Trent and London were the two biggest brewing centres, but beer from Dorset was also highly regarded. In 1788, a wine merchant called William Palmer thought so highly of it that he placed a special advertisement in the *Bath Chronicle*:

DORSETSHIRE BEER

Brewed by Stanning & Co

and sold at their cellars in Bath

by Mr William Palmer on the Borough Walls

and now ready to be delivered at the following prices – viz.:

Mild & Best Beer in Casks fit for Bottling @ twenty pence per gallon

Ditto in bottles at six shillings per dozen.

Guinness also has a distinguished history. In July 1838 the following advertisement appeared in the *Bath Chronicle*:

GUINNESS'S DUBLIN STOUT

A large stock of this excellent stout, in hogsheads, barrels, kilderkins and

bottles, is kept at the Stores, Sawclose, where fresh supplies are received weekly

from Dublin.

Samuel Waring

(Sole Consignee for the Western Counties)

Sawclose, Bath, and 13 King Street, Bristol

But, sadly, brand labels were just as much a target for the unscrupulous entrepreneur in the early nineteenth century as they are today. A few weeks later, Samuel Waring was forced to put another notice in the paper:

Mr Waring, the agent for Guinness's Celebrated Porter, has been under the necessity

of adopting a specific label, in order to guard the public from imposition.

Exaggerated claims were made for the efficacy of certain bottled beers. In 1846, for example, porter from the Oakhill Brewery was advertised for sale at the *Albion Tavern* (now *Flan O'Brien's*) in terms that would make a Trading Standards Officer wince:

Superior Double Stout

OAKHILL PORTER

In Cask, Bottle or Draught,

Which for its Medicinal Quality

and General Utility as a Beverage,

Cannot be Surpassed

In the late eighteenth century, several breweries opened in Bath to cash in on the booming porter market. The first was the Northgate Brewery, founded by Samuel Sayce in the 1770s. His porter sold in Bath for fourpence a quart – a penny less than London brands. In the late eighteenth century, there was even a brewery – Powney & Hannam's – brewing "strong beer, ale and table beer" opposite the Guildhall. In 1780, the opening of Warren's Porter and Amber Brewery, near Walcot Turnpike, was announced in the following terms:

The principal design in erecting this brewery was the production of fine Porter;

and the proprietor flatters himself that he shall be able to convince the public that

Porter brewed at Bath will in every respect be equal to what is manufactured in

London.

But then he blew it by going on to admit that "the brewery is supplied with the river water in its greatest purity, on which account it is peculiarly favourable to the brewing of the most wholesome ale and table beer." Sadly, no amount of spin could alter the fact that the river running through Bath was heavily polluted. Bathonians could see – and smell – it for themselves. When R&J Smith of Walcot Brewery advertised their "Porter, Strong & Table Beer" in 1796, they were at pains to point out that it was brewed "with Spring not River Water."

As breweries opened up, they acquired inns and alehouses, or worked out deals which effectively turned them into tied houses. The independent publican, in a process that has continued to the present day, found him or herself squeezed out by the big boys. Some publicans jumped onto the bandwagon, building little empires of their own, but a relentless process of upsizing, which even today shows no signs of abating, had already begun. When we read of vast multi-nationals making hostile bids for multi-million-pound brewing-cum-leisure consortiums, they are continuing a process which began when eighteenth-century brewers' agents knocked on alehouse doors and made the landlords offers they couldn't refuse.

Despite the growth of brewery empires, small breweries at the back of pubs survived for a surprisingly long time. In 1903, there were still over 30 home-brew pubs in Bath. These included the *Barley Mow* in Bathwick Street, the *Bell* in Walcot Street, the *Burnt House* at Odd Down, the *Devonshire Arms* on Wells Road, the *Green Tree* in Green Street, the *Lamb & Lion* on Lower Borough Walls, the *Long Acre Tavern* on Long Acre, the *Old Farm House* on Lansdown Road, the *Park Tavern* on Park Lane, the *Railway Tavern* on Wells Road, the *Ram*, the *Ring of Bells*, and the *White Hart* in Widcombe, and the *Royal Oak* on Pulteney Road. Most had closed by the 1930s, but two kept going until after the Second World War. Many Widcombe residents still remember brewing going on at the back of the *Ram* in the early 1950s. The last to go, however, was the one at the old *Long Acre Tavern*, which closed in 1956, when the pub was taken over by Wadworth's.

Today, after a period of over forty years without a brewery, beer is once again being brewed in Bath. The Abbey Ales Brewery was opened by Alan Morgan in 1997 at the back of the *Old Farmhouse* on Lansdown Road. Bellringer Beer, first brewed that October, remains the flagship of the company. The history of brewing in Bath is a fascinating one, and far too complex to do justice to here. For those who want to find out more, Mike Bone's article in *Bath History VIII* is a comprehensive introduction to the subject.

Finally, anyone unconvinced of the efficacy of beer should take note of this story, recorded by the antiquarian, John Timbs, and retold in Hackwood's *Inns, Ales and Drinking Customs of Old England*. It has a special relevance to Bath:

> About 1730, Pulteney, afterwards the Earl of Bath, lay for a long time at Lord Chetwynd's house of Ingestre in Staffordshire, sick, very dangerously, of a pleuritic fever. This illness cost him an expense of 750 guineas for physicians; and, after all, his cure was accomplished merely by a draught of small beer. Dr Hope, Dr Swynsen, and other physicians, from Stafford, Lichfield, and Derby, were called in, and carried off about 250 guineas of the patient's money, leaving the malady just where they found it. When two physicians who were Pulteney's

friends arrived they found his case to be quite desperate, and gave him over, saying that everything had been done that could be done. They prescribed some few medicines, but without the least effect. He was still alive, and was heard to mutter, in a low voice, "Small beer, small beer!' They said, "give him small beer or anything!" Accordingly, a great silver cup was brought, which held two quarts of small beer. Pulteney drank off the whole at a draught, and demanded another. Another cupful was administered to him, and soon after that he fell into a profuse perspiration and a profound slumber for nearly 24 hours. In this case the saying was verified, "if he sleep he will do well." From that time forth he recovered wonderfully, insomuch that in a few days the physicians took leave of him.

CHAPTER NINETEEN

BEER AND SKITTLES

Life ain't all beer and skittles, and more's the pity.
George Du Maurier, *Trilby*, 1894

Sports and games have been a part of pub life for as long as there have been pubs. And, despite the buzzing, beeping, burbling machines that gobble up money faster than a parking meter in Milsom Street, many of the games played today go back centuries. A list of popular pub games drawn up over 350 years ago included "Billiard Table, Shovel Board, Cards, Dice, and Ninepins," all of which are still going strong today.

If the Puritans had had their way, however, these pastimes would be as much a part of the dim, distant past as bear baiting and the ducking stool. In the increasingly Puritan climate of the early seventeenth century, traditional leisure pursuits were, one by one, outlawed. It is interesting to note that both James I (in 1617) and Charles I (in 1633) stood out against the growing tide of Puritanism by ordering a Declaration of Sports to be read from every pulpit in the land, giving their subjects the right to indulge in "decent and sober recreation." Unfortunately, they were fighting a losing battle. When the second Declaration of Sports was read out in 1634, the villagers of Dundry, near Chew Magna, took this as the cue to re-erect their maypole (which the curate had made them take down) in the field next to the church. They declared it to be their "ancient right" to revive

> those daies wherein recreations, sportes and playes of severall sortes were used as setting up of maypoles and summer luggs, dancing, sporting, kissing, bullbayting, coyting, bowling, shootinge at butts, cudgleplaying, tennis playing and divers other sportes.

The curate did not agree. It was "not seemly," he declared, "to have a maypole soe neere placed unto the church," nor was it right that his parishioners should use it as an excuse to "so unreverentilie demeasne themselves." The curate won and the maypole came down, this time for good.

Yet, even when Cromwell had taken over, and anything that smacked of fun was a heinous offence, there were still plenty of people prepared to run the risk of having a good time. On the day after Pensford Fair, in April 1656, several people were charged with "riotous behaviour ... at the *George Inn* and afterwards in the street." A few months later, John Templar was charged with selling "a wainload of beer" to between 300 and 400 revellers who had come to see the "cudgell match" at the Timsbury Feast.

One barbaric sport which survived the civil war was cock fighting. Cockpits could be found at several of Bath's more upmarket inns, such as the *Three Crowns* in London Street, the *Lamb* in Stall Street, the *George* in Walcot Street, the *Hare & Hounds* at Mount Pleasant in Widcombe, and the *Coach & Horses* in Twerton. Big money changed hands at cock fights and gentlemen flocked to them from miles around. The following announcement from the *Bath Journal* in 1745 is typical:

> A cock match to be fought at Mr Figg's at the *Lamb Inn* in Bath between the Gentlemen of Somerset against those of Wiltshire, each side throwing 41 cocks in the main, for four guineas a battle, and 40 the odd; also ten cocks each for bye-battles, for two guineas each battle. To weigh on Monday the 29th of April and fight the three following days.

Leaving aside the arcane terminology, one thing is plain. Cock fighting was not a poor man's sport. Four guineas in 1745 was equivalent to around £400 today.

Although cock fighting did not become illegal in England until 1835, it fell out of favour in Bath much earlier. Announcements of cock fights dry up in the mid-1770s, and – although we have found no confirmation of this – it seems that the sport was banned in Bath (as it was in Peterborough in 1792) before it was outlawed nationally. In some parts of the country, however, it continued to the bitter end. The largest cockpit in the country, at Melton Mowbray, was not built till 1826. Even after 1835, illegal cockfights continued. In 1840, for example, James Kempster of the *Packhorse* at Paulton was fined for training cocks and preparing a pit.

The last record we have discovered of an unofficial cock fight in Bath dates from 1809. Barbaric though the sport was, this last gasp of an expiring tradition did have a humorous side to it, and one that today's purveyors of Nostradamian eschatology might do well to ponder:

> On the 30th of March 1809, the destruction of the city of Bath was to have been effected by a convulsion of the earth, which should cause "Beacon Hill to meet Beechen Cliff." This inauspicious junction was said to have been foretold by an old woman, who had derived her information from an angel. This reported prophecy rendered many of the inhabitants truly unhappy, and instigated crowds of visitors to quit the city. The portentous hour, twelve o'clock, passed, and the believers were ashamed of their former fears. The alarm is said to have originated with two noted cock-feeders, who lived near the before-mentioned hills; they had been at a public house, and after much boasting on both sides, made a match to fight their favourite cocks on Good Friday, which fell on this day; but, fearing the magistrates might interfere if it became public, they named the cocks after their respective walks, and in the agreement it was specified that "Mount Beacon would meet Beechen Cliff, precisely at twelve o'clock on Good Friday." The match was mentioned with cautions of secrecy to their sporting friends, who

repeated it in the same terms, and with equal caution, until it came to the ears of some credulous beings who took the words in their plain sense; and, as stories seldom lose by being repeated, each added what fear or fancy framed, until the report became a marvellous prophecy, which in its intended sense was fulfilled; for the cocks of Mount Beacon and Beechen Cliff met and fought, and left their hills behind them on their ancient sites, to the comfort and joy of multitudes, who had been infected by the epidemical prediction.

Once cock-fighting was banned, pubs with cockpits had to find something else to put in them. One popular solution was to hire them out to travelling menageries. These menageries, which combined extravagant showmanship with appalling cruelty, included lions, dolphins, tigers, giraffes, and a whole host of other exotic creatures, all crammed into cages hardly larger than themselves. The *George* in Walcot Street (which stood on the site now occupied by the YMCA) was particularly noted for the quality of its travelling menageries. In 1820, for example, Drake's Royal Menagerie called there. Attractions included "the only black tiger and the only white lion ever seen in England ... a great condor, six lyons, a fiery lynx, a laughing hyaena, an ursine bear and four porpoises ... and the stupendous elephant which, about a year and a half ago, was overturned in coming down Lansdown Road" The Lansdown incident had clearly entered local folklore. Looking at the report of it, which appeared in the *Bath Chronicle* on 21 August 1817, it is not difficult to see why:

> Wednesday afternoon, as a caravan, with the stupendous elephant, was returning from Lansdown Fair, the hind wheels became entangled in the gutter on the steep part of the road just below Spencer's Belle Vue, and the driver, endeavouring to extricate the vehicle by a sudden jerk, it upset, and falling on one of the shaft horses, a valuable animal, killed it almost instantly. The elephant became unmanageable even by its keeper and every effort to lift the caravan being found useless, it remained in its fallen state till midnight, when the elephant was enticed by large pieces of bread and buckets of water into an adjacent coach-house and the caravan was taken away to be repaired.

Other sports involving animals took place – or at least started – at pubs. Pubs called the *Hare & Hounds* or the *Fox & Hounds* got their names because hunts met there on a regular basis. Generally, these were outside the town – such as the *Hare & Hounds* on Lansdown or the long-gone *Hare & Hounds* near Widcombe Old Church – but there was once a *Fox & Hounds* at the Northgate end of Walcot Street, a reminder that, until the eighteenth century, the country started right outside the city walls.

Pigeon clubs were a mainstay of many pubs. The story goes that one landlord at the *Ring of Bells* in Widcombe was so proud of his birds that he kept them in his bedroom. Ratting clubs also met in pubs – an instance of how human resourcefulness could turn the onerous necessity of vermin control into a sport. There were also shooting clubs, the members of which regularly turned out to control the sparrow or pigeon population. These lingered on until after the First World War, when the 1920 Firearms Control Act – a panic measure brought in amid fears that revolution in Russia and Civil War in Ireland would spark off armed insurrection in Britain – restricted gun ownership.

Most pub games were relatively healthy pastimes, if only because they slowed down the rate at which people drank. One spectator sport, which survives to this day with its own section in the *Guinness Book of Records*, is what can best be described as unhealthy eating. Pretty disgusting even now, but when this announcement appeared in the *Bath Journal* in 1744, it must, given the starvation rations many people had to live on, been even more so:

> On Friday next at the *Globe* at Newton ... the noted Sam Gane of the same parish is to eat a shoulder of mutton of eight pounds, half a peck of potatoes, a quarter of a peck of onions, and a threepenny loaf and drink one gallon of beer for a considerable sum of money – to be ready exactly at four in the afternoon.

Many pubs had skittle alleys, although these were not always popular with local residents. A letter, written to the magistrates the day before the licensing session in 1828, graphically describes the misery of living near a disorderly house, in this case the long-gone *Albion Tavern* on the Upper Bristol Road:

> Honor'd sir
>
> Please to excuse my boldness in taking the liberty of writing to you on such a subject but obligation forces me to inform you of the circumstance it is concerning of the *Albion Tavern* now kept by Mr Liquorish (late Mr Evans) he has had a skittle alley made in his under kitchen and it so annoys we neighbours that we can get no rest untill twelve or one o'clock at night owing to its being under ground and back no eye or watchman can see or hear them and the Landlord lets them play so long as they please and of a Sunday he puts them in the alley during the whole of divine service and oftentimes we are awaked up two & three in the morn by the noise of those drunkards just come out of the above Inn & Sir! I trust, tomorrow being Licence day that there will be a stop put to that Alley.
>
> I am
> Sir
> Your Obedient
> & humble servt.
> A Tradesman residing
> near the above Inn.

By the end of the nineteenth century, however, skittle playing was on the way out, eclipsed by a new craze – bagatelle. A report prepared for the licensing authorities in 1903 listed pub after pub in which the skittle alley had been allowed to fall into disuse. Since then, of course, skittles have made a comeback, and many alleys reopened, while bagatelle is all but forgotten. Billiards was also very popular, although only the more upmarket pubs could afford to buy a billiard table and set aside a room for it. The lavish new pubs built in the 1880s and 1890s, however, almost invariably had a well-appointed billiard room.

With the exception of the smaller beerhouses, most pubs had a club room, generally on the first floor or at the back of the building. These were used not only by sporting clubs, but also by friendly societies, political parties and trade unions. Freemasons, Oddfellows and Foresters lodges also met in pubs. Of the numerous *Freemason's Arms*, *Oddfellow's Arms* and *Forester's Arms* that existed in Bath in the nineteenth century, the only one left is the *Forester's Arms* on Combe Down.

Pub football teams still flourish today, just as they did in the nineteenth century. The difference is that, whereas rivalry between today's pub teams is friendly, in the past it often resembled the type of partisan activity which still mars some premiership games. One tradition – happily now abandoned – was for pubs that had fielded a losing team to send a mob of heavies, later the same evening, to the pub whose team had won, to settle the score.

One sport that no longer features in the fixture lists of Bath's pubs is backsword, an eighteenth-century diversion that was more than a little barbaric, as this announcement from 1751 indicates:

> To be played for at Backsword on the Monday next, the tenth of June, at the *New Inn* at Widcombe near Bath . . . a gold-lac'd hat, value one guinea – To begin in the forenoon and leave off at sunset. The first man that breaks a head shall be instituted to the favour.

Boxing too has had a long and distinguished association with pubs. In the seventeenth century there was even an inn called the *Noble Science* in the High Street. More recently, the *Barley Mow* on Margaret's Hill was one of the top boxing pubs in the area, with its own fully-equipped gym. Professional boxing matches were also held at pubs, the most celebrated being that between Tom Sayers and John C Heenan at the back of the *Bear* on Wells Road in 1860. Impromptu bare-knuckle bouts also took place outside pubs until well into the nineteenth century. Although they often stemmed from disagreements or hasty words exchanged after a lengthy drinking session, they were more than mere extensions of the bar room brawl. Betting often took place as to the likely outcome, rules – of a sort – were observed, and the contest was organised into a series of rounds. Despite this, the outcome was sometimes fatal.

Certain pubs were notorious for fighting. The *French Horn*, long since demolished, on Lower Borough Walls, was one such. One night in 1817, a sedan chairman called Brown who had upset one of his colleagues by working for lower rates than those generally agreed, was invited outside. To accommodate the spectators, the fight that ensued was held some distance away on Kingsmead Fields. Unfortunately, during it, the two men fell into a pit full of stones and broken bottles. Although the fight ended with a drink and a handshake, Brown later complained off being short of breath and subsequently died. A few months later, another chairman, Samuel White, was challenged to a fight while drinking in the *French Horn*. This time, the contest took place several days later in the pouring rain at Lansdown Fair. Although White won the fight, he too later died of his injuries.

Five years later, a serious fight, involving at least seven men, broke out in the *Horse & Jockey* in Beau Street. After the landlord, who also happened to be a constable, had broken it up, the combatants adjourned to a piece of waste ground called Collier's Field on the Lower Bristol Road. Again, one of the men died, although this time one of the combatants was charged with manslaughter.

Music has also been a feature of pub life, despite many efforts to suppress it, since the dawn of drinking. It has taken many forms. Pubs called the *Ring of Bells*, the *Six Bells*, or something similar, were so called, not because of their proximity to a church, but because they hosted handbell ringing contests. This advertisement for a contest at the *Six Bells* in Colerne, for example, appeared in the *Bath Chronicle* on 4 April 1757:

> To be rung for at Colerne … on Whit Monday, six hats, value two guineas given by Charles Milsham at the Sign of the *Six Bells* at Colerne, where all persons will be entertained after the like manner. Those who do not use the house will not be allowed to ring for the hats. If the hats are not approv'd of the winners shall have the two guineas.

Singing contests were popular as well, although they were not commemorated in pub names in the same way. In 1774 a contest was advertised in Widcombe:

> To be sung for on Tuesday in Whitsun Week, at the *Hare & Hounds* at Mount Pleasant in the Parish of Lyncombe & Widcombe, six pairs of neat gloves, by six singers of one company, and residing in one parish, which company (or companies) are to sing six songs each – viz. three two-part and three three-part songs.

Much singing was naturally impromptu, but there was often a fiddler on hand to provide an accompaniment. Wandering fiddlers travelled the country, eking out a living by playing on street corners or in pubs. To judge from this description of an eighteenth-century alehouse by William Cowper, the standard of playing frequently left something to be desired:

> Pass where we may, through city, or through town,
> Village or hamlet of this merry land,
> Though lean and beggar'd, every twentieth pace
> Conducts th'unguarded nose to such a whiff
> Of stale debauch, forth-issuing from the styes
> That law has licensed, as makes temp'rance reel.
> There sit involved, and lost in swirling clouds
> Of Indian fume, and guzzling deep, the boor,
> The lackey, and the groom. The craftsman there
> Takes a Lethean leave of all his toil;
> Smith, cobbler, joiner, he that plies the shears,
> And he that kneads the dough; all loud alike,
> All learned, and all drunk. The fiddle screams
> Plaintive and piteous, as it wept and wail'd
> Its wasted tones and harmony unheard.

Not surprisingly, some pubs did not welcome wandering fiddlers. In 1841, for example,

> Francis Comley was fined ten shillings and costs for an assault upon Leonard

Wandering fiddlers travelled the country, eking out a living by playing on street corners or in pubs

Lye. It appeared that on Friday evening the defendant, who is a wandering violin player, went into the house of the complainant, who keeps a house for the sale of intoxicating liquors on Holloway, and expressed an anxiety to "discourse most eloquent music" on his four-stringed instrument. The landlord had a decided objection to the instrumental display, and upon refusing permission, many words ensued, and the defendant suddenly struck the complainant a blow on his face, which materially damaged it. For this conduct a warrant was obtained, and for the assault in question the fine was inflicted.

In the second half of the nineteenth century, pianos supplanted fiddles in pubs. Even small beerhouses acquired cottage pianos, while more upmarket establishments boasted baby grands. A piano was not necessarily a sign of respectability, however. When the vicar of St James's campaigned to have the *Bell* on Lower Borough Walls closed down in 1881, for example, the specific nuisances he complained of were "riots, fighting and piano playing."

Although piano playing has given way, in most cases, to more hi-tec entertainment, live music is still a major attraction at many pubs. Bath is a magnet for musicians and the standard of entertainment in its pubs is second to none. Very few people know, however, that the first ever rock concert took place in Bath. It was way back in February 1847 that "Messrs Richardson's Rock Band" appeared at the Assembly Rooms. The performers, apparently, entertained the assembled company by banging bits of rock together.

CHAPTER TWENTY

THE BELLS OF HELL GO TING-A-LING-A-LING

Drink is doing more damage in the war than all the German submarines put together. We are fighting Germany, Austria and Drink and, as far as I can see, the greatest of these deadly foes is Drink.
Lloyd George, October 1915

In 1903, the licensing magistrates, keen to get to grips with the problem of unruly houses and over-provision, sent Mr E Newton Fuller, the Clerk to the Justices, out to visit "all houses in the City of Bath licensed for the sale of intoxicating liquors" and record his findings. Apart from providing invaluable insights into what individual pubs were like, he also made a few general points:

> A large majority of the houses appear to have been repaired in recent years, and only very few can be said to be in bad condition, while sanitary conveniences have in nearly all cases been provided, though in a few houses the difficulty of finding suitable places appears to have been too great to ensure proper ventilation, and in one or two the conveniences have also to be used by the women of the house.
>
> [There is] an extremely small number at which anything but drink is provided for customers. Probably this is accounted for by the large number of restaurants and eating houses in the city. Another thing which one notices is the large amount of draught ginger beer which is sold, especially at the smaller houses.
>
> A few of the houses have back exits, which must make police supervision very difficult, but this is very exceptional.

At the time of his fact-finding mission, there were 240 pubs in the city (which at that time excluded Twerton and Weston). As Bath had a population of just under 50,000, this meant there was a pub for every 208 residents, well over three times higher than the ratio today.

Armed with Mr Newton Fuller's report, the magistrates embarked on a thoroughgoing closure programme, which saw 44 pubs disappear between 1906 and 1914. Most of those that disappeared did so through redundancy. Policemen were instructed to keep an eye on certain pubs and keep a record of how many people used them during a seven-day period. One of those that fell under their scrutiny was the *Rising Sun* at 2 Circus Mews, which closed in 1913:

> Chief Inspector Bence said the house was not required for the needs of the neighbourhood. There were very few people living there. After about seven o'clock in the evening the place was practically deserted. The trade done there was very small indeed. It was practically a one-man house for six nights, the same man going in each time.

Opening hours remained unaffected throughout the Edwardian period, however. Pubs could open from 6am to midnight, except on Sundays. The strength of beer was much as it had been 50 years earlier and prices remained fairly constant. Drinkers could have been forgiven for thinking that, although the number of pubs was slowly dwindling, on the whole there was not too much to worry about. Then came the Great War.

The war was just four days old when the Government passed the first of its Defence of the Realm Acts, making it illegal for anyone to buy a drink for a serviceman "with intent to make him drunk." In mid-October, pubs across the country were ordered to close at 10pm. A month later the tax on beer was tripled.

Then Lloyd George made his famous speech about the war being lost because munitions workers were spending all day in the pub. He set up a government inquiry, as a result of which opening hours were drastically reduced. Pubs could only open from 11.30am to 2pm, and from 6.30pm to 9.30pm. A year later, beer output was cut by four million barrels a year and brewers were ordered to reduce the strength of their beer.

Despite the crackdown, however, drunken outrages still made the pages of the *Bath Chronicle*. In April 1915, the wives of two men on active service were found drunk in Bath Street one Saturday evening. When arrested, they said they had been knocked down by a tram. The magistrate said that if they were brought before him again, he would see that their War Office allowances were stopped.

Just before Christmas 1915, a young man from Bristol called Stanley Kirwin, who worked as a docker at Avonmouth, caught the train to Bath for a night on the town. All went well until, somewhat the worse for wear, he caught the 1.20am mail train home. The *Bath Chronicle* takes up the story:

> The train was unusually long and it carried about 600 passengers. Consequently the train had to be moved up a little so as to bring the rear portion up to the platform. Kirwin was in a carriage near the front of the train, and when it stopped a second time, his carriage had passed over the River Avon and halted overlooking Claverton Street. Owing to the reduction in the street lighting that part would probably be veiled in darkness at the time; but what happened was that the carriage door opened and Kirwin stepped or jumped out. He may have imagined that there was a platform there, but any theorizing on that point is the merest conjecture. As a matter of fact he pitched over the railway parapet, and landed in the flagged street footpath 25 feet below.
>
> The driver at once reported that a passenger had fallen out of the train

into Claverton Street, and Inspector Bryant, who was in charge of the station, sent a porter to inform the police at Widcombe Station and to summon the city ambulance. Mr Bryant himself followed down in a few minutes, after seeing the train out of the station; but so expeditiously had his orders been carried out that already the man had been picked up by the city motor ambulance and taken to the Royal United Hospital. A remarkable thing in such a terrible fall is that the unfortunate young man lost no blood and broke no limbs, but upon examination at the hospital the doctor found that he had suffered injuries to the spine and that his condition therefore was serious. From the position in which the poor fellow was found lying in the street, it is evident that his descent was more in the nature of a forward jump. Had he fallen vertically from the top of the parapet he must have struck a low wall which separates the street footpath from the railway property; but he was found on the street side of the wall, his head nearly against the wall, and his feet close to the gutter, and he was lying on his back.

As the First World War progressed, the government brought in more and more restrictions on the sale of alcohol. Early in 1916, they brought in the "no treating" rule which stopped a customer in a pub buying a drink for anybody else. In theory, a man could not even buy a drink for his wife. Among the publicans who were prosecuted for allowing treating was the landlord of the old *Beefsteak Tavern* behind the market. The Government even toyed with the idea of total prohibition, but, although two million people signed a petition supporting such a move, they drew back from imposing the ultimate sanction.

Late in 1915, a Licensing Reform Meeting was held in Bath, at which it was proposed to open a "model public house." This was an idea that dated back to the 1890s, when limited liability companies opened pubs where the emphasis was on non-alcoholic drinks, with profits going to the local authority or a charitable trust. The idea had several spin-offs, most notably the takeover by the government of five breweries and 321 pubs in Carlisle in 1916, followed by the immediate closure of four of the breweries and 130 of the pubs. Pubs in Enfield Lock and Invergordon were also nationalised. The reason the government gave for these drastic measures was the large number of munition workers in these areas, but they seem also to have been pilot schemes to assess whether wholesale nationalisation was practicable. State control was, fortunately, not extended, although it lasted in Carlisle until 1971.

The idea of a model public house in Bath came to nothing, but it was clear that many people in the city were keen to reform the city's pubs. In 1916, the Temperance Party called for further restrictions on the sale of alcohol, but the Licensed Victuallers' Association protested that there were enough restrictions already. In the following year, the Licensed Victuallers decided that the best way to silence their critics in the temperance movement was by showing their commitment to the war effort. When one of their members found an ambulance being offered for sale at £127 – considerably below the usual price – they clubbed together to buy it. They presented it to the Red Cross at a fund-raising gala in Sydney Gardens, which also featured the Coronation of George V performed by marionettes, a mystical conjuring display by a "ventriloquial humorist," Egyptian calisthenics by the scholars of St Luke's School, and "Miss Ford reciting 'The Reflections of a Penny.'"

Some idea of the impact the First World War had on Bath's pubs can be gauged from the proceedings of one fairly typical licensing session from February 1916:

Mr JH Knight ... appeared on behalf of the licensee of the *Rising Sun*, Grove Street. He explained that his client, Mr William John Hayman, originally bore the surname "Heizman." Having regard to the present situation, his client had changed his name by deed poll to "Hayman." Before this deed poll could be registered it had to be proved that Mr Hayman was a British subject and well affected towards His Majesty's Government. He had written to the Mayor of Blandford (where Mr Hayman was born) who was a magistrate, and had obtained the necessary confirmation. He now asked to have the name on the license changed from "Heizman" to "Hayman." The application was granted.

The Chairman announced that all the licenses would be renewed with the exception of three classes, consideration of which would be deferred till March 3rd.

The first group to be so deferred consisted of the *Lamb*, Stall Street, the *Waterman's Arms*, Broad Quay, the *South Pole Hotel*, Dorchester Street, the *Bear Inn*, Wellsway, and the *Shakespeare Inn*, Old Orchard Street. In all these cases convictions had been recorded during the year, and the holders must make personal application for the renewal of their licenses.

The second group would be referred for a different reason. In the case of the *Full Moon*, Upper Borough Walls, the *Livingstone Hotel*, Moorland Road, the *Argyle Vaults*, Argyle Street, the *White Horse*, Northampton Street, the *Red Lion*, Kingsmead Street, the *Forester's Arms*, Combe Down, the *King's Arms*, Monmouth Place, the *Bell*, Gloucester Street, the *New Inn*, Monmouth Place and the *Shamrock*, Avon Street, the licensees were away serving their King and country. In order to comply properly with the regulations respecting licensees they would be given an opportunity of transferring their obligations to suitable persons. The justices desired to express their appreciation of the patriotism which had led them to answer their country's call. Every care would be taken by the justices that no undue hardship should be entailed, and it went without saying that the attendance of these licensees would be excused at the subsequent proceedings.

The third group of houses which would be deferred till March 3rd consisted of the *Angel Tavern*, Holloway, the *Half Moon*, Holloway and the *Black Dog*, Walcot Buildings. These would be referred on the grounds of redundancy in order that compensation might be granted.

Mr Graham Simmons applied for a temporary transfer of the license of the *Full Moon*, Upper Borough Walls, from the late Mr AE Cleall, who was killed in the war, to his brother, Mr Wilfred Cleall. Letters of administration had been granted to Mr Cleall's widow who was present. Mr Cleall's widow had been in partnership with his brother, and was purchasing his interest in the business. A temporary transfer was granted.

At the end of the war, the government claimed that its temperance programme had worked wonders. They pointed to the number of convictions for drunkenness as proof of the success of their strategy – down from 3,388 a week in England & Wales in 1914 to 449 a week in 1918. A less partial observer may have concluded that four years of waging all-out war with compulsory conscription and the death of one man in ten under the age of 45 may have had something to do with bringing the figures down. In the all-important 15-24 age group, traditionally responsible for a high proportion of alcohol-related mischief, the death toll had been even higher – one in three.

The opening hours imposed during the war were supposed to be temporary, but in 1921 the government decided that there would be no return to the halcyon days of 1914. Pubs were allowed to open for just eight hours a day – from 11.30am to 3pm, and from 5.30pm to 10pm. This law remained in force, with minor modifications, for most of the twentieth century, only being finally abandoned in 1988.

The magistrates' drive to reduce the number of pubs continued unabated after the war. It was helped by an ongoing programme of slum clearance. Areas which had once been full of pubs were bulldozed and replaced by new developments with no pubs at all. New housing estates in the suburbs also had very few pubs. As a result, the number of pubs in Bath (including Combe Down, Twerton and Weston) fell from 186 in 1918 to 156 in 1938. Only two new pubs opened in the interwar period – the *Englishcombe Inn* on Englishcombe Lane and the *Trowbridge House* on Coronation Avenue.

Beer consumption fell after the First World War, hitting an all-time low of 104 pints per head in 1933. Although beer increased in strength after wartime restrictions were lifted, it never regained its pre-war potency. By 1939, it had crept back up to an average 4% alcohol by volume, before dropping back to 3.2%, when wartime restrictions were imposed once again.

The Second World War did not see a repetition of the savage closure programme of the First World War. The pubs that went owed their demise to the Bath Blitz rather than the Bath magistrates. The *Half Moon* on Holloway, the *Bear* on Wellsway, the *Folly* beyond Hampton Row, the *Red Lion* in Kingsmead Street, the *Circus Brewery* in Circus Mews, the *Oxford Brewery* in Julian Road, and the *Railway Inn* in Twerton were among the pubs either destroyed in two nights of bombing or so badly damaged that it was decided to demolish them. The *Livingstone* in Moorland Road was also destroyed but stayed in business by moving up the road.

Beer doubled in price during the Second World War, from around sixpence a pint to a shilling. Even if you had the money, it did not automatically mean you could get a drink. "No beer" signs were common outside pubs from 1941 onwards and many pubs only opened on certain evenings. Customers were often rationed to a pint or a half, and if you were not a regular you were lucky to get served at all. Draught beer, often of inferior quality or watered down, was the order of the day. Bottled beer was rare, and Guinness virtually unobtainable. It is hardly surprising that the American troops stationed in Britain during the Second World War found the beer warm and unpalatable. The British found it pretty bad as well, but there was a war on, and they put up with it. It is just a pity that the myth of warm beer still survives on the other side of the Atlantic almost 60 years after the end of the war.

After wartime restrictions were lifted, beer got stronger again, but by 1950 it had only managed to creep back up to around 3.5% alcohol by volume. Because it was so weak, it was difficult to keep in prime condition, and draught beer gradually acquired a reputation for unpredictability. As a result, sales of bottled beer soared, and by the end of the 1950s bottles accounted for well over a third of total beer sales. Analysts predicted that bottles were the shape of things to come and draught was on the way out. In the event, of course, it did not happen. By 1984 bottled beer sales had slumped to a mere 9% of the total. Since then they have rallied somewhat, due to the growing popularity of premium lager and real ale in bottles, but still they lag far behind sales of draught.

One thing that put paid to hopes that bottled beer would dominate the market was the rise of canned beer. Virtually unknown in the 1950s, and accounting for only 3% of total beer sales as late as 1970, canned beer has now cornered around a quarter of the market. The big difference between bottled and canned beer is that canned beer is rarely sold in pubs, almost all of it being sold for consumption at home – or on the street.

There was another alternative to draught beer even before the Second World War, however. Although it was not generally available, keg beer, that anathema of the real ale movement, was already three years old by the time Chamberlain told the nation he had not heard back from Herr Hitler. It was in 1936 that East Sheen Tennis Club complained to Watney's that, since their bar only opened at weekends, half-used barrels of beer were going off during the week. Watney's obligingly sent them a barrel of experimental pasteurised beer which would not go off. They liked it so much they placed a regular order. And so it was that Watney's Red Barrel was born.

The first brewer to start large-scale keg beer production, however, was Flower's of Stratford Upon Avon. Flower's Keg was introduced in 1954. The following year came Whitbread Tankard. Soon every major brewer was producing pasteurised, pressurised, predictable keg beer. As late as 1959, keg still accounted for only 3% of total beer sales, and most of that was in the form of lager. The breweries, however, were keen to replace draught beer with keg. It was a change the vast majority of the nation's drinkers accepted willingly. Incredible as it may seem, they were even prepared to pay more for keg. Just as diesel trains were welcomed by people who had only known the misery of dirty, smelly steam trains, so chilled, pasteurised and predictable beer was welcomed by people who had known little except warm, ill-kept, indifferent ale. If it was a penny or so dearer, so what? That was the price of progress. It would have seemed inconceivable that, within a few years, there would be festivals devoted to drinking real ale – or that people would be driving miles to travel behind a steam train.

CHAPTER TWENTY-ONE

THE LAST OF ENGLAND?

When you have lost your inns, then drown your sorry selves,
For you will have lost the last of England.
Hilaire Belloc, 1912

Two pints of lager and a packet of crisps, please.
Splodgenessabounds, 1980

The 1960s was a decade of two halves. To start off with, it was all steam trains, real ale and My Old Man's a Dustman. Rationing was a recent memory and austerity was still the order of the day. Less than ten years later, steam was dead, keg was king and Lucy was in the Sky with Diamonds. Keg beer and lager were part of the brave new world which replaced the dusty misery of the past. The change was orchestrated by the big breweries who carried the majority of drinkers with them, courtesy of a relentless marketing campaign. And the breweries had almost total control over what people drank. In Bristol in 1969, 461 out of a total of 517 pubs were owned by breweries. Over 90% of those 461 were owned by Courage's. It was a similar story in Bath.

Beer not only had carbon dioxide pumped into it, it got weaker as well. By the early 1970s, many beers were so weak that they could have been legally sold in America during prohibition. Remember Ind Coope Superdraught, Whitbread Starbright, or Watney's Starlight? The weakest of the lot was Watney's Special Mild, weighing in with an Original Gravity of 1030.4 – any weaker and it could have been sold to children as a soft drink. Lager was not much better. A report in the *Daily Mirror* in 1972 concluded that Carlsberg and Tuborg were "more suitable for a maiden aunt of moderate habits than a man who uses his muscles."

Strange times: hard toilet paper, Ted Heath, the Golden Shot, Bennie Hill, the Pound in Your Pocket, Horace Batchelor, the Singing Postman, "I'm Backing Britain," Simon Dee, Dave Dee, Dozy, Beaky, Mick & Titch, Mary Whitehouse, Cherry B, hard toilet paper, the Crazy World of Arthur Brown, Jeremy Thorpe, the Black & White Minstrels, black & white television, Babycham, Mungo Jerry, Green Shield Stamps, Hughie Green, Plastic Beatles Wigs, World Cup Willy, Rivers of Blood, the Clitheroe

Kid, Watney's Red Barrel, Vesta Prawn Curry, Alf Garnett, and hard toilet paper.

As the swinging 'sixties shuffled into the sybaritic 'seventies, keg beer and lager swept all before them. By 1976, they accounted for 60% of the market. Bottled beer accounted for another 20%, leaving draught beer – or real ale – with a 17% share. Pubs were ripping handpumps out like there was no tomorrow. It did indeed seem that there would be no tomorrow for draught beer.

Lager only accounted for about a third of keg beer sales in 1976, but it was becoming more popular by the day, shuffling off the maiden aunt image, and being promoted as a drink that did not need to be served up with a dash of lime to disguise its taste. The incredible growth in lager's popularity had as much to do with the market-led growth of a lager-laddish culture as it did with what it tasted like. As time went by, the average lad about town came to view a pint of real ale in much the same way as he viewed snuff, flat caps and whippets. Image was everything. Real ale meant beards, beerguts and boring tirades about specific gravity. Lager meant partying, scoring, having a ball. By 1998, bitter and stout accounted for 46% of draught or keg beer sales. Lager accounted for 51%, with mild just about hanging on with 3%. Today, even lager has become more than a tad passé among younger drinkers, for whom vodka and vodka-based drinks are now the number one tipple.

The fact remains that real ale, properly cared for, is an exceptional drink, with a myriad different variations and nuances. But it is too easy to serve badly. There is no excuse for serving flat, warm, stale beer, but very often that is what drinkers get. And just about anything is preferable to that, even lager or nitro-keg chilled and pasteurised beer.

It was not just beer that got a makeover in the 1960s. Pubs which had not changed for generations were gutted in an orgy of modernisation that has since progressed through theme pub, fun pub, super pub, food pub, and ending, more often than not, in closed pub. In 1970, John Dickson, a Whitbread executive, gave a speech in Durham which summed up the attitude of most breweries "It is high time," he told his audience, "that Andy Capp was given a new suit and a car and took his wife out to one of the many popular north-east pubs where he can still enjoy his pint of beer and Florrie can have a glass of sauterne with her scampi and chips." In other words, breweries wanted to marginalise beer-drinking and beer-drinkers in favour of lines which had a higher profit margin. The idea was to turn pubs into anodyne fooderies, where a throughput of family groups maximised returns on investment and the only concession to a sense of community was a collection of sepia-toned photographs of gnarled rustics clutching mugs of scrumpy. Dead beer, dead conversation, dead atmosphere, dead loss.

One of the main things that has changed in pubs in the last 30 years is the provision of food. It was in the 'sixties that the pub food revolution took off. For a time, chicken in the basket, toasted curry sandwiches, and cellophane-wrapped pies were the order of the day. Remember those pies? They gave rise to stories like this one from Clement Freud:

I went into a pub because the sign said, "beer, pie and a kind word." I paid my money, ate the pie and drank the beer but nothing happened so I waited. Eventually the barman asked me what I was waiting for and I said, "the kind word." "Oh," he replied, "don't eat the pie."

Today, most country pubs rely on food to survive. Some have given up all pretence to be pubs and while they look, from the outside, just as they did thirty years ago, inside they look exactly what they are – restaurants. Anyone just dropping in for a pint is treated much as they would be if they went into a shoe shop, sat down and announced they had only come in to get warm. Town pubs have not suffered to the same extent, and many Bath pubs only serve food at lunchtimes. Some, such as the *Star*, seem to have been untroubled by the food revolution, and sport only a few cheese or ham rolls on a tray, an assortment of crisps and nuts, and a jar of pickled eggs.

In the early 'seventies it looked as though real ale would soon go the way of the steam train. Most people, although they may not have liked the idea, accepted it as inevitable. Then a bunch of troublemakers with a name that could have been invented by PG Wodehouse – the Campaign for the Revitalization of Ale – got together to stick a spoke in the wheels of the brewers' juggernaut. They soon decided to change their name to the Campaign for Real Ale – and a British institution was born. The Campaign for Real Ale has often been vilified for its beer-guts and beards image, but, while some of its members seem keen on promoting this image, CAMRA is much more than a bunch of people wittering on about specific gravity and varieties of hops as a way of legitimising marathon drinking sessions. It has consistently been one of the UK's most successful consumer organisations, mobilising public opinion and forcing the breweries to listen to their customers. They have attracted support from some unlikely quarters along the way. In 1979, only six years after CAMRA was founded, Watney's withdrew Red Barrel, not because anyone had convinced them it was dreadful, but because of a dramatic downturn in sales. Despite all the money they had spent advertising it, by the time it was withdrawn it was associated by most people with just two things – CAMRA's nickname for it (Grotney's) and Eric Idle's inspired rant on *Monty Python's Flying Circus*:

> What's the point of going abroad if you're just another tourist carted around in buses surrounded by sweaty mindless oafs from Kettering and Boventry in their cloth caps and their cardigans and their transistor radios and their Sunday Mirrors, complaining about the tea – "Oh, they don't make it properly here, do they, not like at home" – and stopping at Majorcan bodegas selling fish and chips and Watney's Red Barrel and calamares and two veg and sitting in their cotton frocks squirting Timothy White's suncream all over their puffy raw swollen purulent flesh 'cos they overdid it on the first day. And being herded into endless Hotel Miramars and Belle Vueses and Bontinentals with their modern international luxury roomettes and draught Red Barrel and swimming pools full of fat German businessmen ... And then some adenoidal typists from Birmingham with flabby white legs and diarrhoea trying to pick up hairy bandy-legged waiters called Manuel and once a week there's an excursion to the local Roman remains

to buy cherryade and melted ice cream and bleeding Watney's Red Barrel …

Bath's pubs have faced many crises in recent years. One of the most widely publicised threats came in the early 'eighties, when, if you'd believed the prophecies of doom in the *Bath Chronicle*, two millennia of elegant living were about to fall victim to a tidal wave of punk. Things came to a head in January 1981 when city centre pubs closed their doors to "customers with coloured spiky hair, chains and bondage pants." Two popular punk hangouts, the *Assembly Inn* in Alfred Street and the *Hop Pole* on the Upper Bristol Road, got new landlords who immediately made them punk-free zones. At the *Assembly*, Terry Sullivan informed customers that a reasonable standard of dress was required, while at the *Hop Pole* Harry Derrick made it clear that customers who put their feet on the furniture and sat on the floor were not welcome. Other pubs which imposed a ban included the *Porter*, the *Lamb & Lion*, the *Talbot* (now the *Hobgoblin*), *Smith's Wine Vaults*, the *Devonshire Arms* (now the *Bath Tap*), the *County Wine Vaults* (now *Flan O'Brien's*), the *Griffin*, and the *Bell*. The manager of the *Hat & Feather*, Raymond Newton-Edwards, was more cautious, saying that punks would be served individually, but not in groups, as "their appearance upsets the other customers."

Pat Harris, who ran the *Negative Café* on Lower Borough Walls, emerged as the spokesman for the safety-pin brigade:

> There's always been some resistance to punks, but in the last few weeks it seems to have become a lot worse. When we cannot go into any of the pubs in Bath it is becoming desperate. I think trouble is building up. The punks are left to roam the streets in boredom and frustration if they can't get into pubs. It may be a campaign to get people to be more neat. I don't think they like us and the landlords are very rude about telling us to leave. Punks like to go out in a group so they can talk. There is no work and they are unhappy. When they are turned away from the pubs they are more upset than ever.

A quarter of a century on, although punk cannot be said to have acquired respectability, it has at least come of age. Punk is just one lifestyle option among many, unlikely to raise the eyebrow of even the most staunch traditionalist. Punk's Silver Jubilee, coinciding with the Queen's Golden Jubilee, was just another reminder of how time has moved on. Punk has, however, left a lasting legacy on the streets – or at any rate the windowsills – of Bath. So concerned were some residents, at the height of the punk era, about the number of spiky-haired layabouts cluttering up the windowsills of Bath's Georgian buildings and gobbing at the pigeons, that they put spikes on the windowsills to stop them sitting there. Today the ne'er-do-wells who inspired these adornments are long gone, but the spikes – an iconic, post-ironic echo of the barbed barnets they once sported – remain.

Throughout the 'eighties and 'nineties, drinking laws were slowly relaxed. Bath held out against the tide for a while, turning down an application in 1985 for pubs to stay open until 11pm instead of 10.30pm on Mondays to Thursdays. Three years later, however, the matter was taken out of the local licensing authority's hands, and 11pm closing was imposed nationally.

In 1988 came the most far-reaching change to licensing laws since the First World War. The law forcing pubs to shut in the afternoons, brought in by Lloyd George in 1915, was repealed and pubs were allowed to open from 11am to 11pm. To anyone brought up in the bleak years before 1988, when the heady bliss of a lunchtime session would gradually cloud over as towels were draped over beerpumps, it was the realisation of an impossible dream, like the crumbling of the Berlin Wall. True, the generations that began drinking after 1988 will never know the joy of turning up at a pub at 5.30 just as the lights come on and the bolts are pulled back to a cry of "they're open." But nostalgia can shed a golden glow over even the most miserable memories. All-day drinking may have its drawbacks (as you will know if you have ever stumbled, early one evening, into some unfamiliar dive whose denizens have been drinking steadily since lunchtime) but they are far outweighed by its benefits. Although many pubs still shut in the afternoon, they do so by choice rather than by government decree, and there is always bound to be another one open somewhere nearby.

When all-day opening started, however, some people thought it meant the End of Civilisation As We Know It. Take this report from the *Bath Chronicle* of 26 August 1988:

> Bath publicans are bracing themselves for trouble at the start of the first weekend of all-day drinking. City centre pubs reported a busy week but say most of their daytime customers so far have been tourists and retired people. Today workers leaving for the Bank Holiday were expected to have their first taste of all-day drinking – and some landlords fear it could get out of hand … The *Grapes* landlord in Westgate Street, Clive Prescott, said, "Certain people are drinking more with the longer hours. There is a possibility of having problems tomorrow. We have taken on extra people for tomorrow. We expect to get people coming in at lunchtime and then staying when they used to go home. People will have to learn to control their drinking instead of having their drinking controlled for them." Several publicans said they intended to be extra vigilant over the weekend in refusing to serve customers who are drunk. Some city centre pub landlords were too worried to give their names in case they encouraged youngsters to come to their premises to cause trouble.

Some licensees, however, welcomed the change to all-day opening. The landlady of the *Volunteer Rifleman's Arms*, Beryl Amott, "said she had always had to explain the old afternoon shut-down to puzzled Americans so often in the past and turn away up to 20 tourists after the 2.30pm closure time." Although the overwhelming majority of city centre pubs now stay open all day, over half continued to close in the afternoon when the new licensing law came into force. Problems such as the need to recruit more bar staff and higher overheads were cited as reasons for not staying open. The chairman of the Bath Licensed Victuallers' Association, Robert Godwin, also said that he thought it would "take people a long time to adapt to the new hours," apart from which, they only had "so much money to spend on beer."

Over a decade later, all-day drinking is part of the British way of life. It seems inconceivable that, for the best part of a century, we accepted, with hardly a murmur, a government ban on drinking in the afternoon. Now, pubs with special licences can stay open till the early hours – astounding to those who grew up in the days when you hit the streets running at ten to eleven, and a bone of contention to those who live near one of these late-night boozeries. New proposals to allow pubs to open 24 hours a day, and for licensing to be taken out of the hands of the magistrates and dealt with by local authorities, indicate that, whatever else happens, the battle over licensing hours is not over yet. But if history teaches us anything, it is that, when our rulers have encouraged us to drink more, we have responded with gusto.

Not that we seem to have needed much encouragement. Since 1970, alcohol consumption in the United Kingdom has risen by something like 50%. Somewhat surprisingly, this is not part of a global trend. Although countries as diverse as Japan, Finland, Russia and the Netherlands have also seen big increases in alcohol consumption, countries such as France and Italy have seen equally dramatic falls. It is worth bearing in mind, though, that the French were so far ahead of us to start off with that they are still ahead in the putting-it-away stakes.

Nevertheless, we are in the grip of a mounting crisis – or so we are told. Sir Michael Marmot of University College, London, for example, believes that:

> the country has reached the point where it is necessary and urgent to call time on runaway alcohol consumption. A strategic programme is needed now to curb the nation's escalating level of drinking in the interests of both individual and public health.

Sir Michael has recently contributed to a report by the Academy of Medical Sciences which estimates that alcohol-related crime and public disorder cost the country £6.4bn a year and calls on the Government to tackle the issue by increasing the duty on alcohol.

We have, of course, been here many, many times before. The details may be different, but the basic problem is the same: people are drinking too much, making a nuisance of themselves, and it's time something was done about it. It seems unlikely, however, that the problem of binge drinking, mainly indulged in by young people with a relatively high disposable income in trendy city centre bars, can be dealt with simply by raising the price of drinks. As in the eighteenth century, it is "spiritous liquor," rather than beer, that is the main culprit. This time, however, it is vodka rather than gin, and its devotees are somewhat more affluent than the penniless wretches of Hogarth's *Gin Lane*.

But, just because drunkenness has been a problem for centuries, does not mean that we should just shrug our shoulders and accept its worst consequences as inevitable. Disease, filth, malnutrition, and appalling living standards for the majority of the population were commonplace two centuries ago, just as they always had been. If they had been accepted as inevitable, they would still be with us. And let us not forget that drinking took a nose-dive in the early twentieth century, falling from an average tally of 275 pints a year in 1876 to 104 pints a year in 1933. The First World War – not to mention the Depression which followed – obviously had a part to play in this, but it is clear that large numbers of people, influenced by temperance propaganda, decided that heavy drinking was a bad idea. Today, people no longer need to drink alcohol because water is unsafe, nor – in most cases – because they live in appalling conditions. They drink – as Dr Johnson did – to get rid of the pain of being a man – or a woman.

Getting rid of the pain of being a man in some city-centre superpubs, however, may end up with a trip to the local Accident & Emergency Department. Around 40% of all A&E admissions are due to booze-fuelled fights outside pubs and clubs or drink-related accidents. The proliferation of superpubs, aimed at the youth market, is the main reason for the sharp rise in anti-social drunkenness. "Happy hours" and "all you can drink" promotions merely compound the problem, by encouraging faster consumption. The Government has, so far, held back from a crackdown on superpubs, opting instead for a series of proposals aimed at getting the pub companies to put their house in order. The problem is, of course, that a culture of high consumption is inherent in the concept of the superpub. Turning the superpub culture around, and encouraging customers to drink moderately instead of going on a binge is like giving someone a top-of-the-range car and asking them drive it in third gear.

Somewhat paradoxically, the Government seems to believe that further liberalisation of the licensing laws, effectively paving the way for 24-hour drinking, will help to cut down on binge drinking, by getting rid of the traditional rush to down as many drinks as possible before last orders are called. With so many late-night drinking establishments around, it is difficult to see how this argument holds water. It seems more likely that, with more bars open for longer, binges will get longer and alcohol consumption will continue to rise. One is reminded of the Duke of Wellington's cunning plan to reduce drunkenness by increasing the number of pubs. There were as many people telling him he was wrong in 1830 as there are protesting against 24-hour opening today. He did not listen either.

There have been some minor, and rather half-hearted, attempts to counter the onward march of liberalisation. In 1989, alfresco quaffing took a rap over the knuckles when a controversial booze ban came into effect, making drinking in the streets punishable by a £100 fine. Pubs with tables and chairs outside had to apply for a special permit exempting them from the ban. If it was granted, they had to drill studs into the pavement to mark out a "designated drinking area." The booze ban turned out to be ineffective, but it was not till March 2004 that another law, giving police the power to confiscate cans or bottles from anyone drinking in the street, was passed.

1989 also saw what many hailed as a new dawn for Britain's smaller brewers. The Monopolies and Mergers Commission forced through legislation to break the stranglehold of the big brewers. Licensees of tied houses were given the go-ahead to sell guest beers from small independent breweries. In theory it sounded fine. But things did not work out as planned. In 1989, six breweries controlled three-quarters of the UK beer market. Today that number has dropped to three – Carlsberg-Tetley, Scottish Courage and Interbrew.

At the same time, the pubs once owned by the breweries have been hived off to "pub companies." Take the case of the Unique Pub Company. In 1991, the Inntrepreneur Pub Company was set up, in the wake of the monopoly ruling, by Courage's and Grand Met, as part of a pubs-for-breweries deal. In 1997, Inntrepreneur was bought by the Nomura Principal Finance Group of Japan, who, in the following year, set up the Unique Pub Company and transferred most of the pubs in the Inntrepreneur portfolio to it. No disrespect intended, but you have to wonder if a group of Japanese financiers – or Danes or Belgians, for that matter – are really the best people to entrust with the future of a unique British institution. Imagine the outcry if English Heritage was sold off to a foreign business consortium and rebranded as the Unique Heritage Company (UK) Ltd.

It won't happen, of course. But, in the brewing industry, it seems as if the battle may already have been lost. It is the same everywhere you look. For most people, the name of Whitbread is synonymous with brewing. The history of the company goes back over 250 years, to when Samuel Whitbread established the first purpose-built mass-production brewery in the world. Although Whitbread is still a large, successful company, it stopped brewing beer in 2000 and sold off its pubs a year later. Clearly, its directors were of the opinion that its other operations – including Beefeater, Bella Pasta, Café Rouge, Pizza Hut, TGI Friday, Travel Inn, Marriott, Costa Coffee, David Lloyd Leisure Clubs and Brewer's Fayre – offered more hope for the future than traditional pubs and traditional beer.

In an interview late in 2002, David Thomas, Whitbread's Chief Executive, proudly described the child-friendly Brewster Restaurants he had introduced, barely drawing breath when he described their facilities:

We will take your children away from you, entertain them and keep them safe while you eat!

Then, banging the table for emphasis, he declared:

I wish I could show you the picture of Brewster the Bear who comes out to play in the fun factory every hour!

Anyone who remembers Whitbread Starbright may not consider Whitbread's decision to stop brewing and sell off its pubs as much of a tragedy. Yet it is a sad reflection of the state of the industry that Whitbread's chief executive enthuses not about brewing the perfect pint, nor yet about how much beer he has sold, but about a picture of someone dressed as a bear.

The battle lines are drawn, between traditional, small, street-corner locals (which the multi-nationals want to close) and the superpubs (which they want to open). If we do not praise them for anything else, we must praise local councillors for resisting the tide towards mega-get-it-down-your-neck, fun-and-fast-food joints. If the multi-nationals had their way, many of Bath's most cherished old pubs would have become shops or houses years ago and the city centre would be swamped by booze barns.

In July 1997, B&NES planning officers made a report to the council's planning, transportation and environment committee dealing with the "proliferation of pubs, wine bars and restaurants in Bath city centre." This was followed by a policy paper four months later which highlighted the concerns of local residents:

> The main focus for such concern is the impact of such uses on the amenities of nearby residential occupiers. The planning system can exercise little control over this, save by refusing to approve the use in the first place, and by careful restriction of hours of operation. Clearly, the larger the establishment, the greater the potential for noise and disturbance to arise.

They concluded that the concentration of pubs in the city had reached saturation point.

The most famous superpub battle was that over the former King Edward's School in Broad Street. Despite being given the go-ahead by the planners, the licensing authorities refused permission for Samuel Smith's to turn the old school into a pub. Others schemes did get through, though, as the *Bath Chronicle* reported a year later:

> Two new superpubs opened last month – *Baty's* in George Street and the *Rat & Parrot* in Westgate Street, which its owners say is the largest bar in the area. The new pubs have fuelled criticism that there are too many similar watering holes in the city centre. But the proliferation of city superpubs may have reached its peak, according to a report by the Bath office of commercial property agents King Sturge. The report says: "While there has been much concern regarding the growth of these new venues in Bath, it is very difficult to see where further developments could take place other than in the Sawclose area by the Theatre Royal, already identified by Bath and North East Somerset Council for leisure development, as there is a very finite supply of suitable buildings and locations in which this type of development is permitted." The report adds that the decline in superpubs is part of a national trend ... Fuller's last month submitted another application to develop the Environment Centre in Milsom Street. The first was thrown out by councillors after many protests.

The second application was also thrown out, after nearby residents "complained about the area being part of a drinking circuit, with people vomiting and urinating in the streets," and the police warned it could become "like Bristol's notorious Whiteladies Road." A further application to turn it into "an ale and pie house" was also thrown out. Although the company appealed to the Secretary of State, the council's decision was upheld. The inspector who conducted the appeal said afterwards that:

> the unique character of Bath and its status as a World Heritage City made this a matter of particular importance. I heard a lot of evidence from local residents concerning current levels of late-night noise and disturbance, damage to property and the anti-social behaviour of people leaving the public houses at closing time. I saw, on my late-night visit, broken glass on the pavement and streams of urine from doorways and I noted various groups of noisy and boisterous young people making their way through the residential streets for up to an hour after closing time. While city-centre residents must expect a degree of disturbance from late-

night activity, this must be within reasonably acceptable limits. From the evidence before me, and from what I have seen, I believe these limits have been reached. Eventually the building became the Loch Fyne Seafood Restaurant.

However, other superpubs continued to be approved. In 1999, the *Slug & Lettuce* in the Royal York Hotel and *Bar Karanga* in Manvers Street, both got the go-ahead. Late in 2002, the ground floor of the revamped Tramshed in Walcot Street opened as the *Ha! Ha! Bar*, part of a chain with no real ale and an emphasis on food, and a claim to be the biggest bar in Bath. In January 2001, however, plans by Surrey Free Inns (who had turned a former bank into the 400-capacity *Litten Tree* on George Street) to open a 550-capacity *Bar Med* pub in part of the former Co-op Living Store in Westgate Buildings received the thumbs down after a vigorous residents' campaign, even though B&NES planning officers initially recommended acceptance. It was pointed out that there were 22 licensed premises within 200 metres of the proposed pub.

A report on superpubs and circuit drinking in the *Bath Chronicle* early in 2001 concluded with these words:

> It is gravely disturbing to note that those attending a recent meeting in the Pump Room prior to forming a residents' association of people living in the neighbourhood of the abbey, unanimously took the view that the city centre is no longer safe or peaceful.

At the same time that the multi-portfolioed multinationals who now control the bulk of the licensed trade press for more superpubs, the traditional local is increasingly under threat. Society is changing faster than ever before. Expectations are higher. It is clear that, in an increasingly competitive market, some pubs are failing to make a go of it. Without exception, those that are failing are the ones that belong to major chains – glum, old-fashioned boozers which have been gutted, sanitised, themed, de-themed and made over so often that every last trace of character or individuality has been squeezed out of them. Mass-produced menus, mass-produced decor, indifferent food, indifferent beer, indifferent service, muzak and anonymity. While superpubs ride high on a tide of mass consumption, patronised by those with high disposable incomes, hell-bent on having a good time, many old pubs lie stranded like old hulks on a sandbank of corporate cynicism, unloved, unwanted and uncared for. They are to the traditional local what Richard Claydermann is to music. Perhaps their passing would be no great cause for sorrow, for, in a sense, they have already been lost. But it would be sad, none the less.

While they dwindle away, however, other pubs are thriving as never before. Take two obvious examples – the *Star* and the *Old Green Tree*. Some may dismiss their appeal as mere nostalgia, but their success rests on far stronger foundations than that. Their furnishings and decor, although impressive, would not entice drinkers back if their standards of service were poor and their sense of community lacking. Indifferent bar staff, lousy beer, and a take-it-or-leave-it attitude would soon ensure that their hallowed portals were unsullied by all but the least discriminating drinker or the unsuspecting visitor.

They are only two examples, but there are many other pubs, which are just as successful, and for the same reasons. Classic architecture and period fittings are not a prerequisite for a successful pub. Take the *Bell* in Walcot Street. Although old, it is architecturally undistinguished and has none of those accoutrements, like the little wood-panelled rooms to be found at the *Star* or the *Old Green Tree*. Yet it is one of the most popular pubs in the city, winner of the *Venue* 2002 Award for Bath's best pub, local CAMRA pub of the year 2004, serving the widest range of real ales in the city, booking some of the best bands, and firmly at the heart of the community. That is because it is run and staffed by people who genuinely care about it, and try to make it the sort of pub they like to drink in. It is not the product of some Japanese or Dutch accountant's idea about how maximum throughput can be achieved, nor are its fittings the product of some leisure chain marketing manager's attempt to jump on whatever new bandwagon the style gurus and sociological spin-doctors have dreamed up. Nor are its barstaff resentful that they have to stand behind a bar and serve you when they could be out having a good time somewhere else.

Someone who has done more than anyone else to expose the seamy underside of pub life in the twenty-first century is Al Murray a.k.a. the Pub Landlord. Off stage, he believes that "the refitting and theming of pubs is the most hideous and ridiculous thing. Soon every pub will be the same. To the breweries, they aren't community places, but simply retail outlets for them to squeeze every last red cent out of." For him, the most worrying thing of all, is that, after performing at a function for brewery and pub-chain executives, they were falling over themselves to get him to come and run a pub for them. They had totally missed the point. Not only did they believe he was just a pub landlord who told jokes. They also thought he was just the sort of man they wanted in one of their pubs. That, as they say in the movies, really *is* scary.

But, to round off this odyssey through Bath's bibulous past, just ponder the awesome thought that, if all those who have ever frequented the city's pubs – Celts and Romans, monks and weavers, Saxons and Normans, Royalists and Roundheads, prostitutes and Puritans, beaux and bohemians, night watchmen, night soil men, lager louts, gin wives, navvies, sedan chairmen, and old Dr Johnson and all – stood in a long (and no doubt swaying) line, it would take a hell of a long time to get served.

APPENDIX ONE:

BATH PUBS IN 1776

This was the first year in which licensing records for Bath included pub names. Prior to that they only listed the name of the licensee and the street in which the pub stood. This list only covers licensed premises within the city, which at that time did not include Bathwick, Twerton, Weston, Widcombe or most of Walcot. (Although licensing records for these parishes are available for this period, they do not include pub names.) Pubs which are still open are indicated by an asterisk.

Angel Inn*	Westgate Street	Now the Rat & Parrot
Artichoke	Broad Street	Precise location unknown
Bath Arms	Horse Street	Demolished
Bath Side House	Near the King's Bath	Demolished
Bear Inn	Cheap Street	Demolished
Beefsteak Tavern	Newmarket Row	Demolished
Bell	Monmouth Street	Now the Raincheck Bar
Bell	Stall Street	Demolished or rebuilt
Bell*	Walcot Street	Building survives
Birdcage	Avon Street	Demolished
Birdcage*	Westgate Street	Now Flan O'Briens (rebuilt)
Black Boy	Kingsmead Square	Precise location unknown
Black Horse	Broad Street	Demolished
Black Swan	Broad Street	Demolished
Boar's Head	Westgate Street	Demolished
Bottle & Glass	St James's Street	Demolished
Bunch of Grapes	Broad Street	Precise location unknown
Bunch of Grapes*	Westgate Street	Building survives
Butcher's Arms	Lot Lane	Demolished
Castle & Ball	Northgate Street	Demolished
Catherine Wheel	Parsonage Lane	Demolished
Chairmen	Bridewell Lane	Demolished
Chequers	Avon Street	Demolished
Chequers	Beauford Square	Precise location unknown
Chequers	Kingsmead Street	Demolished
Chequers*	Newmarket Row	Now the Rummer
Chequers	Quay	Demolished
Chequers	Queen Street	Precise location unknown
Chequers	Stall Street	Precise location unknown
Chequers	Wine Street	Demolished
Christopher*	High Street	Now All Bar One
Coach & Horses	Near the Cross Bath	Demolished

Coach & Horses	Horse Street	Demolished
Coffee House	Stall Street	Precise location unknown
Cross Keys	High Street	Demolished
Crown	Avon Street	Demolished
Crown	High Street	Demolished
Crown	Stall Street	Precise location unknown
Crown & Cushion	Bridewell Lane	Demolished
Duke of Cumberland	Orchard Street	Precise location unknown
Fountain	Horse Street	Demolished
Fox & Hounds	Walcot Street	Demolished
Full Moon*	Upper Borough Walls	Now Sam Weller's
Full Moon	Horse Street	Demolished
Gallon Pot	Avon Street	Demolished
Gardener	Horse Street	Demolished
George Inn	Walcot Street	Demolished
George Inn	Near the Cross Bath	Demolished
Globe	Kingsmead Square	Building survives (No 5)
Golden Lion	Horse Street	Demolished
Green Man	Broad Street	Precise location unknown
Green Tree*	Green Street	Building survives
Greyhound	High Street	Demolished
Griffin*	Monmouth Street	Building survives
Grove Coffee House	Orange Grove	Demolished
Hand & Shears	Walcot Street	Demolished
Heart & Compass	Off Monmouth Place	Demolished
Hole in the Wall	Avon Street	Demolished
Horse & Groom	Bell Tree Lane	Building survives (No 2, Beau St)
Horse & Groom	Princes Street	Building survives (No 9)
Joiner's Arms	Horse Street	Demolished
Jolly Footman	Kingsmead Street	Demolished
King Bladud	Parsonage Lane	Demolished
King's Head	Bartlett Street	Building survives (No 2)
King's Arms*	Monmouth Place	Building survives
King's Arms	Orchard Street	Now Bath Spiritualist Church
King's Arms	Walcot Street	Building survives (No 5)
Lamb	Avon Street	Demolished
Lamb Inn	Stall Street	Substantially rebuilt
Leek	Horse Street	Demolished
Leg of Mutton & Cauliflower	Wine Street	Demolished
Mason's Arms	Lear Lane	Demolished
Mug	Walcot Street	Precise location unknown
New Inn	Kingsmead Square	Demolished
New Inn*	Rivers Street	Now the Chequers
Noah's Ark	Newmarket Row	Demolished
Old Darby	Cottell's Lane	Demolished
Orange Tree	Walcot Street	Building survives (No 70)
Packhorse	Northgate Street	Demolished
Parade Coffee House*	Terrace Walk	Now the Huntsman
Pelican	Walcot Street	Demolished
Pipes	Horse Street	Demolished
Plough	Horse Street	Demolished
Plume of Feathers	Horse Street	Demolished

Plume of Feathers	Quiet Street	Precise location unknown
Post Boy	Trim Street	Precise location unknown
Prince Frederick	Beauford Square	Demolished and rebuilt.(No 3)
Queen Charlotte	White Hart Lane	Demolished
Queen's Head	Cheap Street	Demolished
Raven	Abbey Green	Now Evans' Fish Restaurant
Red Lion	Kingsmead Street	Demolished
Ring of Bells	Stall Street	Precise location unknown
Ring of Bells	Orange Grove	Demolished
Roebuck	Quiet Street	Precise location unknown
Rose	Avon Street	Demolished
Rose & Crown	Northgate Street	Demolished
Royal Oak	Upper Borough Walls	Building survives (Central Wine Bar)
Royal Oak	Stall Street	Demolished
Rummer	Horse Street	Demolished
Saracen's Head*	Broad Street	Building survives
Seven Stars	Upper Borough Walls	Building survives (Nos 2 & 3)
Shakespeare's Head	Westgate Street	Precise location unknown
Ship	Horse Street	Demolished
Smith's Arms	Avon Street	Demolished
Spread Eagle	Avon Street	Demolished
Squirrel	Upper Borough Walls	Demolished
Star*	Guinea Lane	Building survives
Star & Garter*	Lilliput Alley	Now back part of the Huntsman
Stile	Horse Street	Demolished
Stile Head	Kingsmead Square	Precise location unknown
Sun	Orange Grove	Demolished
Talbot	St James's Street	Demolished
Thatched House	Walcot Street	Precise location unknown
Three Black Birds	Frog Lane	Demolished
Three Crowns	Quiet Street	Precise location unknown
Three Tuns	Stall Street	Demolished
Three Tuns & Crown	Marchant's Passage	Demolished
Turk's Head	Broad Street	Building survives (No 14)
Unicorn	Northgate Street	Demolished
Wheatsheaf	Stall Street	Precise location unknown
White Hart	Avon Street	Demolished
White Hart	Stall Street	Demolished
White Lion	High Street	Demolished
White Swan	Walcot Street	Precise location unknown
York House*	York Buildings	Now Rat & Parrot
York Tap House*	Lansdown Road	Now Mandalyn's

NOTES: Horse Street is today known as Southgate Street, Bell Tree Lane as Beau Street, Orchard Street as Old Orchard Street, and Cottell's Lane as Julian Road. White Hart Lane was roughly where Bath Street is today, and Frog Lane has been replaced by New Bond Street.

APPENDIX TWO

BATH PUBS IN 1808

By 1808, the practice of including pubs names in licensing records was standard throughout Somerset. It has been possible, therefore, to include pubs in Bathwick, Charlcombe, Combe Down, Twerton, Weston, Widcombe and Walcot Out Parish in this list. Pubs which are still open are indicated by an asterisk.

CITY (including Walcot In Parish)

Angel*	Westgate Street	Building survives (Rat & Parrot)
Bath Arms	Horse Street	Demolished
Bath Arms	Kingsmead Street	Demolished
Beefsteak Tavern	Newmarket Row	Demolished
Bell	Monmouth Street	Building survives (Raincheck Bar)
Bell*	Walcot Street	Building survives
Birdcage*	Westgate Street	Rebuilt (Flan O'Briens)
Black Swan	Broad Street	Demolished
Bladud Inn	Walcot Street	Building survives (No 90)
Butcher's Arms	Boatstall Lane	Demolished
Carpenter's Arms	Chatham Row	Building survives (No 14)
Castle & Ball	Northgate Street	Demolished
Catherine Wheel	Walcot Street	Building survives (No 70)
Chequers	Chandos Buildings	Building survives
Chequers	Newmarket Row	Demolished
Chequers	Peter Street	Demolished
Chequers	Stall Street	Precise location unknown
Chequers	Wine Street	Demolished
Christopher Inn*	High Street	Building survives (All Bar One)
Coach & Horses	Barton Street	Building survives (Walrus & Carpenter)
Cross Keys	High Street	Demolished
Crown & Thistle	Avon Street	Demolished
Crown	High Street	Demolished
Darby & Joan	Guinea Lane	Building survives (No 16)
Dolphin	Broad Street	Demolished
Duke of York	Quay	Demolished
Elephant & Castle	Monmouth Street	Demolished
Exeter Inn	Horse Street	Demolished

Fountain	Avon Street	Demolished
Fox & Hounds	Walcot Street	Demolished
Fox & Raven	Quiet Street	Demolished
French Horn	Lower Borough Walls	Demolished
Full Moon	Horse Streeet	Demolished
Full Moon*	Upper Borough Walls	Building survives (Sam Weller's)
Gallon Pot	Kingsmead Square	Precise location unknown
Garrick's Head*	St John's Court	Building survives
George Inn	Walcot Street	Demolished
Glass Chair	Bridewell Lane	Demolished
Golden Lion	Horse Street	Demolished
Green Tree*	Green Street	Building survives
Greyhound	High Street	Demolished
Griffin*	Monmouth Street	Building survives
Grove Tavern	Orange Grove	Demolished
Hand & Shears	Walcot Street	Demolished
Hart & Compass	Cumberland Row	Demolished
Hope & Anchor	Horse Street	Demolished
Horse & Groom	Barton Street	Demolished
Horse & Jockey	Bell Tree Lane	Building survives (No 2 Beau St)
Jolly Coachman	Upper Borough Walls	Demolished
King's Arms	Orchard Street	Building survives (Spiritualist Church)
King's Arms	Walcot Street	Building survives (No 5)
King's Arms*	Monmouth Place	Building survives
King's Head	Bartlett Street	Building survives (No 2)
King's Head	Lilliput Alley	Building survives (No 3)
Lamb Inn	Stall Street	Demolished
Lansdown Arms*	Lansdown Road	Building survives (Mandalyn's)
Lord Nelson	Avon Street	Demolished
Marlborough Tavern*	Marlborough Buildings	Building survives
Mason's Arms	Peter Street	Demolished
New Inn	Horse Street	Demolished
New Inn*	Rivers Street	Building survives (Chequers)
Newmarket Tavern	Newmarket Row	Demolished
Pack Horse	Northgate Street	Demolished
Parade Coffee House*	North Parade	Building survives (Huntsman)
Pelican	Walcot Street	Demolished
Plough	Horse Street	Demolished
Plume of Feathers	Horse Street	Demolished
Prince Frederick	Beauford Square	Rebuilt (No 3)
Prince of Wales	Bridewell Lane	Demolished
Raven	Abbey Green	Building survives (Evan's)
Raven	Quiet Street	Demolished
Red Lion	Kingsmead Street	Demolished
Ring of Bells	Orange Grove	Demolished
Rodney Arms	Westgate Place	Demolished
Rose & Crown	Horse Street	Demolished
Royal Oak	Upper Borough Walls	Building survives (Central Wine Bar)
Rummer*	Newmarket Row	Building survives
Sadler's Arms	Stall Street	Demolished
Saracen's Head*	Broad Street	Building survives

AWASH WITH ALE

Seven Stars	Upper Borough Walls	Frontage survives (Nos 2-3)
Ship & Nelson	Horse Street	Demolished
Smith's Arms	Avon Street	Demolished
Spread Eagle	Horse Street	Demolished
Star & Garter	Lilliput Alley	Building survives (Rear of Huntsman)
Star*	Guinea Lane	Building survives
Still	Horse Street	Demolished
Sun	Orange Grove	Demolished
Talbot	St James's Street	Demolished
Theatre Tavern	Monmouth Street	Demolished
Three Blackbirds	Little Stanhope Street	Rebuilt
Three Cups	Northgate Street	Demolished
Three Tuns & Crown	Marchant's Passage	Demolished
Three Tuns	Stall Street	Demolished
Turk's Head	Broad Street	Building survives (No 14)
Unicorn	Northgate Street	Demolished
Westgate House	New Westgate Buildings	Demolished
Weymouth Arms	Cottles Lane	Demolished
Wheatsheaf	Broad Street	Building survives (No 27)
White Hart	Lower James Street	Demolished
White Hart	Stall Street	Demolished
White Lion Tap	Bridge Street	Demolished
White Lion	High Street	Demolished
York House Hotel*	York Buidings	Building survives

BATHWICK

Argyle Tap	Argyle Street	Building survives (No 17)
Argyle Wine Vaults*	Argyle Street	Building survives (Boater)
Crown*	Bathwick Street	Rebuilt
Ostrich	Grove Street	Demolished
Pulteney Arms*	Daniel Street	Building survives
Rising Sun*	Grove Street	Building survives
Sydney Gardens Tap	Sydney Gardens	Building possibly survives

CHARLCOMBE

Hare & Hounds*	Lansdown	Building survives

COMBE DOWN

Brassknocker Inn	Brassknocker Hill	Building survives
Carriage Inn	The Avenue	Building survives

TWERTON

Crown*	High Street	Building survives
George	High Street	Building survives (No 132)
White Hart	High Street	Building survives (Nos 142-4)

WALCOT OUT-PARISH

Barley Mow	Margaret's Hill	Demolished
Bell	Balance Street	Demolished
Belvedere Coffee House*	Belvedere	Building survives
Gloucester Inn	Somerset Buildings	Demolished
Hanover Hotel*	London Road	Building survives (Piccadilly)

Hat & Feather*	London Street	Rebuilt
Larkhall Inn*	Larkhall	Building survives
Managed Horse	Julian Road	Demolished
Porter Butt*	London Road	Building survives
St James's Hotel*	St James's Street	Building survives
Three Crowns	London Street	Rebuilt
White Horse Cellar	Somerset Buildings	Demolished

WESTON

Blathwayt Arms*	Lansdown	Rebuilt
Crown*	Weston	Building survives
Dolphin*	Lower Weston	Building survives
King's Head*	Weston	Building survives

WIDCOMBE

Angel Inn	Holloway	Demolished
Angel Inn Tap	Holloway	Demolished
Bear*	Bear Flat	Rebuilt
Cooper's Arms	Claverton Street	Demolished
Cross Keys*	Midford Road	Building survives
Greyhound	Claverton Buildings	Building survives (No 18)
Half Moon	Holloway	Demolished
New Inn	Widcombe Hill	Demolished
Old Fox	Holloway	Demolished
Packhorse	Claverton Street	Demolished
Red Lion*	Wells Road	Relocated (part of old building survives)
White Hart*	Widcombe Hill	Building survives
Young Fox	Holloway	Demolished

APPENDIX THREE

BATH PUBS IN THE 1850S

The 1830 Beer Act led to an explosion in the number of licensed premises in Bath. The 1850s probably represents the high point as far as the number of pubs in the city goes. Thereafter, new legislation and the transfer of control for all licensed premises back to local magistrates saw the numbers start to fall. The information in this list is taken from a variety of sources for the period 1850-58, when pubs were opening and closing with a rapidity that even the licensing authorities found it hard to keep up with. It has, therefore, proved impossible to draw up a definitive list for a particular year. All the pubs listed below were, however, open at some time during the 1850s. No distinction has been made between beerhouses and fully licensed premises. Pubs in Bathwick, Walcot Out Parish and Widcombe (which became part of Bath in the 1830s) are included in the listings for the city. Again, an asterisk indicates the establishment is still in business today.

CITY (including Bathwick, Walcot Out Parish & Widcombe)

Name	Location	Status
Abbey Wine Vaults*	Stall Street	Rebuilt (Roundhouse)
Albion Brewery	Corn Street	Demolished
Albion Tavern*	Westgate Street	Rebuilt (Flan O'Briens)
Angel Inn*	Westgate Street	Building survives (Rat & Parrot)
Angel Tavern	Holloway	Demolished
Angel & Crown	Lower Bristol Road	Demolished
Argyle Wine Vaults*	Argyle Street	Building survives (Boater)
Bacchus	Corn Street	Demolished
Bargeman's Tavern	Sydney Wharf	Precise location unknown
Barley Mow*	Bathwick Street	Building survives (Barley)
Barley Mow	Margaret's Hill	Demolished
Bath Arms	Kingsmead Street	Demolished
Bathwick Tavern	Sydney Buildings	Building survives (No 13)
Bear*	Wells Road	Rebuilt
Beaufort Arms	Princes Street	Building survives (No 8)
Beefsteak Tavern	Newmarket Row	Demolished
Beehive	Belvedere	Building survives (Grappa)
Beehive	Walcot Street	Building survives (No 66)
Bell	Gloucester Street	Building survives (No 5)
Bell	Lower Borough Walls	Building survives (Faerie Shop)
Bell	Lower Bristol Road	Demolished
Bell*	Walcot Street	Building survives
Belvedere Arms	Caroline Place	Building survives (No 6)
Belvedere Wine Vaults*	Belvedere	Building survives
Belvoir Castle*	Lower Bristol Road	Building survives
Black Horse	Kingsmead Square	Building survives (No 9)

Black Swan	Broad Street	Demolished
Bladud's Head	Walcot Street	Building survives (No 90)
Blucher	Southgate Street	Demolished
Boatman's Arms	Waterloo Buildings, Widcombe	Demolished
Borough Wine Vaults*	Westgate Buildings	Building survives (DYMK)
Bridge Tavern	Claverton Street	Demolished
Britannia	Piccadilly	Building survives (Piccadilly)
Broadley's Wine Vaults	Gascoyne Place	Building survives
Bunch of Grapes	Morford Street	Building survives (No 23)
Butcher's Arms	Boatstall Lane	Demolished
Cabinet Maker's Arms	Trim Street	Demolished
Caledonian	Trim Street	Building survives (No 16)
Californian Tavern	Dover Terrace, Snow Hill	Demolished
Canal Tavern	Ebenezer Terrace, Widcombe	Demolished
Castle	Northgate Street	Demolished
Catherine Wheel	Walcot Street	Building survives (No 70)
Chandos Arms	Westgate Buildings	Building survives
Chatham House	Chatham Row	Building survives
Chequers	Chandos Buildings	Demolished
Chequers	Peter Street	Demolished
Christopher*	High Street	Building survives (All Bar One)
Circus Tavern	Circus Mews	Demolished
Claremont Arms	Claremont Buildings	Demolished
Claverton Brewery	Claverton Street	Demolished
Cleveland Arms	Cleveland Wharf	Building survives
Coach & Horses	Barton Street	Building survives (Walrus & Carpenter)
Coachmaker's Arms	Snow Hill	Demolished
Cooper's Arms	Claverton Street	Demolished
Corn Street Brewery	Corn Street	Demolished
County Wine Vaults*	Westgate Street	Building survives (Flan O'Brien's)
Cross Keys	High Street	Demolished
Cross Keys*	Midford Road	Building survives
Crown*	Bathwick Street	Rebuilt
Crown	Claremont Row	Demolished
Crown	High Street	Demolished
Crown	New Orchard Street	Demolished
Crystal Palace*	Abbey Green	Building survives
Darby & Joan	Guinea Lane	Building survives (No 16)
Devonshire Arms*	St James Parade	Building survives (Bath Tap)
Devonshire Arms *	Wells Road	Building survives
Dolphin	Broad Street	Demolished
Don Cossack	Walcot Street	Demolished
Dorset House	Morford Street	Demolished
Druid's Arms	Philip Street	Demolished
Duke of York	Quay	Demolished
Edinburgh Castle	Newark Street	Demolished
Exeter Inn	Southgate Street	Demolished
Folly	Beyond Hampton Row	Demolished
Fountain	Avon Street	Demolished
Fox & Hounds	Walcot Street	Demolished
Freeman's Arms	Monmouth Street	Demolished

AWASH WITH ALE

Freemason's Tavern	Abbey Green	Building survives (Evan's)
French Horn	Lower Borough Walls	Demolished
Full Moon	Southgate Street	Demolished
Full Moon*	Upper Borough Walls	Building survives (Sam Weller's)
Fuller's Wine Vaults	Southgate Street	Demolished
Gardener's Arms	Lower Bristol Road	Demolished
Garrick's Head*	St John's Place	Building survives
Gay's Hill Tavern	Gay's Hill	Demolished
George Inn	Walcot Street	Demolished
Gloucester Inn	Somerset Buildings	Demolished
Golden Fleece	Pulteney Road	Building survives
Golden Lion	Southgate Street	Demolished
Grapes*	Westgate Street	Building survives
Green Park Tavern*	Lower Bristol Road	Building survives
Green Tree*	Green Street	Building survives
Green Tree*	St James Parade	Building survives (Hobgoblin)
Greyhound	Claverton Buildings	Building survives (No 18)
Greyhound	High Street	Demolished
Griffin*	Monmouth Street	Building survives
Grove Tavern	Newmarket Row	Demolished
Half Moon	Half Moon St, Snow Hill	Demolished
Half Moon	Holloway	Demolished
Hampton Museum	Hampton Row	Building survives (No 14)
Hat & Feather*	London Street	Rebuilt
Heart Encompassed	Cumberland Row	Demolished
Heart in Hand	Ambury	Demolished
Hooper's Arms	Highbury Terrace	Building survives (No 1)
Hop Pole*	Upper Bristol Road	Building survives
Hope & Anchor	Somerset Buildings	Demolished
Horse & Jockey	Beau Street	Building survives (No 2)
Institution Wine Vaults*	North Parade	Building survives (Huntsman)
Jolly Sailor	Claverton Street	Demolished
King William	Thomas Street	Building survives
King's Arms*	Monmouth Street	Building survives
King's Arms	Walcot Street	Building survives (No 5)
King's Head	Bartlett Street	Building survives (No 2)
King's Head	Lilliput Alley	Building survives (No 3)
Kingsmead WineVaults	Kingsmead Street	Demolished
Lamb	Brookleaze Place, Larkhall	Demolished
Lamb	Hampton Row	Building survives (No 9)
Lamb	Stall Street	Building survives (No 26)
Lamb & Lion*	Lower Borough Walls	Building survives
Lambridge Tavern	Lambridge Street, Larkhall	Demolished
Lansdown Arms	Richmond Place	Building survives (No 37)
Lansdown Arms*	Lansdown Road	Building survives (Mandalyn's)
Lansdown Brewery	Lansdown Road	Demolished
Larkhall Inn*	Larkhall	Building survives
Live & Let Live	Lampard's Buildings	Demolished
Long Acre Tavern*	Long Acre	Rebuilt
Malakoff Tavern	Claverton Street	Demolished
Malt & Hops	Corn Street	Demolished
Manage Horse	Cottles Lane	Demolished

Manver's Arms	Manvers Street	Demolished
Marlborough Tap*	Marlborough Buildings	Building survives
Mason's Arms	Ferry Lane, Dolemeads	Demolished
Mason's Arms	Peter Street	Demolished
Mason's Arms	Widcombe Parade	Demolished
Nelson Arms	Beechen Cliff Place	Building survives (Nelson House)
Nelson & Victory	Southgate Street	Demolished
New Cornwell Brewery	Walcot Street	Demolished
New Inn	Charlotte Street	Demolished
New Inn	Juda Place, Snow Hill	Demolished
New Inn*	Rivers Street	Building survives (Chequers)
New Inn	Southgate Street	Demolished
New Inn	Widcombe Hill	Demolished
New Moon	Upper Borough Walls	Building survives (Central Wine Bar)
Newbridge Tavern	Lower Bristol Road	Demolished
Newmarket Tavern	Newmarket Row	Demolished
Newmarket Tavern	Walcot Street	Demolished
Nightingale	Walcot Street	Demolished
Norfolk Tavern	Upper Bristol Road	Demolished
North Pole	Margaret's Place, Hedgemead	Demolished
Oddfellow's Arms	Ainslie's Buildings, Hedgemead	Demolished
Oddfellow's Arms	Ashman Place, Dolemeads	Demolished
Oddfellow's Arms	Avon Street	Demolished
Oddfellow's Arms	Upper Bristol Road	Demolished
Old Fox	Holloway	Demolished
Old Monmouth Arms	Monmouth Street	Demolished
Old Pack Horse	Northgate Street	Demolished
Old Standard	Claremont Buildings	Demolished
Ostrich	Grove Street	Demolished
Oxford Tavern	Cottles Lane	Demolished
Pack Horse	Pulteney Road	Demolished
Painter's Arms	St James's Street South	Demolished
Park Tavern*	Park Lane	Building survives
Plasterer's Arms	Corn Street	Demolished
Plough	Wells Road	Demolished
Porter Butt*	London Road	Building survives
Porter Stores*	Miles's Buildings	Building survives (Porter)
Porter Stores	New Bond Street Place	Building survives (V. Rifleman's Arms)
Portland Brewery	Portland Place	Demolished
Post Office Tavern	Broad Street	Demolished
Prince Frederick	Beaufort Square	Rebuilt (No 3)
Pulteney Arms*	Daniel Street	Building survives
Queen Square Tavern	Barton Street	Demolished
Queen Sq. Wine Vaults	Chapel Row	Building survives (No 11)
Queen Victoria	Hampton Row	Building survives (No 1)
Queen's Head	Walcot Street	Demolished
Railway Tavern	Newark Street	Demolished
Railway Tavern	Wells Road	Rebuilt
Rainbow Tavern	Upper Borough Walls	Demolished
Raven	Quiet Street	Demolished
Red Lion	Kingsmead Street	Demolished
Red Lion*	Odd Down	Building survives

Ring of Bells*	Widcombe Parade	Building survives
Rising Sun	Circus Mews	Demolished
Rising Sun*	Claremont Terrace	Building survives
Rising Sun*	Grove Street	Building survives
Rising Sun	Richmond Place	Building survives (No 39)
River's Arms	Upper Camden Place	Building survives (No 25)
Rose & Crown	Little Corn Street	Demolished
Rose & Crown	Marchant's Passage	Demolished
Rose Tavern	Morford Street	Demolished
Royal Hotel*	Manvers Street	Building survives
Royal Oak*	Pulteney Road	Building survives
Royal Sailor	Holloway	Demolished
Rummer Tavern*	Newmarket Row	Building survives
Sadler's Arms	Stall Street	Demolished
Saracen's Head*	Broad Street	Building survives
Sawclose Tavern*	Sawclose	Building survives (Delfter Krug)
Sedan Chair	Bridewell Lane	Demolished
Seven Dials	Westgate Street	Demolished
Seven Stars	Upper Borough Walls	Frontage survives (Nos 2-3)
Shakespeare	Old Orchard Street	Building survives (Spiritualist Church)
Ship	St James's Street South	Demolished
Smith's Arms	Avon Street	Demolished
Smith's Arms	Winifred's Terrace, Dolemeads	Demolished
Somerset Arms	Pulteney Place, Dolemeads	Demolished
Somerset Arms	Somerset Street	Demolished
Somerset Arms	Winifred's Lane	Building survives
South Pole	Dorchester Street	Demolished
Spread Eagle	Southgate Street	Demolished
St James's Brewery	Corn Street	Demolished
St James's Hotel*	St James's Street	Building survives (St James's Wine Vaults)
St James's Tavern	St James's Parade	Building survives (No 31)
Stag's Head	Widcombe Parade	Demolished
Star*	Guinea Lane	Building survives
Sterling Tavern	Gallaway's Buildings	Building survives (No 4)
Sun	Orange Grove	Demolished
Sydney Porter Stores	Bathwick Stores	Building survives (No 35a)
Theatre Tavern	Monmouth Street	Demolished
Three Blackbirds	Little Stanhope Street	Rebuilt
Three Crowns	London Street	Rebuilt
Three Cups	Walcot Street	Demolished
Trafalgar Tavern	Calton Road	Demolished
Traveller's Rest	London Road	Demolished
Trinity*	James Street West	Rebuilt
Turk's Head	Broad Street	Building survives (No 14)
Unicorn	Northgate Street	Demolished
Union Tavern	Union Passage	Building survives (No 5)
Union Tavern	York Street	Building survives (No 10)
Vaults*	Cleveland Place	Building survives (Curfew)
Victoria Tavern	Bridewell Lane	Demolished
Victoria Tavern	Monmouth Street	Building survives (No 29)
Walcot Wine Vaults	Walcot Street	Building survives (No 114)

Waterman's Arms	Quay	Demolished
Westgate House	New Westgate Buildings	Demolished
Westhall Inn*	Upper Bristol Road	Building survives (New Westhall)
Weymouth Arms	Cottles Lane	Demolished
Wheatsheaf	Broad Street	Building survives (No 27)
Wheelchair	Kingsmead Square	Building survives (No 7)
White Hart	James Street West	Demolished
White Hart	Stall Street	Demolished
White Hart*	Widcombe Hill	Building survives
White Horse Cellar	Somerset Buildings	Demolished
White Horse*	Northampton Street	Building survives (Dark Horse)
White Lion	High Street	Demolished
White Lion	Lambridge Buildings, Larkhall	Building survives (No 1)
White Lion	Lower Bristol Road	Demolished
White Lion Tap	Bridge Street	Demolished
White Swan	Lower Bristol Road	Demolished
Widcombe Brewery	Pulteney Road	Demolished
Wine Vaults*	York Street	Building survives (Alehouse)
Worcester Tavern	St Saviour's Road, Larkhall	Building survives
York House*	York Buildings	Building survives (Slug & Lettuce)
York House Tap	Broad Street	Building survives (Below York House)
Young Fox	Holloway	Demolished

CHARLCOMBE

Hare & Hounds*	Lansdown	Building survives

COMBE DOWN

Brassknocker	Brassknocker Hill	Building survives
Carriage Inn	The Avenue	Building survives
Hadley Arms*	North Road	Building survives
Horseshoe*	Raby Place	Building survives
King William IV*	Combe Down	Building survives
Mason's Arms	North Road	Building survives
Rock (Davidge's)	Rock Lane	Building survives

TWERTON

Anchor		Precise location unknown
Boot		Precise location unknown
Clothier's Arms		Precise location unknown
Crown*	High Street	Building survives
George	High Street	Building survives (No 132)
Golden Fleece*	Avon Buildings	Building survives
Queen	Waterloo Buildings	Demolished
Railway Inn	Avon Buildings	Demolished
Ring of Bells	High Street	Building survives (No 4)
Royal Oak	Lower Bristol Road	Building survives
Seven Stars	Avon Buildings	Rebuilt (Tramways Club)
Swan		Precise location unknown
Wheatsheaf	High Street	Building survives (Carpet Shop)
White Hart	High Street	Building survives (No 142-4)

WESTON

Blathwayt Arms*	Lansdown	Rebuilt
Crown*	Lansdown Place	Building survives
Crown & Anchor*	High Street	Building survives
Dolphin*	Locksbrook Road	Building survives
Globe	High Street	Building survives (No 82)
King's Head*	High Street	Building survives
Mason's Arms	High Street	Precise location unknown
Queen's Head	Trafalgar Road	Building survives (No 1)
Summerhill Tavern	Primrose Hill	Building survives
White Lion	High Street	Demolished
Windsor Castle	Upper Bristol Road	Rebuilt

BIBLIOGRAPHY

Much of the information in this book is from primary sources, in particular Alehouse Recognizances and Licensing Records held in the Bath and Somerset Record Offices. Other documents consulted include Coroner's Reports, Council Minutes, Information Concerning Vagrants, Surveying Committee Minutes, and Watch Committee Records held in the Bath Record Office.

Old newpapers were also a major source of information. These included the *Bath Journal*, the *Bath Herald*, the *Bath Chronicle* and the *Bath & Cheltenham Gazette* (all held in Bath Central Library), and *Farley's Bristol Newspaper* (held in Bristol Reference Library). Other material consulted in Bath Central Library included papers in the Boodle Collection and scrapbooks of miscellaneous material.

Other works consulted include:

A Record of the Great Floods in Bath and the Surrounding District, November 13 & 15, 1894 (Reprinted from the Bath Herald), Bath 1894

Old English Coffee Houses, London, 1954

Bath and Bristol Guide, Bath, 1755

Kegs & Ale: Bath and the Public House, Bath, 1991

Tables of Revenue, Population, Commerce, Etc, Compiled from Official Returns, London, 1835

Amis, Kingsley, *Lucky Jim*, London, 1953

Aspinall, A, ed., *Mrs Jordan & her Family, Being the Unpublished Letters of Mrs Jordan and the Duke of Clarence, later William IV,* London, 1951

Bickerdyke, John, *The Curiosities of Ale & Beer*, London, 1889

Bold, Alan, *Drink to Me Only: The Prose and Cons of Drinking*, London, 1982

Bone, Mike, "The Rise and Fall of Bath's Breweries, 1736-1960," in *Bath History, VIII*, Bath, 2000

Boston, Richard, *Beer and Skittles*, London, 1976

Brand, John, *Observations on Popular Antiquities, Chiefly Concerning the Origin of Our Vulgar Customs, Ceremonies and Superstitions*, London, 1900

Brown, Malcolm & Judith Samuel, "The Jews of Bath," in *Bath History, Volume 1*, Gloucester, 1986

Brown, Pete, *Man Walks into a Pub: A Sociable History of Beer*, London, 2003

Butler, Richard, *Bath City Police: A Brief History*, Bath, 1985

Chisholm, Kate, *Fanny Burney*, London, 1998

Clark, Peter, *The English Alehouse: A Social History, 1200-1830*, London, 1983

Cornell, Martyn, *Beer: The Story of the Pint,* London, 2003

Crawford, Anne, *Bristol and the Wine Trade*, Bristol, 1984

Crowden, James, *Cider: The Forgotten Miracle*, Somerton, 1999

Davenport, Peter, *Medieval Bath Uncovered*, Brimscombe Port, 2002

Davis, Dorothy, *A History of Shopping*, London, 1966

Davis, Graham & Penny Bonsell, *Bath: A New History*, Keele, 1996

Davis, Graham, *Bath Beyond the Guide Book: Scenes from Victorian Life*, Bristol, 1988

De la Beche, Sir Henry, *Report on the City of Bath & Its Sanatory Condition*, London, 1845

Dillon, Patrick, *The Much Lamented Death of Madam Geneva: The Eighteenth-century Gin Craze*, London, 2002

Disney, Francis, *Shepton Mallet Prison*, Shepton Mallet, 1992

Dixon, Roger & Stefan Muthesius, *Victorian Architecture*, London, 1978

Egan, Pierce, *Walks Through Bath*, Bath, 1819

Fagan, Garrett G, *Bathing in Public in the Roman World*, Ann Arbor, 1999

Fawcett, Trevor, *Voices of Eighteenth-century Bath*, Bath, 1995

French RV, *Nineteen Centuries of Drink in England*, London, 1884

Fryer, Peter, *The Man of Pleasure's Companion*, London, 1968

Gilmour, Ian, *Riots, Risings and Revolution: Governance and Violence in Eighteenth Century England*, London, 1992

Girouard, Mark, *Victorian Pubs*, London, 1975

Grafton, Frank, *Tipple & Temperance*, Unpublished article, Bath Record Office

Hackwood, Frederick, *Inns, Ales and Drinking Customs of Old England*, London, 1985 (reprint)

Harman, Claire, *Fanny Burney*, London, 2000

Harrison, Brian, *Drink and the Victorians*, London, 1971

Haydon, Peter, *Beer & Britannia: An Inebriated History of Britain*, Thrupp, 2001

Hecht, J Jean, *The Domestic Servant in Eighteenth-Century England*, London, 1980

Honan, Park, *Jane Austen, Her Life*, London 1987

Hudson, Thomas, *Temperance Pioneers of the West*, London, 1887

Hunt, Henry, *Memoirs*, 3 vols., London, 1820

Hutt, Christopher, *The Death of the English Pub*, London, 1973

King, FA, *Beer Has a History*, Hutchinson, 1947

Lane, E, "The Police and Crime in Bath, 1850-1860," Unpublished essay, 1980, in Bath Record Office

Langland, William, *Piers Plowman*, done into Modern English by the Rev Professor Skeat, London, 1905

Longmate, Norman, *How We Lived Then*, London, 1971

Mainwaring, Captain Rowland, *Annals of Bath from the Year 1800 to the Passing of the New Municipal Act*, Bath, 1838

Manco, Jean, "Saxon Bath," in *Bath History VII*, Bath, 1998

Manco, Jean, *The Spirit of Care: The 800 Year Story of St John's Hospital, Bath*, Bath, 1998

Marwick, Arthur, *Britain in Our Century*, London, 1984

Melville, Lewis, *Bath Under Beau Nash*, London, 1907

Morris, Dr Claver, *The Diary of a West Country Physician*, ed Edmund Hobhouse, London, 1934

Neale, RS, *Bath: A Social History, 1650-1850, or A Valley of Pleasure, yet a Sink of Iniquity*, London, 1981

Paston-Williams, Sara, *The Art of Dining*, Oxford, 1993

Peach, REM, *The Annals of the Parish of Swainswick*, London & Bath, 1890.

Pearce, Fred, *The Critical Guide to Bath Pubs,* Bristol, 1976

Penrose, Rev John, *Letters from Bath, 1766-1767*, ed. Brigitte Mitchell & Hubert Penrose, Gloucester, 1983

Pound, Christopher, *Genius of Bath: The City & its Landscape*, Bath 1986

Pudney, John, *A Draught of Contentment: The Story of the Courage Group*, London, 1971

Robertson, Charles, *Bath: An Architectural Guide*, London, 1975

Scott, GR, *The Story of Baths and Bathing*, London, 1935

Shickle, Rev CW, ed., *Ancient Deeds Belonging to the Corporation of Bath*, Bath, 1921

Simond, Louis, ed. Christopher Hibbert, *An American in Regency England*, London, 1968

Skinner, John, *The Journal of a Somerset Rector*, ed. Howard & Peter Coombs, Oxford, 1971

Smollett, Tobias, *Humphrey Clinker*, London, 1771

Southey, Robert, *Letters from England*, London, 1807

Stone, Barbara, *Bath Millennium*, Bath, 1973

Sydenham, S, *Bath Tokens of the Seventeenth Century*, Bath, 1905 YES

Symons, Katherine E, *The Grammar School of King Edward VI, Bath, and Its Ancient Foundation*, Bath, 1934

Trench, Richard, *Travellers in Britain: Three Centuries of Discovery*, London 1990

Ward, Ned, *A Step to the Bath*, London, 1700

Watney, John, *Beer is Best: A History of Beer*, London, 1974

Wilcox, Ronald, "Bath Breweries in the Latter Half of the Eighteenth Century," in *A Second North Somerset Miscellany*, (pp. 23-31), Bath, 1971

Wood, John, *Description of Bath*, London, 1749

Woodforde, James, *Diary of a Country Parson*, ed. John Beresford, 5 vols., Oxford, 1924-31

Wroughton, John, *Stuart Bath: Life in the Forgotten City, 1603-1714*, Bath, 2004

Wroughton, John, *A Community at War: The Civil War in Bath and North Somerset, 1642-1650*, Bath, 1992

Wroughton, John, ed., *Bath in the Age of Reform*, Bath 1972

INDEX

AWASH WITH ALE

THE GREAT BATH PUB CRAWL

You've read the book – now take the tour. Guided walks start from the *Old Green Tree* in Green Street throughout the summer. Party bookings – tailored to your requirements – can be arranged throughout the year. Devised by Kirsten Elliott and Andrew Swift, the **Great Bath Pub Crawl** is a leisurely ramble through 2000 years of Bath's history – with an emphasis on the raising of the wrist. And when the tales of beerhouses, gin epidemics, boozy Bathonians and ghostly goings-on get too much, there's the chance to sample some of the ales brewed in local breweries. For the real ale enthusiast or for anyone who wants to hear some of the tales that don't get into the history books, the **Great Bath Pub Crawl** provides a unique and unforgettable introduction to one of the world's most fascinating cities.

For more information, ring 01225 310364 or visit www.greatbathpubcrawl.com.

ALSO AVAILABLE FROM AKEMAN PRESS

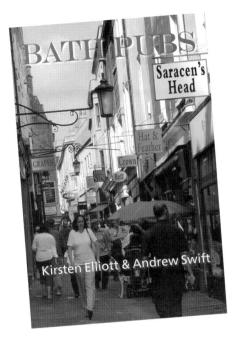

BATH PUBS

by Kirsten Elliott & Andrew Swift

The history of all Bath's surviving pubs, lavishly illustrated, with the story of brewing in Bath and a look at the thorny question of which is the city's oldest pub.

Price: £12.99   ISBN: 0-9546138-0-5

Available from all good Bath bookshops or direct from Akeman Press, 58 Minster Way, Bath BA2 6RL (post free).

Forthcoming publications from Akeman Press:

ALL ROADS LEAD TO FRANCE: Bath in the Great War
by Andrew Swift
To be published Autumn 2004

A CANDLE FOR WILLIAM: In the Footsteps of William Beckford
by Kirsten Elliott
To be published in 2005

BATH'S LOST PUBS
by Kirsten Elliott & Andrew Swift
To be published in 2005

A bit about the team that brought you this book.

The authors
Kirsten Elliott first came to live in Bath in 1960, while (she adds hastily) still at school. With a teenager's usual enthusiasm for all things educational, the history of Bath made little impression upon her. Her chief memories are chucking her hat in the river after taking O-levels, dancing in the streets during the early Bath Fringe Festival, and belonging to the Berni Royal Jazz Club. However, four years after her return in 1981, she became a guide to the city and discovered the delights of digging in dusty documents to uncover previously unknown facts. She has published a book of walks in Bath and, with co-author David Purchase, a book of countryside walks, as well as numerous articles. She is also the author of "BATH", a new introductory history, illustrated by photographer Neill Menneer.

One little known fact about Kirsten Elliott is that she once ran a Fantasy League football team under the pseudonym of Billy Beckford.

Andrew Swift is a man of whom the rest of the team is in awe. It's not just his academic credentials, which are impressive – a BA in English, an MA in Fine Arts, and a PhD in English Literature – but his ability to multitask that puts the rest in the shade. Writer and journalist, postcard dealer, walking encyclopaedia on railways, on which he has published several books, photographer of everything from quaint to quirky, and a mean keyboard player (he was once part of a group called The Heavers), he has been known to produce the odd (and we mean odd) radio programme. He is also Beer Taster in Chief for the Great Bath Pub Crawl. He says he starting drinking at an early age and has always looked back.

Arriving in Bath in 2001, Andrew Swift quickly turned his academic talents to researching Bath's history, and in 2003 formed Akeman Press with Kirsten Elliott.

The illustrator
Julian Landau works as an illustrator, musician, "poetic licensee", actor, tour guide and raconteur. He graduated from Cardiff School of Fine Art in 1999 and in 2001 was awarded the prestigious title of Bard of Bath for his anthology of nonsense verse, 'Imagine A Menagerie'. As Jonah Flatfoot he is the lead vocalist & guitarist for the delightfully original 'swingska' group, The Zen Hussies, who perfume their inimitable hybrid of goodtime musical stompositions at pubs, clubs & festivals all over Europe. The Zen Hussies can be found out about via their website (www.zenhussies.com) or through the infamous "Communal Viper" scandal sheet of which Landau is Addertor.

A tour guide for The Great Bath Pub Crawl, he wishes his epitaph to be "One can never do worse than to shirk thirsty work", and desires to be embalmed in his favourite "five yard suit".

The designer
Niall Allsop was once described in the tabloid press as a 'bearded Irishman with an earring' … two of which still apply. In the interests of balance it is worth detailing the qualities and idiosyncracies omitted in this peculiar publication.
Career One: Born and bred in an untroubled Belfast where he trained as a teacher; moved to England to educate the natives (and help the likes of Andrew achieve academic success); at the tender age of 27, became Britain's youngest Headteacher.
Career Two: Decided to give someone else a chance, stamped on his chalk and went on the dole; became a freelance photo-journalist while living on a narrowboat; became the editor of a national inland boating magazine; wrote a few books on boating and canals; got bored with boats.
Career Three: Learnt to typeset in Manchester, discovered Apples (the computers, that is); became a graphic designer; bumped into Kirsten and Andrew; never looked back …
Career Four: Wins national lottery …